AMERICAN INDIAN STUDIES

AMERICAN INDIAN STUDIES

NATIVE PHD GRADUATES GIFT THEIR STORIES

EDITED BY
MARK L. M. BLAIR,
MARY JO TIPPECONNIC FOX,
AND KESTREL A. SMITH

THE UNIVERSITY OF
ARIZONA PRESS
TUCSON

The University of Arizona Press
www.uapress.arizona.edu

We respectfully acknowledge the University of Arizona is on the land and territories of Indigenous peoples. Today, Arizona is home to twenty-two federally recognized tribes, with Tucson being home to the O'odham and the Yaqui. Committed to diversity and inclusion, the University strives to build sustainable relationships with sovereign Native Nations and Indigenous communities through education offerings, partnerships, and community service.

ISBN-13: 978-0-8165-4437-0 (paperback)

Cover design by Leigh McDonald
Cover photos of graduates courtesy of the University of Arizona American Indian Studies program: Gregory Redhouse, 2016 (top); Tarissa Spoonhunter, 2014 (bottom left); Michael Lerma, 2010 (bottom right)
Typeset by Sara Thaxton in 10/14 Warnock Pro with Irby WF and Helvetica Neue LT Std

Publication of this book is made possible in part by the proceeds of a permanent endowment created with the assistance of a Challenge Grant from the National Endowment for the Humanities, a federal agency.

Library of Congress Cataloging-in-Publication Data
Names: Blair, Mark L. M., 1972- editor. | Fox, Mary Jo Tippeconnic, editor, writer of preface. | Smith, Kestrel A., editor. | Nicholas, Sheilah E. (Sheilah Ernestine), writer of foreword.
Title: American Indian Studies : Native PhD graduates gift their stories / edited by Mark L. M. Blair, Mary Jo Tippeconnic Fox, and Kestrel A. Smith.
Other titles: Native PhD graduates gift their stories
Description: Tucson, Arizona : The University of Arizona Press, 2022. | Foreword by Sheilah Nicholas (Hopisino). Preface by Mary Jo Tippeconnic Fox (Comanche/Cherokee). | Includes bibliographical references and index.
Identifiers: LCCN 2021037134 | ISBN 9780816544370 (paperback)
Subjects: LCSH: University of Arizona—Graduate students. | University of Arizona. American Indian Studies Program. | Indians of North America—Education (Graduate)—Arizona—Tucson. | Indian college students—Education (Graduate)—Arizona—Tucson. | Doctoral students—Arizona—Tucson. | Indians of North America—Study and teaching (Graduate)—Arizona—Tucson. | LCGFT: Biographies.
Classification: LCC E97.65.A6 A44 2022 | DDC 378.1/982970791776—dc23
LC record available at https://lccn.loc.gov/2021037134

Printed in the United States of America
♾ This paper meets the requirements of ANSI/NISO Z39.48-1992 (Permanence of Paper).

This book is dedicated to the past, present, and
future members of the AIS community.

We respectfully acknowledge the University of Arizona is
on the land and territories of Indigenous peoples. Today,
Arizona is home to twenty-two federally recognized
tribes, with Tucson being home to the O'odham and
the Yaqui. Committed to diversity and inclusion, the
University strives to build sustainable relationships with
sovereign Native Nations and Indigenous communities
through education offerings, partnerships, and
community service.

CONTENTS

Foreword by Sheilah E. Nicholas (Hopisino)   *ix*

Preface by Mary Jo Tippeconnic Fox (Comanche/Cherokee)   *xv*

Introduction   3
KESTREL A. SMITH

FAMILY AND KINSHIP

1. Nan Ikhvnanchi, Nan Ikhvnanchi, Keyu Hokma Pi Illachi
    (Educate, Educate, or We Perish)   16
    ALISSE ALI-JOSEPH (OKLAHOMA CHOCTAW)

2. T'áá shí ànísht'éego t'éiyá ádoolnííł   29
    GEORGINA BADONI (DINÉ)

3. "Bidiishkaal": Putting Forth Effort   41
    ARESTA TSOSIE-PADDOCK (DINÉ)

MENTORSHIP

4. Who's Watching the Boy? Creator's Watching Him   53
    MICHAEL LERMA (P'URHÉPECHA)

5. Warrior   74
    FERLIN CLARK (DINÉ)

6. Transfer of Knowledge   90
    TARISSA SPOONHUNTER (ARAPAHO/BLACKFEET)

SERVICE AND GIVING BACK

7. "Keep Pluggin'": New Generations Need Strong
    Shoulders to Stand On   107
    MICHELLE L. HALE (NAVAJO, LAGUNA,
    CHIPPEWA, ODAWA)

8. No Madness for a Nomad   127
    GREGORY I. REDHOUSE (DINÉ)

9. THINKING BIG: "The Goddamn White Man Took
    Everything, but He Can't Take Away Your Education"   148
    LOUELLYN WHITE (KANIEN'KEHÁ:KA
    [MOHAWK]/AKWESASNE)

    Conclusion   164
    MARK L. M. BLAIR (ANISHINAABE)

    Contributors   175
    Index   181

FOREWORD

Native people know their own stories, and thus are the best equipped
to tell those stories. And, the best interest of the peoples is the primary
value. This is an essential indigenous concept—individuals are linked
inextricably to the people who birthed them, and thus have an obligation
to that people.

—KEMPER (2010, 6)

This book is a *gift*. I am deeply humbled by the invitation to write the foreword for this *gifting* of stories. I accept the invitation as one who is "linked
inextricably" to the Indigenous contributors who story our collective journey. Thus, I embrace the obligation to speak/write responsibly and with responsibility in a way that honors each storyteller who unapologetically and
boldly story authentically lived experiences of going to, through, and beyond
the academy. In *American Indian Studies: Native PhD Graduates Gift Their
Stories*, Indigenous storytellers representing tribal nations—Kanien'kehá:ka
(Mohawk), Diné/Navajo, Choctaw, P'urhépecha, Arapaho/Blackfeet—
poignantly affirm that they remain tethered to, or have (re)membered themselves to, the People who birthed them and now are fulfilling obligation(s)
to those People/Indigenous Peoples. At the heart, this is *relational* work
(Kovach 2009).

For a number of the volume storytellers, a prominent draw of American Indian Studies (AIS) at the University of Arizona as their chosen academic pathway was to be lucky enough to be in the company of Indigenous
"legends"—the "greatest scholars of all time"—Vine Deloria Jr. (Standing

Rock Sioux), N. Scott Momaday (Kiowa), Robert K. Thomas (Cherokee), Robert Williams (Lumbee), James Anaya (Apache/P'urhépecha), and Tom Holm (Cherokee). Coupled to an "awesome caliber of American Indian faculty steeped in various disciplines"—Luci Tapahonso (Diné), Mary Jo Tippeconnic Fox (Comanche), Tsianina Lomawaima (Mvskoke Creek), Jay Stauss (Jamestown S'klallam), Manley Begay (Diné), and Robert Martin (Oklahoma Cherokee)—who comprised the "'dream team' of respected scholars" and made for "an exciting time to be a student there!" (Clark, page 76, this volume). For Tarissa Spoonhunter, AIS fulfilled an aspiration "to attend a good graduate school where there were lots of Indians" (page 97, this volume). As such, AIS is an exemplar of *Indigenous community* within the academy.

Not only do these storytellers revel in having been "surrounded by the best Indigenous minds in the world" (Lerma, page 63, this volume), they describe AIS as a community inclusive of and encompassing faculty, external mentors, family, and others providing "manifold forms of support" (Red-house, page 127, this volume)—all "[who] wanted us to do well once out in the world with our AIS graduate degrees" (Hale, page 123, this volume). It is a manifold of support that emanates "from a vision of working *with* Native Americans toward a participatory goal of emancipation and empowerment" (Kirkness and Barnhardt 1991, citing Tierney), manifesting distinctly in the humanizing aspect of this goal—student and faculty-mentor interpersonal relationships—expressed in the following testimonies. Louellyn White describes Dr. Tsianina Lomawaima as "brilliant and no-nonsense" but "gentle when I needed it and [who] pushed when I was ready," and more poignantly writes, "She believed in me and I will forever be grateful" (page 160, this volume). Michael Lerma recalls that Dr. Manley Begay's words, "You are the cream of the crop," voiced in the first class of the semester, "did more to boost my esteem" (page 63, this volume) as recognition of the potential and promise he and each of his classmates represented. As well, for Michael, Dr. Tom Holm stands out as a fervent student advocate—someone who "had the guts to stand up for me." He reflectively writes, "Had it not been for Holm, maybe I would not be where I am now" (Lerma, page 61, this volume). These relationships of support and advocacy are testament that AIS has established a culture within the academy that offers instrumental value to Indigenous students—privileges students' aspirations and cultural predispositions—in their pursuit of higher education. This is a commitment Kirkness and Barnhardt describe as attending to the four R's: "*respects* them for who they are, that is *relevant* to their view of the world, that offers *reciprocity* in their relationships with others, and that helps them exercise *responsibility* over their own lives" (1991, 14, emphasis added). It is strongly upheld by Lerma, who writes that when he was admitted to the AIS doctoral program, "A heavy weight was lifted from my shoulders. . . . I finally felt [at] home. . . . They made a space for me at their fire" (page 63, this volume).

Seated in their rightful spaces around the AIS fire, the "fire" itself illuminates the academic aspirations and cultural predispositions that all the storytelling alumni brought to the AIS fold. With each story, I became *vicariously involved* in their lived experiences; more often than not, their stories were my stories. I envisioned each storyteller as standing at the crossroad of a life journey, "pausing" first to gaze *back* at the journey—at those stepping-stones that created the pathway of experiences to this juncture. This gaze back into memory also precipitated a "look within" or "going within" (Kovach 2009), an emancipatory (re)searching and self-(re)discovery of one's purpose in the maze of life. The late Tohono O'odham artist Leonard Chana's words, shared posthumously in *The Sweet Smell of Home: The Life and Art of Leonard F. Chana*, express the significance of the maze-of-life symbol as an apt metaphor:

> I use the maze of life . . . because it is considered the life of the person or the group. *They say* you are born. That is where you enter. You start going through the maze of life, and every turn you make, a major event happens in your life as you go. And then as you go along, you learn about yourself, how you do things. . . . By the time we get down here at the center, *they say*, you stop and look back at what you have accomplished in your lifetime, what you learned of the O'odham [ancestral] ways. (Chana, Lobo, and Chana 2009; italics added)

Chana acknowledges and references ancestral voices and knowledge with the words *they say*, premised in generations of accumulated lived experiences of the O'odham People through the maze of life. This process of (re)membering oneself to ancestral voices and knowledge—listening and hearing—is to know who you are, where you come from so that you know where you are going—a reverberating theme across these stories of a collective Indigenous journey.

Thus, not only are these stories autobiographies, they also are commentaries on the "context that we've inherited" (Justice 2016, 30) born of the shared legacy of imperialism and ongoing colonialism (Moreton-Robinson 2016)—when we became "disconnected from cultural traditional teachings" (Archibald 2008, ix). They are an unhindered, poignant, powerful, and critical storying of hidden truths of stories not told or heard. Stó:lō scholar Jo-ann Archibald describes Indigenous stories as life lessons learned the "hard" way (2008) and entails "'researching back', claiming, remembering, and rewriting as well as celebrating survival" (Kuokkanen 2007, 142) of the resurgent power of Indigenous resilience, integrity, and persistence captured by Ferlin Clark, who writes: "I discovered ancient truths for a modern world" (page 84, this volume).

Indigenous storying allows an exploration and unveiling of our oppression and thus offers accessibility to/into the experiences and pain of Indigenous historical trauma. Reciprocally, Indigenous stories produce critical insight about Indigenous lives and epistemes—*Indigenous embodied knowledges*—"guided by and extending the work of our intellectual ancestors to offer locations of engagement that place, provoke, and entice our thinking beyond the familiar and comfortable" (Moreton-Robinson 2016, 9–10). Embracing of these stories and storytelling as gifts is to affirm that they have found a respectful place in education and the academy.

—Sheilah E. Nicholas (Hopisino)
AIS Alumna, 1991, 2008

References

Archibald, J. 2008. Indigenous Storywork: Educating the Heart, Mind, Body, and Spirit. Vancouver: UBC Press.

Chana, L. F., S. Lobo, and B. Chana. 2009. *The Sweet Smell of Home: The Life and Art of Leonard F. Chana*. Tucson: University of Arizona Press.

Justice, D. H. 2016. "A Better World Becoming: Placing Critical Indigenous Studies." In *Critical Indigenous Studies: Engagement in First World Locations*, edited by A. Moreton-Robinson, 19–34. Tucson: University of Arizona Press.

Kemper, K. 2010. "Who Speaks for Indigenous Peoples? Tribal Journalists, Rhetorical Sovereignty, and Freedom of Expression." *Journalism and Communication Monographs* 12 (1): 3–58. https://doi.org/10.1177/152263791001200101.

Kirkness, V. J., and R. Barnhardt. 1991. "First Nations and Higher Education: The Four R's: Respect, Relevance, Reciprocity, Responsibility." *Journal of American Indian Education* 3 (30): 1–15.

Kovach, M. 2009. *Indigenous Methodologies: Characteristics, Conversations, and Contexts.* Toronto: University of Toronto Press.

Kuokkanen, R. 2007. *Reshaping the University: Responsibility, Indigenous Epistemes, and the Logic of the Gift.* Vancouver: UBC Press.

Moreton-Robinson, A., ed. 2016. *Critical Indigenous Studies: Engagements in First World Locations.* Tucson: University of Arizona Press.

PREFACE

Education, once used as a tool to assimilate American Indian youth, today is a means to strengthen and rebuild Native Nations.* In this book, *American Indian Studies: Native PhD Graduates Gift Their Stories*, Native PhD graduates from American Indian Studies (AIS) at the University of Arizona (UArizona), the first such program to offer a freestanding degree, share stories about their educational experiences and how doctoral education has shaped their identities, lives, relationships, and careers.** Their stories reflect a broader emphasis in the field of AIS in which many scholars count themselves as activists both in scholarship and practice in and outside the academy because their central focus is service to Native communities (James 2016).

This book originated as an idea of co-editor Mark Blair during his doctoral coursework and the writing of his dissertation, which was reinforced during the twentieth-anniversary celebration of the UArizona American Indian studies doctorate program in 2017. Mark, a graduate of Dartmouth College, was familiar with the book *First Person First Peoples* by Andrew Garrod and Colleen Larimore (1997), which I used in my American Indian higher education class. The book was a model for our publication. Our goal for this book is to help Native students aspiring to a PhD in AIS, or another

---

American Indian, Native American, First Nations, Indian, Native, and *Indigenous* are used interchangeably to refer to the Indigenous Peoples of what are now known as the United States and Canada.

**The terms *UArizona* and *UA* are used interchangeably in this book to refer to the University of Arizona, Tucson, Arizona.

graduate program, get a realistic picture of what it takes to earn the degree and how the PhD can impact one's life. It is also a contribution to the sparse scholarship that is currently available on American Indian graduate students.

The editors asked Native UArizona AIS PhD graduates to write about their educational experiences earning their doctorates using storytelling, a traditional means of passing knowledge and information for Native Peoples. In the resulting chapters, nine Native graduates who hold the highest scholarly degree in the academy from the first AIS program highlight their personal voices and stories, sharing their messages, lessons, and advice as gifts to future American Indian graduate students.

Personal stories of mentorship, networking, relationships, reciprocity, sacrifices, commitment, challenges, and triumphs shape this book. These stories are unique to the individuals, their families, and their communities. Their narratives provide insight into the journeys of American Indian graduate students pursuing advanced degrees and their experiences after earning the degree. We (co-editors) hope that giving voice to the AIS Native doctoral graduates in these stories will inspire future generations of American Indian students to follow in their footsteps—stories that are realistic so Native students are better prepared to succeed.

The AIS program at the UArizona has a rich history of leadership in the field, especially in graduate education with the creation of the first free-standing AIS master's degree in 1982 and first PhD in the United States in 1997. This program is a place where students interested in Native cultures, Peoples, and experiences can earn degrees in AIS instead of a concentration or minor in ethnic studies, American studies, political science, anthropology, or other disciplines. To date, the AIS doctoral graduates from the University of Arizona number over fifty.

Many individuals contributed to the creation and success of the AIS doctoral program at UArizona during its development. The degree would not have happened without the hard work and input of faculty, staff, students, and administrators at the time, especially the core faculty who revised and finalized the PhD proposal and guided it through the necessary academic channels to become a reality with the arrival of the first class in fall 1997. The core faculty included Drs. Jay Stauss, director/head; Tom Holm; K. Tsianina Lomawaima; Michelle Grijalva; Mary Jo Tippeconnic Fox; Nancy Parezo; Mary Willie; and many other affiliate faculty from across the university, such as Dr. Ofelia Zepeda, Robert Williams, Dr. N. Scott Momaday, Emory

Sekaquaptewa, and Dr. Larry Evers. Luci Tapahonso, Dr. Bob Martin, Eileen Luna-Firebaugh, Dr. Franci Washburn, and Dr. Manley Begay joined the AIS faculty in the early years of the doctoral program. Most of these faculty are now retired or have moved on, but their contribution to the development and success of AIS remains. Many of these faculty and staff are mentioned by the individual chapter authors as impacting their education and lives while students before and after graduation.

We want to thank the nine Native American AIS doctoral graduates who contributed to this book by sharing their unique personal stories. They are some of the first to hold a PhD in AIS, which is significant in itself. These graduates hold positions across the country in higher education (mainstream universities and tribal colleges and universities); tribal, state, federal, and local governments; Native organizations; business; and other areas. Their stories, lives, and careers are truly inspirational; we appreciate their contributions to the scholarship on Native American Indian graduate students and American Indian studies.

Wa do

Uh-dah-ko (Thank you)

—*Mary Jo Tippeconnic Fox, PhD*
(Comanche/Cherokee)

References

Garrod, Andrew, and Colleen Larimore, eds. 1997. *First Person First Peoples: Native American College Graduates Tell Their Life Stories*. Ithaca: Cornell University Press.

James, Jesse. 2016. "Scholarship as Activism in the Field of Native Studies." *International Journal of Conflict Engagement and Resolution* 4 (1): 90–103.

AMERICAN INDIAN STUDIES

Introduction

KESTREL A. SMITH

Past, Present, Future: Celebrating Twenty Years of Doctoral Education

On November 2 and 3, 2017, colleagues, advocates, and constituents of the University of Arizona's (UArizona) American Indian Studies (AIS) program gathered to celebrate the twentieth anniversary of the first AIS PhD program in the United States. Navajo Nation Poet Laureate Luci Tapahonso's (2008) poem, *A Blessing*, set the agenda in motion, offering words of encouragement and appreciation for the AIS graduates at UArizona:

> May the words we speak go forth as bright beads
> of comfort, joy, humor, and inspiration.
> We have faith that the graduates will inspire others
> to explore and follow their interests. (45–47)

These two days of celebration and commemoration included panels and presentations by UArizona AIS faculty, alumni, and affiliates on issues surrounding Native law and policy, education, natural resources, and literature. Doctoral graduates shared stories of how they have utilized the knowledge and experience acquired from the UArizona AIS program in their careers, and the contributions they are now making to the fields of academia, Native and non-Native governments, and public services. Together, their journeys illustrate the collective power of change made possible by the AIS program in supporting and shaping the educational, political, economic, cultural, and social well-being of Native communities across North America.

American Indian Studies: Native PhD Graduates Gift Their Stories provides a forum for nine of these Native doctoral graduates to share the impact the UArizona AIS program has had in their personal and professional lives with a broader audience. I am grateful to have attended the AIS PhD program at UArizona alongside several of the contributors in this book. The friendships and collegiality built during our shared time in the AIS program has remained as we each charted our own paths following graduation. Contributing alongside all of the authors in this collection is a privilege and honor. Their successes are essential to highlight considering that the number of Native doctoral graduates in the United States, in any field of study, has seen little growth over the last decade (Blair 2015; National Science Foundation 2018; Patel 2014). According to the National Science Foundation *Survey of Earned Doctorates* (2018), the percentage of the American Indian or Alaska Native population graduating with doctoral degrees remained under 1 percent between 2006 and 2016:

Doctorates earned by underrepresented minority U.S. citizens and permanent residents: 2006–16

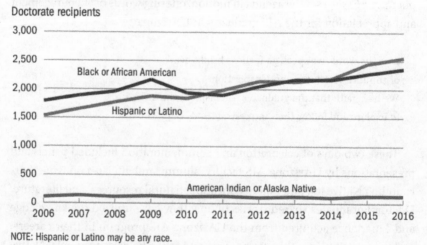

NOTE: Hispanic or Latino may be any race.

Source: National Science Foundation 2018, 3.

The personal narratives of struggle and success shared throughout this book help to reduce the invisibility of Native doctoral students and graduates in the larger mainstream dialogue that result from such statistics (Blair 2015; Brayboy et al. 2012; Shotton et al. 2013). While each student has their own path to walk, these stories can also serve to empower others to reach their own educational goals, whether it be in an AIS program or other field of study.

Origins of AIS in Higher Education

As an academic field, AIS is a relatively new addition to mainstream higher education compared to the more "traditional" STEM disciplines of science, technology, engineering, and mathematics. Having roots in student-led political activism of the 1960s and 1970s civil rights movement, AIS emerged out of a heightened awareness of the proportionately low numbers of African American, Hispanic, and Native students in mainstream U.S. institutions of higher education (Kidwell and Velie 2005; Champagne and Stauss 2002). However, whereas the majority of the country was primarily focused on the first two groups referenced above, the AIS movement had its own agenda as it related to Native communities, experiences, and sovereignty. Specifically, these efforts focused on integrating unique Native perspectives and objectives into the mainstream academic framework in order to foster an intellectual space for Native Peoples to explore, promote, and revitalize their traditional and contemporary cultures and knowledges on their own terms.

Interdisciplinary in nature, AIS blends multiple subjects otherwise seen as stand-alone disciplines in mainstream academia, such as law and policy, natural sciences, education, economics, and literature, and connects them through the lens of the lived Native experience. Perhaps the most unique aspect of AIS as an academic field is the way in which the inherent sovereignty of Native Nations acts as the common thread that weaves through these disciplines, uniting them to create a distinct field of study. Among the earliest pieces of literature used in AIS curricula were *House Made of Dawn* (Momaday 1968), *Custer Died for Your Sins: An Indian Manifesto* (Deloria 1969), *Bury My Heart at Wounded Knee: An Indian History of the American West* (Brown 1970), and *Black Elk Speaks: Being the Life Story of a Holy Man of the Oglala Sioux* (Black Elk and Neihardt 1932) (Kidwell and Velie 2005). According to Kidwell and Velie (2005, 6), "Up until *House Made of Dawn* appeared in 1968,

TABLE I.1 Native American studies programs by region

Eastern United States	28
North Central United States	45
Western United States	43
South Central United States	6
Alberta, Canada	4
Ontario, Canada	11
British Columbia, Canada	6
Manitoba, Canada	3
New Brunswick, Canada	1
Nova Scotia, Canada	1
Saskatchewan, Canada	3
Quebec, Canada	4

Source: Nelson 2018, 2–3.

Indians had published only nine novels in the United States"; however, these early texts spurred growth in the area of Native-authored literature and collectively began to build the AIS canon from within. In doing so, it cultivated a space for Native Peoples and communities to have a more prominent voice in the academic and political landscapes that had habitually omitted them in the past. Among the earliest institutions to begin creating such a presence included the University of Arizona, the University of California at Berkeley, and the University of Minnesota (Blair 2015; Kidwell and Velie 2005); the first serves as the focus of this book.

Over five decades later, the field of AIS, including Native American studies and Indigenous studies programs, has expanded to include numerous undergraduate and graduate programs across the United States and Canada. The *Guide to Native American Studies Programs in the United States and Canada* edited by Robert M. Nelson (2018) attempts to present a comprehensive list of academic institutions in the United States and Canada that offer at least one major or minor undergraduate, graduate, or certificate program in this field of study. This database includes over 150 programs across North America, listing multiple campuses of the same institution individually, such as the University of Wisconsin–Green Bay and the University of Wisconsin–Madison. According to this guide, the UArizona AIS program is one of forty-three total programs in the "Western U.S. Region" (Nelson 2018, 2–3).

Most of these programs are offered under the umbrella of a broader discipline such as ethnic studies, American studies, or anthropology, rather than as a "pure" program where a degree is awarded in American Indian studies/Native American studies/Indigenous studies (Blair 2015). The UArizona AIS program, however, is currently one of only three "pure" doctoral programs in the United States, the other two being from the University of California, Davis's Native American Studies program and the University of Alaska

Fairbanks's Indigenous Studies program (Blair 2015). While the terminology of each program differs, their foci are similar in their concentration on the experiences and sovereignty of the communities, nations, and cultures indigenous to North America.

History of AIS at UArizona

The UArizona Tucson campus resides on the traditional homelands of the Tohono O'odham and Pascua Yaqui nations. Located in a state with twenty-two reservations, and only an hour's drive from several of them, UArizona is situated in a place that presents great potential to positively impact both on- and off-reservation Native communities. The campus's close location to large reservations such as the Navajo Nation is one reason why the AIS program attracts a high number of Diné (Navajo) students; a trend reflected in the fact that five out of the nine chapter authors in this book identify as Diné. The desire to remain close to home often influences Native students' decisions on where to attend college. As a land-grant institution, UArizona is charged with the responsibility of serving the population within the state, approximately 5 percent of which is "American Indian and Alaska Native, alone" (U.S. Census Bureau, n.d.). The development of the AIS program at UArizona is one way in which the institution can serve this population by facilitating an appropriate space for Native Peoples to engage their own unique perspectives within academic dialogue and scholarship. In doing so, the AIS program also creates a more welcoming and familiar intellectual environment for many Native students who otherwise considered mainstream academia to be too foreign or intimidating, thus helping to increase Native college student enrollment in the United States.

The AIS program at UArizona began to materialize in 1968 with the submission of an official program proposal largely spearheaded by Edward P. Dozier (Tewa), the first Native PhD anthropology graduate in the United States (Stauss, Tippeconnic Fox, and Lowe 2002). Together with other faculty and staff at UArizona, Dozier worked to develop an academic framework centered on traditional and contemporary knowledges and experiences of Native Peoples and communities. By 1970, these collaborations led to the creation of the groundbreaking American Indian Studies program at UArizona, of which Dozier was the first chair (Stauss, Tippeconnic Fox, and Lowe 2002). Unfortunately, Dozier passed away in 1971, only one year after taking on this new role and only two months before the university was awarded a five-year, $500,000 grant by the Ford Foundation to support the creation and growth of the new AIS program (Stauss, Tippeconnic Fox, and Lowe 2002). Among the goals for this grant, "the university committed itself to expanding Indian faculty and staff; . . . increasing scholarship aid to Indian students; . . . [and] improving retention by expanding Indian student counseling services" (Stauss, Tippeconnic Fox, and Lowe 2002, 86).

Following Dozier's death, Emory Sekaquaptewa (Hopi) served as chair of the UArizona AIS program from 1971 to 1976, followed by Jay Stauss (Jamestown Band S'Klallam) from 1976 to 1978 (Stauss, Tippeconnic Fox, and Lowe 2002). The AIS program experienced growing pains in these early years, particularly with regard to issues of hiring Native faculty members through the 1971 Ford Foundation grant. Although the grant led to the hiring of seven new faculty members at UArizona, Stauss was the only Native faculty member out of these preliminary hires. Additionally, none of the seven were full-time AIS faculty, as they were all cross affiliated with other departments at the university (Stauss, Tippeconnic Fox, and Lowe, 2002). This lack of new Native faculty hires ultimately led to the termination of the Ford Foundation grant, as UArizona was not fulfilling one of the commitments it had initially made to increase the number of Native faculty and staff at the institution (Stauss, Tippeconnic Fox, and Lowe 2002). However, despite these early challenges in obtaining Native faculty, the AIS program did succeed in establishing an AIS BA minor as well as increasing the number and variety of AIS courses available to students at the university during this time (American Indian Studies Research Center 1991).

In 1978, Vine Deloria Jr. (Standing Rock Sioux) assumed the role of AIS director and led efforts to develop graduate-level AIS courses and degrees at UArizona. These plans were set in motion in 1979 through the formation of an AIS concentration within the already-established political science MA program at the university with the goal of yielding graduates knowledgeable in federal Indian law and policy issues (Stauss, Tippeconnic Fox, and Lowe 2002). In 1981, Robert K. Thomas (Cherokee) became director of the AIS program and continued on with these early efforts, leading to the launch of an independent AIS MA program in the fall of 1982. This milestone was significant not only as the first degree program of its kind in the United States but also in the recognition it brought the entire AIS field of study as an indication of its validity within mainstream academia (Stauss, Tippeconnic Fox, and Lowe 2002). The MA program saw swift growth in student enrollment, further demonstrating its capacity to act as a leader in this evolving field. In its third year (1985–1986), the AIS MA program had sixteen students actively enrolled, the single largest AIS graduate student body in the United States at the time (American Indian Studies Research Center 1991). By the 1991–1992 academic year, the AIS MA program student enrollment had increased to thirty, including Native and non-Native students from both the United States and Canada (American Indian Studies Research Center 1991).

The number of Native scholars joining UArizona as cross-listed AIS faculty also increased during this time, such as N. Scott Momaday (Kiowa) and Leslie Silko (Laguna Pueblo), both with the English Department; Thomas Holm (Creek-Cherokee) with the Political Science Department; and Alice Paul (Tohono O'odham) with the College of Education (Thomas 1984). The expanding scope of faculty expertise in the AIS program also led to the development of additional course subjects during this time. The MA program grew from its original political science focus to include additional areas such as American Indian education, linguistics, societies, and literature. The addition of these new classes not only helped to meet the academic needs and interests of students already enrolled in the program but also facilitated increased enrollment of additional students with more diverse backgrounds and goals.

The growth of the AIS program did not stop with the MA degree and in fact saw rapid progress follow. In 1984, the UArizona Graduate College approved a PhD minor in AIS, and by the 1988–1989 academic year there were four doctoral students minoring in the program (American Indian Studies Research Center 1991; Stauss, Tippeconnic Fox, and Lowe 2002). Additionally, internal AIS negotiations began in the 1992–1993 academic year to formulate a proposal for a full PhD program in AIS (Stauss, Tippeconnic Fox, and Lowe 2002). Two years later (1994–1995), the AIS program made a move from the College of Social and Behavioral Sciences to the UArizona Graduate College to enable more self-control over its future direction (Stauss, Tippeconnic Fox, and Lowe 2002). That same academic year, the AIS program revised its PhD proposal and had it approved by the Graduate College during the 1996–1997 academic year, welcoming its first students in the fall 1997 semester (Stauss, Tippeconnic Fox, and Lowe 2002). The UArizona AIS doctoral program was designed to prepare

> graduate students for academic careers; to conduct advanced and applied scholarly research from a cross-cultural perspective; to develop innovative theories, methodologies, and research tools appropriate for and useful to

sovereign tribes; and to educate students to assume leadership and policy making roles in higher education, tribal communities, the state and nation. (Tippeconnic Fox, Nelson, and Stauss 2001, 56)

Currently, the AIS PhD program plan of study requires the successful completion of a minimum of sixty-six credits, encompassing forty-eight coursework credits and eighteen dissertation credits (University of Arizona, n.d.). The program offers five concentration areas: education, environment/ natural resources, law and policy, society and culture, and literature. All doctoral students are required to take at least fifteen credits within one concentration area as well as at least one course in two other concentration areas to ensure a broad yet balanced education on issues impacting Native communities (University of Arizona, n.d.).

As the first PhD in AIS in the United States, this program holds distinction as producing the nation's first doctoral graduates in AIS and remains a leader in graduating students who go forth to support Native communities in a variety of ways (Stauss, Tippeconnic Fox, and Lowe 2002; Blair 2015; Kidwell and Velie 2005; Tippeconnic Fox, Nelson, and Stauss 2001). According to Blair (2015, 147), "With over 300 alumni, UA[rizona] AIS graduate programs boast the largest network of any of the graduate programs in AIS." Outside of the AIS program, the University of Arizona/Sloan Indigenous Graduate Partnership (UA/SIGP) was established, aimed at increasing the number of Native graduate students in the STEM (science, technology, engineering, and mathematics) fields at UArizona. However, although the UA/SIGP "gets most of the attention and credit for UA[rizona] being the number one institution granting PhDs to Native American students, AIS is responsible for approximately 40% of those Native American doctorates" (Blair 2015, 145). These statistics demonstrate the significant and meaningful scale at which the AIS program positively impacts the Native student body at the university as well as more broadly throughout Native communities via students' postgraduation efforts and careers.

Footsteps of Success: Graduating from the Nation's first PhD Program in AIS

The first cohort of UArizona AIS doctoral students consisted of four women, three of whom were Native. They started classes in the fall 1997 semester, joining the already-existing AIS graduate student body of over fifty MA students at the university (Stauss, Tippeconnic Fox, and Lowe 2002). These four students served as "contemporary warriors setting the stage for others to follow" (Tippeconnic Fox, Nelson, and Stauss 2001, 56). Indeed, they were joined the next fall semester by two additional female students, and again in the fall 1999 semester by five more students, two of whom were the program's first male students (Stauss, Tippeconnic Fox, and Lowe 2002). In its fourth year (fall 2000), the UArizona AIS doctoral program had enrolled a total of fourteen students, ten of whom were female, establishing a pattern of a primarily female student body, which has continued into the present. Notably, ten of these first fourteen AIS PhD students were Native, demonstrating the program's ability to attract and support Native students, a trend that also continues to the present (Stauss, Tippeconnic Fox, and Lowe 2002).

Four and a half years after the creation of its groundbreaking PhD program, the UArizona AIS program awarded its first doctoral degree in the fall 2001 semester (Stauss, Tippeconnic Fox, and Lowe 2002). This milestone was also significant in that it was the first degree of its kind to be awarded in the United States. The first Native PhD graduate of the AIS program ensued in the spring 2005 semester. Following in the footsteps of these first graduates, the AIS program has since conferred over fifty additional doctoral degrees, over thirty of which have been to Native graduates. Furthermore, the AIS program has awarded nearly thirty PhD minors to students majoring in disciplines such as education, natural resources, law, and nursing, further enabling them to blend AIS-related knowledge and experience with other fields of study and resultant careers.

Student enrollment in the UArizona AIS doctoral program has steadily increased nearly every year since its

TABLE 1.2 UArizona AIS PhD enrollment

Academic Year	PhD Enrollment
1999–2000	16
2000–2001	14
2001–2002	17
2002–2003	24
2003–2004	25
2004–2005	25
2005–2006	24
2006–2007	28
2007–2008	30
2008–2009	27
2009–2010	28
2010–2011	29
2011–2012	31
2012–2013	33
2013–2014	34

Source: Blair 2013.

creation. By the 2013–2014 academic year, the program had reached a total of thirty-four actively enrolled students, the largest enrollment to that date.

During these years student interest and enrollment in the AIS BA minor also continued to grow, and in fall 2015 the AIS program launched its BA major (Blair 2015). This additional degree option rounded out the UArizona AIS program, now offering degrees at all levels of higher education and further increasing its potential impact within Native communities. Additionally, the AIS program also offers three AIS graduate certificates in Native Nation Building, Renewable Natural Resources, and Higher Education.

In Their Own Voice

American Indian Studies: Native PhD Graduates Gift Their Stories is a collection of personal narratives from nine Native graduates of the UArizona AIS doctoral program. Here, these alumni tell their own stories of endurance and resiliency, hardship and struggles, and accomplishment and success in their own words. Not only do their perspectives provide insight into the diverse and dynamic experiences of Native doctoral students but they also serve as role models of encouragement for those following in their footsteps. In all ways, they illustrate the extensive benefits of having an AIS program at a mainstream academic institution, not just for the students enrolled but for Native communities as well.

While there is an undeniable interconnectedness among many of the experiences, challenges, and successes within the nine authors' stories, three overarching themes emerge in ways that more strongly connect certain chapters together: (1) family and kinship (Ali-Joseph, Badoni, and Tsosie-Paddock); (2) mentorship (Lerma, Clark, and Spoonhunter); and (3) service and giving back (Hale, Redhouse, and White). Chapters are organized in this way, and a more thorough discussion of each theme follows these nine chapters in the conclusion. For each graduate, the University of Arizona served as a focal point in their journey to a meaningful career. While each of their stories is uniquely their own, they all share one common thread: the educational benefits that the American Indian Studies PhD program at the University of Arizona provides to those who walk through their doors. These are their stories, narrated in their own voices.

Current Positions of the Nine UArizona PhD Chapter Authors

Alisse Ali-Joseph, PhD (Oklahoma Choctaw)
Assistant Professor, Applied Indigenous Studies
Faculty Athletics Representative, Office of the President
Northern Arizona University

Georgina Badoni, PhD (Diné)
Assistant Professor, Native American Studies
Department of Anthropology
College of Arts and Sciences
Borderlands and Ethnic Studies Program Affiliated Faculty
New Mexico State University

Aresta Tsosie-Paddock, PhD (Diné)
Assistant Professor
Department of American Indian Studies
Department of Linguistics
University of Arizona

Michael Lerma, PhD (P'urhépecha)
Dean of the School of Business and Social Science
Diné College

Ferlin Clark, PhD (Diné)
President
Bacone College

Tarissa Spoonhunter, PhD (Arapaho/Blackfeet)
Associate Professor, American Indian Studies
Central Wyoming College

Michelle L. Hale, PhD (Navajo, Laguna, Chippewa, Odawa)
Assistant Professor, American Indian Studies
Honors Faculty, Barrett, the Honors College
Senior Sustainability Scholar, Global Institute of Sustainability (GIOS)
Arizona State University

Gregory I. Redhouse, PhD (Diné)
Assistant Professor of Economics
School of Business and Social Science
Diné College

Louellyn White, PhD (Kanien'kehá:ka [Mohawk]/Akwesasne)
Associate Professor
First Peoples Studies Program
Concordia University

References

American Indian Studies Research Center. 1991. *Academic Program Review: Self Study*. Tucson: University of Arizona.

Black Elk, and J. G. Neihardt. 1932. *Black Elk Speaks: Being the Life Story of a Holy Man of the Oglala Sioux*. New York: W. Morrow.

Blair, M. 2013. *American Indian Studies Annual Program Review*. Tucson: University of Arizona.

Blair, M. 2015. "Taking the Next Step: Promoting Native American Student Success in American Indian/Native American Studies Graduate Programs." PhD diss., University of Arizona. http://hdl.handle.net/10150/556961.

Brayboy, B. M. J., A. J. Fann, A. E. Castagno, and J. A. Solyom. 2012. *Postsecondary Education for American Indian and Alaska Natives: Higher Education for Nation Building and Self-Determination*. Hoboken: Wiley.

Brown, D. 1970. *Bury My Heart at Wounded Knee: An Indian History of the American West*. New York: Holt, Rinehart, and Winston.

Champagne, D., and J. Stauss. 2002. "Introduction: Defining Indian Studies Through Stories and Nation Building. In *Native American Studies in Higher Education: Models for Collaboration Between Universities and Indigenous Nations*, edited by D. Champagne and J. Stauss, 1–15. New York: AltaMira.

Deloria, V., Jr. 1969. *Custer Died for Your Sins: An Indian Manifesto*. New York: Macmillan.

Kidwell, C. S., and A. Velie. 2005. *Native American Studies*. Lincoln: University of Nebraska Press.

Momaday, N. S. 1968. *House Made of Dawn*. New York: Harper and Row.

National Science Foundation. 2018. *2016 Doctorate Recipients from U.S. Universities*. Alexandria, Va.: National Science Foundation. https://www.nsf.gov/statistics /2018/nsf18304/static/report/nsf18304-report.pdf.

Nelson, R. M., ed. 2018. "A Guide to Native American Studies Programs in the United States and Canada." Accessed September 14, 2021. https://cpb-us-w2.wpmucdn .com/sites/uwm.edu/dist/f/241/files/2018/07/guide-1dq2hx4.pdf.

Patel, V. 2014. "Why So Few American Indians Earn Ph.D.'s, and What Colleges Can Do About It." *Chronicle of Higher Education*, May 27, 2014. https://www.chronicle .com/article/Why-So-Few-American-Indians/146715.

Shotton, H. J., S. C. Lowe, and S. J. Waterman, eds. 2013. *Beyond the Asterisk: Understanding Native Studies in Higher Education*. Sterling, Va.: Stylus.

Stauss, J., M. J. Tippeconnic Fox, and S. Lowe. 2002. "American Indian Studies at the University of Arizona." In *Native American Studies in Higher Education: Models for Collaboration Between Universities and Indigenous Nations*, edited by D. Champagne and J. Stauss, 83–96. New York: AltaMira.

Tapahonso, L. 2008. *A Radiant Curve: Poems and Stories*. Tucson: University of Arizona Press.

Thomas, R. K., ed. 1984. *Memorandum: Unit History for American Indian Studies Program*. Tucson: University of Arizona.

Tippeconnic Fox, M. J., C. E. Nelson, and J. H. Stauss. 2001. "American Indian Studies Programs at the University of Arizona." *Indigenous Nations Studies Journal* 2 (1): 55–69.

University of Arizona. n.d. *Doctor of Philosophy in American Indian Studies: Ph.D. Degree Guidelines*. https://ais.arizona.edu/sites/ais.arizona.edu/files/PhD%20 Guidelines12_13_0.pdf.

U.S. Census Bureau. n.d. "Quick Facts: Arizona." Accessed July 14, 2021. https://www .census.gov/quickfacts/AZ.

CHAPTER 1

Nan Ikhvnanchi, Nan Ikhvnanchi, Keyu Hokma Pi Illachi (Educate, Educate, or We Perish)

ALISSE ALI-JOSEPH

(OKLAHOMA CHOCTAW)

On May 31, 1968, my grandfather, Albert Ali, lay in a hospital bed dying, blinded by a disease that would soon take his spirit to another place. Over the telephone he heard a gymnasium filled with hundreds of people present to honor him as a man, husband, father, athlete, teacher, and friend. Over the loudspeaker he heard the gym dedicated to him in thanksgiving for his love and devotion to athletics, his sportsmanship on and off the court, and his kind and generous demeanor as a coach, teacher, and friend. On March 31, 2012, forty-four years later, my grandfather was inducted into the Northern California Sports Hall of Fame. Sport has long been present and important to my family and has also served as the driving factor in my pursuit of college.

The community bestowed these honors because my grandfather epitomized important qualities of life: humility, kindness, unconditional love for his family and friends, resiliency, and the ability to create positive outcomes from hardships and challenges for the entire community.

Albert Ali was a man who, through his athletic talents and sportsmanship, was recognized as a sports phenomenon in the 1930s and 1940s. Athletics offered him the opportunity to share his passions and talents and the chance to give them back to the ones he loved and who loved him. He exemplified that organized team and individual sport transcend the playing field and can serve as a guide for how to live our lives with health and dignity. His teachings and passion for athletics became important to me and they have provided a model of what a healthy, well-balanced life should be like.

Walking down Ali Avenue at the local high school, playing high school basketball in the gym named after my grandfather, and receiving the Albert Ali Sports Award, which is presented to the most accomplished male and female senior athlete every year at my high school, are gifts, experiences, and memories that I cherish. In each, I feel his presence and his desire for life. When a sixty-year-old man hugs me and cries after finding out I am Albert Ali's granddaughter, I feel awe. I do know that my Grandpa Ali epitomizes the tribute "a true champion is one who remains calm in situations that unnerve the ordinary." His talents and personal attitude stretched far beyond the county line and are treasured by those who knew him and who have heard his story. I know it was sport and athletic activities that provided him with the discipline, the knowledge, the confidence, and the skills to be able to impart his wisdom to others, including to me. Sport is important. Sport enables.

I begin with remembering my Grandpa Ali because my journey through higher education is imbued with a collage of role models, triumphs, fails, and stories of resilience. I would not have overcome the difficult times, and continued to feed off my successes, without my family and friends and their unwavering love. I see my story beginning with the marriage of my Grandpa Ali and Grammy Robinson. I find strength in both of their own individual stories and the kind, generous, and loving people they were. I often find myself marveling in their resilience and how their hard work has allowed me to reach my personal and professional goals.

I entered a faculty position at Northern Arizona University (NAU) in the Applied Indigenous Studies Department in 2013, where I specialize in the importance of sports and physical activity as a vehicle for empowerment, resilience, cultural identity, health, and educational attainment for American Indian People. I was appointed by the president of NAU as the faculty athletics representative in fall 2015. In this role, I work with the athletic department to maintain academic integrity with student-athletes and faculty, and to ensure the overall well-being of student-athletes. Both of these positions mirror my grandparents and their love of education, athletics, and the importance of giving back to the community.

I have long considered myself an athlete; athletics has been a part of my daily life for as long as I can remember. Whether it was hearing these stories of my remarkable grandfather, playing basketball with my brothers, catching a baseball with my dad and uncle, or spending endless hours hitting ground strokes with my mom on the tennis court, I lived and breathed sports as I grew up. My grandmother relocated from Choctaw territory in Oklahoma to Northern California in the 1940s, along with a number of other American Indians during and after World War II. Here she met my Grandpa Ali. My grandparents soon established a home in California. As Grandpa Ali became the local sports star and Grammy had two daughters, they were embraced by the local community. With such strong and deep roots created by my grandparents, my mother and aunt decided to remain in California and raise their children there, since a majority of our Choctaw family had relocated there as well. With little to do besides school, sport became my life.

My dad was a tennis professional at the local racket club and my mom coached the high school women's tennis team, so I grew up on the tennis court and, luckily, I loved it. I often played against boys who were older and better than I was, a situation that forced me to excel, to strive harder to be the best given my ability. Participating in tennis, basketball, and softball as a youth and adolescent gave me many benefits, both physically and mentally, as well as academically, allowing me to earn a scholarship and play tennis in college. The game has also defined who I am and how I see myself; it helps me know my capabilities are greater than I think and how hard work and resolution can aid me in achieving my goals. Pursuing a college degree was a goal I set for myself growing up. In my Choctaw culture, education has historically been very important. We have a saying, "Nan ikhvnanchi, nan ihvnanchi, keyu hokma pi illachi," which means, "Educate, educate, or we perish."

In 1815 Choctaws invited missionaries into Mississippi for the sole purpose of educating their children in American ways and English. Tribal leaders felt the only hope for our People lay in the education of the young and the adoption of European institutions. Although the use of formalized schooling was an instrument to transform the Choctaw culture for some, and while some resisted this change, many Choctaw leaders and tribal members welcomed schooling as necessary for their national survival. In the Treaty of Dancing Rabbit Creek, they negotiated funding for schools in Oklahoma as part of the removal agreement. Soon after arriving in Oklahoma as a result of the Trail of Tears in 1838, Choctaws set up their own school systems. Tribal leaders favored schools because they believed Euro-American education would protect them from federal and state governmental policies as well as the intrusion of white settlers. Thus, we see that the importance of education was embraced by the Choctaw People, and this is one reason why it is so imperative to them today (Crum 2007).

However, the passion driving me toward college was not solely obtaining a degree, knowledge, or a skill that would help me and my community; it was also playing collegiate tennis. During high school, tennis motivated me to seek a college education. This meant playing tennis for four hours a day, waking up at 4:00 a.m. in order to go for a run and work on my endurance, and staying up well into the night studying to earn a 4.0 GPA, which would give me a better chance to receive a collegiate scholarship. I also knew that competing under pressure and performing well in front of others was as important as hitting the ball forcefully and accurately if I wanted to be recruited. I spent weekends traveling to tournaments around California, earning a top-ten ranking in the Northern California Juniors in 1998, an accomplishment that caught the eye of college coaches. My time and dedication proved successful; I won the Northern California San Joaquin Sections during my senior year in high school and received scholarship offers from four universities in California. My dream, which I had had since the first day I picked up a tennis racket at six years old, had come true. Doors had opened; *a good path*, as my Choctaw ancestors would say, was before me.

After much reflection, I decided to attend the University of California, Davis (UC Davis). There were many reasons for this decision; one was the possibility of mentorship. It was there that I had felt the strongest connection with the coach and team during the recruiting trip. One of the deciding factors for me to attend UC Davis was the tennis coach, Bill Maze. His kind demeanor, sense of humor, and knowledge of and respect for the game all contributed to my choice; the fact that he played tennis at Stanford with the former number-one player in the world, John McEnroe, as his doubles partner was also a perk. Since both my mom and dad coached me growing up, I understood the importance of teaching others and the influence a positive instructor can have on a player's life. When I met Billiam (as I grew to call him) we had an instant bond, and throughout my college career he became a solid friend and supporter. The respect that I held for him contributed to my success on the tennis court and in the classroom. His coaching enhanced my tennis skills, and his keen awareness that I was a student first and a tennis player second reinforced the importance of excelling academically. Additionally, the campus was only an hour and a half away from home and family, and interaction with my family was and has remained very important to me.

Academically, UC Davis had a Native American Studies program, a major I was interested in pursuing in order to work for and give back to my Choctaw community. I made the right choice.

Throughout my four years at UC Davis, I played collegiate tennis on a full scholarship where my coach and teammates became a huge factor in my success and persistence through college. But, as happens for some collegiate athletes, it was never my entire life. My new community called. I became actively involved with the Native American Student Association and served as chair of the Native American Culture Days and Powwow on campus. I was also elected president of the Student Athlete Advisory Committee, where I acted as the liaison between all student-athletes and the UC Davis president's office, making sure the student-athlete voice was heard around campus. Volunteering for these positions ultimately balanced my college experience, so I gained greater awareness and confidence in fostering dialogue between the different sectors of my college life. My positions gave me the opportunity to bring in Billy Mills as the main speaker for the Native American Culture Days in 2001. Mills, a Lakota man, was a star runner at Haskell Indian College in 1955–57 and went on to win the gold medal in the 10,000-meter run at the 1964 Olympic Games in Tokyo. The audience was filled with people affiliated with Native American Studies and student-athletes. This would be one of many times that Mr. Mills and I would promote academics and athletics together. In 2016 he was the keynote speaker in Resilience and Culture Through Sport, a program that I founded at NAU and which will be discussed later in my story.

These personal experiences made me realize that college did not have to be the isolating experience for American Indian students that I have often read about, nor must student-athletes be primarily submerged in sport for them to succeed. Balance is important. It also became apparent that there was a lack of American Indian representation in contemporary college athletics. Mills noted this in his talk and discussed the responsibilities of athletes like himself, and by extension all in the audience. Billy Mills emphasized the importance of the American Indian athletic role models fostering change in our youth and communities. This began to spark my passion for empowering more American Indian People to pursue the sport they love in college. In 2003 I earned a bachelor's degree in Native American Studies. Tennis had allowed me to compete in a sport I love and to remain physically active; it also had introduced me to the Native American collegiate community and provided an educational pathway that has led me to encourage other Native youth to pursue their dreams using sports as a means of access and vehicle for empowerment. The enjoyment of sport runs deeper than the notion of "winning": it fostered a sense of belonging and self-efficacy. It is a part of who I am and how I think of myself. Sport was a huge factor in my decision to pursue both my master's and doctoral degrees in American Indian Studies (AIS) at the University of Arizona (UA).

After earning my bachelor's degree, I knew my educational journey had just begun. Although I wanted to remain at UC Davis to be close to home for my master's degree, my professors encouraged me to seek graduate degrees at an alternative university in order to increase my "employability" once I completed. I am beyond grateful they recommended UA's AIS graduate program. Once I was accepted and visited Tucson, Arizona, it was love at first sight. I moved to Tucson in August 2004, and this is where I would spend the next nine years of my life. Tucson is where I earned my master's and doctoral degrees, reconnected with my Choctaw community, met lifelong friends and colleagues, and fell in love with my husband and father of my two daughters. Tucson became another "home."

The first day on campus at UA I knew I was home. The faculty, staff, and fellow students in the AIS Department became instant companions and friends. I soon found that graduate school was very different from undergraduate, but I was fortunate that my time in the classroom at UC Davis prepared me for graduate school. I had to become accustomed to being just a "student" and not a "student-athlete," as well as being fourteen hours away from home.

As previously mentioned, I grew up in California, away from my Choctaw community in Oklahoma. While I had a connection with my community, I continued to have a nagging void of how I could give back and contribute to my People. Ironically, as Western education historically separated American Indian People from their communities, my educational experience strengthened my relationship with my Choctaw community. I decided to write my master's thesis on Choctaw higher education, since we have historically placed high value on Western education and a relatively high portion of Choctaw People pursue higher education. Writing the history of education within our community as it had never been written was a means to give back, especially since Choctaw was, in part, helping pay for my graduate education. I spent a summer in Durant, Oklahoma, working in the Choctaw Higher Education Department as part of the internship requirement for the master's program. During this time I reconnected with family, created new relationships, and found a space for myself as an active member of my tribe.

This connection furthered my desire to continue my own education and pursue a PhD in AIS. It also heightened my desire to become a professor myself. After earning my master's in 2006, I immediately began the PhD program in AIS at UA. Initially, I was going to continue to research higher education within different communities as the foundation of my doctoral dissertation, but I continued to feel that something was missing. It was not until my first year of the doctoral program, while taking American Indian Higher Education with Dr. Mary Jo Tippeconnic Fox, that I realized the missing piece was athletics. Nanabah Brewer, a fellow student, presented a paper on American Indian collegiate athletes. She highlighted a chart from the 2002–3 National Collegiate Athletic Association race and ethnicity report in order to show the low numbers of American Indian collegiate athletes. As a collegiate tennis player during that time, I recognized that there were only two American Indian collegiate tennis players charted. I immediately raised my hand and proclaimed that those statistics represented my brother and me. Although it was intriguing to recognize my contribution to sport and that my Grandpa Ali would be pleased with his grandchildren, it also saddened me. With all the benefits playing a college sport has to offer, too few American Indians have the opportunity to take advantage of this experience. Perhaps sports today, with its "multiple meanings," as noted by Bloom (2000), can offer hope and a positive means for American Indian Peoples to achieve a higher education. American Indians have long used sport as a means to achieve a sense of pride, self-esteem, respect, spiritual connection, self-determination, and sovereignty (Bloom 2000, xvii). Just as my grandfather acted as a role model on and off the playing field, American Indian student-athletes alike have the ability to foster hope and change in their communities. After this revelation, and with guidance from my supportive faculty members, my focus shifted toward researching the experiences of American Indian student-athletes and how sport aided in their own educational goals.

My personal experience has led me to believe that sport is and can be a pathway to college for American Indian students who participate in individual or team sports. Sport can be a vehicle by which American Indian athletes obtain educational opportunities through scholarship support, which lessens their financial burdens. Because collegiate sport is valued, there are thousands of athletes who earn university degrees while participating in the sport they love. Yet, why are there so few American Indian collegiate athletes?

I come from a family that has benefited from earning an education through sport. My youngest brother played basketball at California State University, Stanislaus, and has had the opportunity to gain financial support and to travel around California as well as compete and stay physically healthy throughout his college career. My oldest brother won a Division III National Tennis Championship at the University of California, Santa Cruz. Moreover, I have spoken with or heard about hundreds of Native American collegiate athletes across the United States and Canada, yet these numbers are still small. Historically, American Indian individuals have pursued college degrees via sports. Many of these persons are famous and are nationally recognized. Yet, we still see very few American Indian People participating in sport at the collegiate level. In 2019–20, American Indians accounted for only seven-tenths of a percent of athletes (0.3 percent for American Indian men and 0.4 percent for American Indian women) in all three of the National Collegiate Athletic Association (NCAA) divisions, indicating that American Indians/Alaskan Natives account for the lowest percentage of student-athletes. While one would expect low numbers given the American Indian population size in the United States, American Indian collegiate athletes are below parity. Moreover, given the talent of American Indian athletes and popularity of sports within Native communities, the numbers are, unfortunately, low. Between 1999 and 2020, both American Indian men and women represented the lowest percentage of student-athletes in NCAA Divisions I, II, and III (Lapchick 2020).

Based off my personal experience and this alarming data, the purpose of my dissertation, "American Indian Collegiate Athletes: Accessing Education Through Sport," was to gain a more comprehensive understanding of the experiences and motivations of American Indian collegiate athletes. By allowing American Indian collegiate athletes to share their own experiences, this study aimed to explore whether sport is perceived as a mechanism to obtain a college degree and how cultural ties to sport strengthen identity and foster resilience within American Indian communities. My goal was to listen to their stories and to create a platform for change. I was able to interview ten amazing American Indian student-athletes and share their stories. The experience of working with these student-athletes was by far the highlight of my educational career at the University of Arizona.

The foundational education I obtained in the classroom, and the guidance and support from the faculty in AIS to pursue research that I am personally and professionally passionate about, continues to afford me opportunities. I earned my PhD in AIS in April 2013. The morning of my graduation, I remember reflecting upon my experience during my nine years in Tucson. While earning a doctorate was something to be very proud of, I find it second to another experience while in Tucson. Here is where I feel it necessary to talk about myself as a recovering alcoholic. Throughout my graduate education, alcohol had become a controlling factor in my life. Controlling in the sense that it had control of me. For years I continued to tell myself that someone like me (I come from a great family, I am educated, I am an athlete) could not be an alcoholic. Every time I told myself this, I enabled myself to justify my actions by thinking, "I am still in college, everyone drinks." The difference was that I would drink every day, sometimes in the morning and throughout the night. In reality, it was a problem, one that I had for many years. Honestly, I contemplated writing about my struggles with alcohol in this chapter. I then realized how selfish it would be of me to not include it in my story. Being an alcoholic is part of who I am. In fact, today I see being a recovering alcoholic as one of the most positive aspects of who I am as a person. By sharing this, I continue to heal myself and aim to help others in their own healing process.

While growing up, I had a very negative experience with alcohol in my life. My father (who is now sober) was an alcoholic and experiencing him drunk was a normalcy in my childhood and teenage years. I vowed to myself that I would never drink like him, and throughout high school and much of my undergraduate years, alcohol was something that did not interest me. However, things changed at the end of my time at UC Davis and when I moved to Tucson. I will be the first to say that I have a very "addictive" personality. Growing up I was "addicted" to being the best athlete, and I believe this mindset helped earn me a collegiate tennis scholarship. However, when my tennis career came to an end, I had more time on my hands and alcohol became a normal part of my daily routine. My addiction evolved while in Tucson, and although I earned a master's degree with a 4.0 GPA and was halfway through a doctoral degree, alcohol was controlling my life. Luckily, with the support of my wonderful mom and family, I was able to take a year off school, move home, and seek help.

Leaving school was one of the hardest decisions that I have ever had to make, but it was a decision that saved my life. While contemplating the decision, one of my professors told me, "Alisse, education will always be here to come back to. You need to go take care of yourself and come back strong and healthy." I really took this to heart and continue to live off this motto. Unless we take care of ourselves, we cannot be helpful or be a role model to others. Today, I am over eleven years sober and there is not a day that goes by that I am not grateful for this experience. After a year of being away, I moved back to Tucson, met my future husband, graduated with my PhD, accepted a teaching job at NAU and had a beautiful daughter. My time in Tucson was life changing.

The March before I graduated, a job opened in the Applied Indigenous Studies Department at NAU. While putting the final touches on my dissertation, I applied for the position and was fortunate enough to join the Applied Indigenous Studies faculty in August 2013. This marked a huge transition in my life. In the time span of four months, I earned my doctorate degree, got married, became pregnant with my first daughter, moved to Flagstaff, Arizona, and began a new job as a professor. When I look back at this time, I think of how fortunate I was to experience all of these positive things in such a short time. I joined a department whose mission is to "provide students with the knowledge and tools to contribute to the sustainability of indigenous communities in the 21st century" (Northern Arizona University, n.d.). My work environment feels more like family and is a space that my now seven-year-old daughter, Homma, and three-year-old daughter, Chulla, visit on a weekly basis. My colleagues are their aunties and uncles, and my students beg me to bring them to class to babysit anytime my husband (who is also a professor at NAU) and I need an extra hand.

After two years at NAU, another opportunity arose. The faculty athletics representative position became vacant. This position is held by a faculty member who is appointed by the president of NAU and serves to assist in ensuring institutional oversight of the Department of Intercollegiate Athletics, student-athlete welfare, and maintenance of a culture of academic integrity within the athletics program. Below is an excerpt from the cover letter in my application for the faculty athletics representative position:

> It is with passion and great excitement that I write this cover letter to express my interest in the Faculty Athletic Representative position at Northern Arizona University. When I first received the FAR position announcement, I felt like the position was specially designed for me and my research interest

as a faculty member in the Applied Indigenous Studies Department at NAU. The main reason that I am so enthusiastic about this position, and one of my strongest assets that I would bring to the position, is my ability to relate to being both a student-athlete, as well as a faculty member that advocates for the academic success of student-athletes.

My athletic experience also sparked my academic goals. My experience as a student-athlete naturally led to my academic research and goals of exploring the under-represented number of American Indian collegiate athletes within the NCAA. Athletics afforded me the opportunity to play the sport I love while earning an education. My ultimate goal has been to help other youth obtain this same experience. My dissertation, "American Indian Collegiate Athletes: Accessing Education through Sport," explored the impact of sports on American Indian collegiate athletes to determine the factors that both inspired and inhibited them from the pursuit of athletics in college. My research provided the first in-depth look at several American Indian collegiate athletes and how sport helped them reach their educational and professional aspirations.

I believe that the fortunate people that get to work with student-athletes on a daily basis have the best job in the world. I hope to be a part of the NAU Athletic family and support our phenomenal student-athletes as the Faculty Athletic Representative.

I include this cover excerpt because it not only embodies my professional goals and aspirations but also expresses how my upbringing, educational experiences, and personal love of education and sport infiltrate my professional career. Just as my long tenure as a student was motivated by my Choctaw culture and my athletic abilities, my time as a faculty member has been influenced from various channels. My time as a student and an athlete did not have to be separated but could complement each other. Similarly, my various roles as a faculty member at NAU do not need to be "compartmentalized." I was hired to teach in the Applied Indigenous Studies Department in part due to my research surrounding health, wellness, and sport. As highlighted in the excerpt above, I was appointed as the faculty athletics representative because I was a former student-athlete and because of my research surrounding American Indian collegiate athletes. My role as a faculty member in Applied Indigenous Studies and as the faculty athletics representative complement each other not only because of my research but also, and more importantly,

because they both act as spaces to elicit positive change and to build charac-
ter in young peoples' lives. In April 2016, I asked Mr. Billy Mills to serve as
the keynote speaker for the second annual Resilience and Culture Through
Sport Day. As a gold medalist and Lakota man, his presence at NAU elicited
excitement and bridged the athletic and American Indian communities.

In my Choctaw culture, education has historically been very important.
The saying *"Nan ikhvnanchi, nan ikhvnanchi, keyu hokma pi illachi"* *(Educate, educate, or we perish)* is something that gives me strength on a daily
basis. I remember the sacrifices that my People made in order to afford me
the opportunities I have today. My hope is to also leave a footprint for my
beautiful daughters to follow. Sport has impressed a work ethic, health maintenance, and overall balance into my life as a past collegiate tennis player. For
me, sport goes beyond the playing field and permeates other aspects of my
life. My story is, in part, a story of becoming. In this process of becoming,
we can begin to see ourselves as role models, educators, and social agents of
change. Today, a common misconception about American Indian People is
that their race, ethnicity, family structure, and economic status are the major
factors affecting their success or failure in school and, ultimately, in life. This
misconception leads educators and others to view Native People as coming
from such deficient circumstances that they cannot be expected to thrive. I
refuse to accept this misconception and instead see American Indian People
as resilient.

Resilience is a word used to define a set of qualities that foster a process of
successful adaptation and transformation despite risk and adversity (Benard
1995). Persons who are resilient have the capacity to withstand, overcome,
or recover from serious threat (Masten 2001). Simply put, resilience is the
ability to bounce back from adversity. Resilience in the face of adversity is
not new to American Indian People; they have survived numerous genocidal
practices, including removal from homelands, the imposition of the reservation system, and the implementation of boarding schools, which aimed to
destroy Indigenous identity and culture. American Indian People have with-
stood drastic changes in sociopolitical, cultural, and physical environments.
Through my years as a student, athlete, and now college professor, I continue
to see how talented and resilient students and student-athletes act as role
models on and off the playing field and have the ability to foster hope and
change within their communities. I have great admiration for my faculty, fellow students, and experiences within the American Indian Studies program

at the University of Arizona. My time in Tucson embodied strength, growth, family, and a love for education. It is my hope that those reading this chapter will find strength in pursuing their own hopes and dreams.

References

Benard, B. 1995. *Fostering Resilience in Kids: Protective Factors in Family, School and Community*. Portland, Ore.: Western Center for Drug-Free Schools and Communities.

Bloom, J. 2000. *To Show What an Indian Can Do: Sports at Native American Boarding Schools*. Minneapolis: University of Minnesota Press.

Crum, S. 2007. "The Choctaw Nation: Changing the Appearance of American Higher Education, 1830–1907." *History of Education Quarterly* 47 (1): 49–68.

Lapchick, R. 2020. *The 2020 Racial and Gender Report Card*. Orlando, Fla.: Institute for Diversity and Ethics in Sport. https://www.tidesport.org/racial-gender-report -card.

Masten, A. S. 2001. "Ordinary Magic: Resilience Processes in Development." *American Psychologist* 56 (3): 227–38.

Northern Arizona University. n.d. "Welcome: Mission." Applied Indigenous Studies. Accessed July 26, 2021. https://nau.edu/ais/.

CHAPTER 2

T'áá shí ànísht'éego t'éiyá ádoolnííł

GEORGINA BADONI (DINÉ)

For my mother.

I was up at 4:00 a.m. in the morning completing my readings for class. Do you know trying not to wake up the toddler sleeping next to you makes it difficult to highlight key ideas and scribble notes in the margins? When I applied to the American Indian Studies PhD program at the University of Arizona, I had anticipated the challenges of having children and carrying a full-time course load while being a graduate assistant. I realize now I knew little of it. My journey to receiving a PhD begins with who I am, where I come from, and where I have been, and ends with where I am going. The title of my narrative is a Diné expression that my parents would say to me. T'áá shí ànísht'éego t'éiyá ádoolnííł ("The only way it will happen is if I work at it myself") is a fitting expression for a doctorate's journey after the efforts, determination, and desire to seek it.

Shí eí Nát'oh Dine'é Táchii'ni nishłį́, Kinłichii'nii báshíshchíín, Biih Bitoodnii dashicheii, Kinyaa'aanii dashinalí. I am Mountain Tobacco Clan, born for the Red House Clan, my maternal grandfather is Deer Springs Clan, and my paternal grandfather is Tower House Clan. I am from Tiis Yá Tóó, or Blue Canyon, located northeast of Tuba City, Arizona. I grew up in a traditional hogan, not the contemporary ones you see today with windows and flooring and built with drywall. The hogan was built with juniper wood and mud, with red-dirt floors and a barrel welded in half for a stove. The juniper tree that grew next to the hogan was a jungle gym for the kids, and the adults used the branches to hang the butchered sheep. When my cousins would return for the weekend or summer, we would gather under the juniper tree and play peyote meetings. We would have the sick patient, the roadman, someone carrying the drum, and the fire chief. We would put rocks in an empty soda can with a stick for the gourd and sing peyote songs for the instruments. Only Native kids play peyote meetings for fun.

My homeland was acres of painted desert with piñon-juniper trees. The painted desert, known for its vibrant colors and geological topography, to me was where I carved toy trucks out of mudstone and would swim in the muddy puddles that collected on the rez roads from summer monsoon showers. It was where I learned to ride a bike and got my scar on my arm from falling from the juniper tree, but I also witnessed tribal disputes between Navajos and Hopis over land and livestock.

My mother and father are both traditional Diné People; they came from medicine men for fathers and traditional women who practice the Holy People's beliefs and customs. My mother is from Dínebiito, and my father was from Blue Canyon. My mother is Natoh' Dine'é Tachííní; she is born for the Biih Bitoodnii, her maternal grandparent was Kinyaa'aanii, and her paternal grandparent was Tabaaha. Her parents were both traditional Diné; her mother tended to the home, and her father was a medicine man. At an early age, my mom would travel with her father to families that needed his assistance in healing and prayers. He was known to perform specific healing ceremonies.

Like many Native American children, my mom was taken from her home at a young age without her parents' consent to start school. She said the school officials came by one day and picked her up and took her away. She remembers them cutting her long hair and giving her a typical short cut with bangs like you see in boarding school books. If she or other children spoke Navajo, they forcibly had to stand in the corner with soap in their mouths. My mom attended Tuba City Boarding School; there, she lived in the female dormitory. Boarding school rules included being prompt for all meals, no speaking your native language, having to make your bed correctly with no creases and tightly tucked corners, and if you did not do it correctly, your bed was stripped, and you had to do it over again. She said at times she would be crying because she could not do it right. My mom endured punishments for breaking other rules, such as being late, talking back, or questioning teachers. Lice-picking was the worst form of punishment; she said they had to use their fingernails and pick lice strand by strand and put them into a cup. She would speak Navajo, herd sheep, and go to ceremonies at home, but on Sunday nights, she would cry when dropped off.

After the Tuba City Boarding School, my mother went to the Sherman Indian School in Riverside, California. The following year, she had the opportunity to participate in the Indian Placement Program. The Mormons were making frequent visits to homes on the reservation. They would try talking to her mother about the Book of Mormon and attempt to convert her family. My grandmother did not adopt the Mormon faith but saw the placement program as an opportunity for her daughter to receive an education that would prepare her for the future. Her mother reassured her that life on the reservation was tough and did not offer much of a future. With encouragement and permission from her mother, my mom left for Orem, Utah, to begin living with her Mormon family. Though her placement family was pleasant and caring, my mom was bored and missed her mother. After planning with a friend, she purchased a bus ticket to go home. Once home, she refused to go back to the placement program and requested to finish her education at Intermountain High School. The Intermountain curriculum differed from other educational institutions, offering technical training, job placement opportunities, and Native American classes. She graduated from Intermountain.

After hearing about my mother's boarding school history, I did not want to know about my father's boarding school experiences. What I do know is my father went to Tuba City Boarding School but dropped out of school. His father's passing forced him to take on the role of the family's caretaker and get a job to support his younger siblings and mother. He did tell me the story of the boarding school aide that would sternly abuse the boys if they were not following the rules. He recalled being beaten by the dorm aide. Many years after leaving boarding school, my dad said that the same dorm aide who brutally beat the boys when they were children was attacked when he was an older man by some of the boys he beat.

My boarding school experience was different compared to my parents. I was fortunate to come home every night and not stay in the dorms. Though I did not stay in the dorms, the harsh treatment of boarding schools still existed. The boarding schools' negative experiences were tolerable if you had your family; having my cousins attend the same school made the days bearable. Having family gave you security during those bad days, but it was rough on the days you had no one to support you. My grandmother would braid my hair for school; sometimes, she would get fancy with my braids. I remember the day she braided my hair with four strands. The same day a group of older girls from the dorms chased me into the bathroom and circled me to unravel my fancy braided hair. I was left with crimped waves of hair and tears. While at boarding school, the joy I experienced was learning to sing songs in Navajo and cultural enrichment activities.

I was in a boarding school for one year when we were forcibly relocated due to the Navajo-Hopi land dispute and moved to Flagstaff, Arizona, where many others also would relocate. We would return to our home on the reservation on the weekends, but we lived in Flagstaff during the week. I was enrolled in public schools with very few students of color and even fewer kids that looked like me. Public school was the first time I experienced discrimination and racism from teachers and students. I did not know the term for it at a young age, but I felt it. In the first grade, my classroom teacher would send me out of the classroom to receive special education services. I would enter a small room and recite words listed on a wall. Each time I would go to the small room, I was encouraged to read the words and make attempts to go further every time. If I successfully read the words with few or no mistakes, I would pick a small toy from the treasure box. I would try to reach the end of the word list, not to earn a toy but instead not to come back to the small room again. That was the only year I was tested.

Attending public school stirred a new emotion of discomfort being in my skin. At home, we spoke Navajo and English, sometimes interchangeably. We participated in traditional ceremonies and lived by Navajo values. I was taught traditional ways of being from my grandmother, my parents, and extended family members. It was at school where I was treated differently. In the second grade, I got in my first fight. It was with a non-Native boy. It was not a "fight" fight, but the first time I was called racist names. After bombarding me with slurs, he threatened to attack me. I confided in my teacher because that is what we were told to do in schools. I was ignored. I told my dad what happened that day, sharing with him the name-calling and how I would get beaten up. The next day, he walked me to school and demanded to see the principal. I did not sit in on the meeting, but I know my dad. He made it clear that my safety and protection were their jobs on Indian land. Whenever he feels a smidge of injustice or prejudice, my father will remind you that Native Americans were here first, which is our land. The boy never attacked me or called me names again.

The racial name-calling continued throughout elementary school. In the fifth grade, another boy would harass me during class, at recess, in the lunch-room, and at any other opportunity to give me a nasty glare and spew names at me. The day it got unbearable; I locked myself in a bathroom stall over-come with self-hatred. At ten years old, I understood racism. Having those early encounters made it easier to identify racism, but it also made it easier for me to tolerate ignorance.

We were forced to demolish our hogan during high school and remove any evidence we lived on our homelands. The Public Law 93-153 Navajo-Hopi land dispute impacted more than where we lived on the weekends. It impacted our livelihood and how we conducted ourselves as Diné People. Flagstaff became our permanent residence, no weekend trips to the rez. For ceremonies we had, we used relatives' land and homes. The disconnection with our lands was also discontinuation with our language, culture, and identity. At the time of removal, I did not realize the impact relocation had on shaping my Navajo identity. During the years I was removed from the homelands, I had become acclimated to white culture. English became my primary language, Navajo was used infrequently, and switching between the two diminished. When I spoke Navajo, I could hear how detached I had become from my language.

My livelihood's removal influenced relationships with family, participat-ing in ceremonies, school interest, and primarily ensuring identity. I was going to school, but I was barely getting by. I did not take an interest in academics or sports; I lacked the ambition and commitment to further my education. During those four years in high school, I managed to get by with passing grades, but I had no plans after graduation. Most students were plan-ning to attend universities and leaving Flagstaff to go off to college. High school counselors or teachers did not take any interest in my future; they probably did not think of me as a collegiate student. I am positive my friends and some family assumed the same. When I shared with high school ac-quaintances that I graduated from college with my MA and was pursuing my PhD it shocked people. They thought of me as the dumb Navajo girl or the drunk Indian. The drunk Native girl does not shock people. However, a Native woman in higher education does.

Before being a PhD student, I primarily taught on Native American reservations in the Arizona Southwest and the Pacific Northwest in K–12 and tribal college settings for ten years. I started my postsecondary educational path at community college, with courses of interest like painting and art history. After two years were completed and art credits were piling up, I decided to transfer to Northern Arizona University. I knew I wanted to pursue a career in the arts, but I lacked a practicing artist's artistic talent. I considered a bachelor's program in art education, and after much reflection on my personal education experiences, I applied to the teaching program. As part of the application package that I submitted to the program, I shared my educational narrative of the lack of agency, representation, and safety in K–12. I named my teacher that humiliated and terrified me in my account. Thinking back, I vowed not to become that teacher.

Continuing my education past my MA degree was influenced by an incident in the public school system during my first year teaching in a non-Native school. One of my students asked, "Guess what I am, Ms. Badoni!" I replied to the third grader on Halloween day after overlooking her costume, "A hippie?" She responded, "No, I am an Indian." She was wearing a headband with triangles and circle shapes around her head, jeans and a T-shirt with feathers, and faux moccasins with fringe. Indians did not create this image; mainstream culture created a subjective interpretation of what Indians look like. I took this as a sign that my work in Indian education was not done.

Before I applied, I asked a friend who completed her doctoral program at another mainstream institution some questions that weighed heavily on my decision. I did not ask about the difficulty level or if it was worth it. I wanted to know about completing a doctoral program with a child. I wanted to know if it would be manageable; I asked how she balanced coursework and family life. See, my friend knew the answers to some of my questions because she is a mother, and he was a toddler when she started her doctoral program. She asked if I had support from family and friends who would assist in taking care of children while I was studying, reading, and attending classes. She stressed having a support system established while she focused on her studies helped her succeed.

Family support I knew I had. I was fortunate to have my parents take early retirement to take care of my one-year-old son. When I discussed the possibility of returning to school with my parents, they did not seem surprised.

Both parents have always supported my academic endeavors; my mother especially urged me to pursue a doctorate. They encouraged me to apply and reassured me my son would be taken care of. They strongly reiterated in the Navajo language that the education I would be receiving would make my family stronger as we moved forward.

I was the first in my family to earn a bachelor's degree and master's degree, and now am the first to start a PhD program. When I did get accepted, it was exciting and frightening at the same time. The first thought was about how to pay for it; the second was about putting my family through deliberate poverty. Another hard decision I had to make was leaving a profession I loved very much and entering a new study field. I conflicted with myself over this decision until the week classes started. It was a choice between teaching an art position in the Pacific Northwest or beginning a PhD program. It was a struggle to relinquish the art teacher identity I had created for many years. After many discussions and changing my mind back and forth, I decided to pursue a PhD. It was my husband who reassured me that with a PhD degree, I would reach more people.

I began my coursework in the fall of 2014. I took two required courses and was appointed a graduate teaching assistant position. During the first semester as a doctoral student, I needed to develop a schedule that would meet my academic needs and meet my family's needs. My son had become accustomed to staying at home with his cheii (grandfather) and his grandmother, and it was the attention he needed from me at home I needed to solve. I accepted my position as a doctoral student, like accepting a job; I came in daily from 8:30 to 4:30 and scheduled Mondays and Wednesdays to complete my graduate teaching assistant assignment. On Tuesdays, Thursdays, and Fridays, I would work on my coursework. Like I said at the beginning, I would spend early morning hours reading for class while my son slept next to me.

However, some events parents cannot plan for, like a sick kid or broken leg. I was in an evening class in my second year when my son broke his leg. He was jumping on a jumping castle when he landed on his left leg as the pillow was coming up. I got the text message in class from my husband that our son might have a sprained knee. The momma-bear instinct kicked in immediately, and I walked out of class and took my son to the emergency room. I called my parents from the ER and let them know he broke his leg and it would be a couple of days before he would get a cast. They came the following day to help take care of him while I continued to go to school. My parents would often visit to help take care of my son if he was sick or had a doctor's appointment, or help for the weekend so I could finish finals.

At the beginning of my second year as a PhD student, I was at a doctor's appointment for a knee injury when the nurse told me I could not get an X-ray since I was pregnant. Yes. Pregnant. My older son had just turned three when we were pregnant again. Flashes of his milestones came back to me, along with the other memories of sleep schedules, breastfeeding, and child-care. I immediately began to worry about managing my coursework, keeping my teaching position, and graduating on time while rearing a three-year-old.

At the time, I was teaching an undergraduate general education class of thirty-five students. The students were primarily white males and white fe-males, with minimal students of color. In the first week of class, we were assigned a reading from *The People's History of the United States* by Howard Zinn. I recall students' reactions to the reading as eye-opening mixed with little interest. I also remember a feeling, the presence of an unfamiliar class-room climate I had never experienced before. The first time I taught a course to predominately white students on course content challenged what students knew of Native Americans. The mood turned out to be white students chal-lenging what I knew of Native Americans. My previous racial experiences had always been based on my appearance, me being Native American. This would be the first time my knowledge, teaching experiences, and life exper-tise were challenged.

The young man was a white male; he was a first-year student. After com-bating me with questions over the assigned Zinn reading during the lecture, he requested another teaching assistant. He stumbled over his words and even failed to make eye contact with me when he said it was not me, but it was a time conflict. I knew his actual conflict was with having a Native Amer-ican teacher. The feeling was all too familiar from the many years of white males challenging me. What was different is how he tested my intellect. The student was denied switching to another teaching assistant. Knowing this student did not want me as his instructor left me feeling bothered. I was a Native American woman, and I could not change that.

Nevertheless, what it did do was push me to work harder on my lectures and to overprepare. My attempt was not to win the student over or blanket the race issue. I also was not trying to give in to my fears or appear helpless. I did follow the prepared course syllabus and deliver basic concepts of Na-tive American cultures, structured to give students a holistic educational introduction to Native Nations and Tribes of North America. He was the only student who regularly came to my office hours to discuss grades, clarify assignments, or discuss class topics. On the last day of class, after he handed me his final exam, he wrote me a note that thanked me for working with him during the semester, and he hoped to take another class from me again.

The second year of the program and the last semester of coursework were when I scheduled my comprehensive exams. In my head, I imagined my round belly as I prepared for written and oral exams. I was right. During the time of my written exam, I was five months along. I waited to share my news with colleagues, school friends, and faculty because I was unsure of the support or judgment I would receive. It was strange how my mind, an Indigenous mind, would come from that viewpoint. From the Diné outlook, we celebrate children. It is how the future is carried on. The non-Native perspectives on pregnant women in higher education look at us with concern if we might drop out or take a break and not return. We were having another boy; his predicted delivery date was July. For those of us in academia, a summer baby before the academic year begins is ideal. Both of my children were of concern when taking my comprehensive exams. The baby I was carrying needed rest, nutritious food, and minimal stress. The three-year-old needed attention. I asked other students who completed their comprehensive exams how they prepared for them. What made my situation unique was trying to write with a three-year-old in the house. I knew the only way to conquer my written exams was to send the family on vacation to LEGOLAND. I recruited my parents to join my husband and son for a week in California.

On day one of written exams, my son, husband, and parents left for California. I waited impatiently for an email with my four questions. The committee tells you one question, but it is a general question with many other components and subparts. I approached my questions with the most difficult or time-consuming questions first and the questions that would not take up much time last. I had spent the week before comps organizing books and articles into four piles by content. I went through all materials on reading lists and color coded them by discipline, and cross-color tagged them with Post-it notes. During the week of writing, I shut the social world out. I did not check or update my Facebook, did not check emails, did not go to the grocery store, and made the only phone calls to my son. I became so disengaged that it was overwhelming when I interacted with the public and seemed starved for interaction.

Sitting at the kitchen table writing, I would rub my baby belly and talk to my son. Any names or words that came across in text I would consider for a baby name. Only those in American Indian education would appreciate names like Brayboy or Cajete. Furthermore, the name Trudell is a lot to live up to. While working on my comprehensive exams, both written and orals, I like to think that my son was absorbing that information with me. He also has an understanding of Native womanhood and historical and contemporary nuanced Indian education. We passed both the written and oral comprehensive exams in the spring of 2016.

At the end of the spring semester, my parents returned home to Flagstaff to tend to their home, and my mother could go to IHS (Indian Health Service) for a cold she had been fighting since she returned from California in March. We encouraged her to see a doctor not from IHS, because they are known for not being thorough with patients. My mother was diagnosed with multiple illnesses. Cancer, valley fever, and hepatitis C. These diseases, we would find out, seemed to impact each other, and the treatment for each was dependent on the others. Hepatitis C had been contracted long ago when she received a blood transfusion, which developed into a tumor on her liver because it was left untreated for over twenty years. The valley fever she contracted during her stay here in Tucson from exposure to the desert environment. Her symptoms from valley fever initiated her to seek medical treatment, and test results indicated her other illnesses.

After I collected myself, I explored the option of returning to Flagstaff and taking a leave from school to help care for my mom. When that was not feasible, what would we do for childcare once the baby was born? For Navajos, for us, my mother was to take care of our children. She was not only teaching them to speak Navajo but also was raising them with Navajo beliefs and traditions. My parents caring for my children was not about free childcare; it helped raise my children with Navajo philosophies and teachings.

I gave birth to my son a month before classes started in August. I did not take time off from school or graduate teaching following his birth. I did make accommodations to my academic environment to support motherhood, like creating space for breast pumping. I also did have honest conversations with my advisor/mentor around balancing course load, teaching position, and dissertation writing to ensure I stayed on the path to graduate. We did not name him after an American Indian education scholar or American Indian activist or writer. We gave him my last name as his middle. My last name, like many other Natives, has significant importance to us. When the federal government assigned names to the Navajos, names they could spell phonetically, our family was named Badoni. I like being reminded of my family's history, the challenges we faced, and our survival. My last name reminds me of those before me, and I want to make sure our story continues.

After reassessing our needs and my mother reassuring me she would beat her illnesses, we decided I should apply for jobs and write a dissertation simultaneously. With comprehensive exams completed and ABD status, I was driven to apply for job positions. To be honest, the ABD status gave me confidence and an ego boost. I thought my chances for a teaching position were likely. However, the rejection emails and not making final consideration left me uninspired and unmotivated. Applying for higher education positions provided the mixed emotions of self-loathing and self-doubt, rounded out with more self-loathing. The first couple of positions I applied for, I was hopeful, and it almost seemed possible that I could become a final candidate. Nothing prepares you for the rejection email. It is a blow to the academic ego. No class prepared me for the disappointment and lows that followed when seeking employment. I was turned down by two fields: one, the art education world I was trying to depart from; and two, the American Indian education field I was trying to get in. I interviewed for two positions, one in each field, and was rejected by both.

In my last year in the UA AIS program, I wrote my dissertation and completed the final draft by April to graduate in May 2017. I made conscious efforts to complete my program on time for my children. As a Native woman in a PhD program, I have experienced academia's high demands—challenges I have overcome with the support of my family, partner, colleagues, and my advisor/mentor. My mother and father returned to Tucson to temporarily help us in order to give me more time to complete my dissertation. My mother's health has improved, and she is making efforts to recover fully. We chose as a family to combine our efforts to push me to complete my program. I spent my birthdays in my windowless office, I didn't take spring break in two years, and I gave up every weekend until I finished. In May 2017, I was the first in our family to graduate with a PhD. With my children, parents, siblings, cousins, and more cousins watching the ceremony, I was overcome with gratitude. A doctoral degree was not an individual effort; it was our families' collective contributions. Therefore, the doctoral degree is not mine to claim; it belongs to our family. However, the only way it will happen is if you work it yourself.

Soon after graduation, our family moved to Seattle, Washington, where I worked as a consulting teacher with the Native Education Program with Seattle Public Schools for two years. In the fall of 2019, I accepted a position as an assistant professor in Native American Studies at New Mexico State University in Las Cruces, New Mexico. The previous work with Seattle Public as a Native American consulting teacher provided me with the skills for collaboration with local school districts that I now utilize in New Mexico, including professional development for teachers to strengthen culturally responsive teaching. My work in New Mexico now incorporates both teaching Native American Studies undergraduate and graduate courses, as well as working with charter and public schools in southern New Mexico as an Equity Council member.

CHAPTER 3

"Bidiishkaal"

Putting Forth Effort

ARESTA TSOSIE-PADDOCK (DINÉ)

Yá'át'ééh, shí 'éí Naakai dine'é / Tó aheedlíínii nishłį́, Bįįh bitoo'nii 'éí bá shíshchíín, Tł'ízí łání 'éí dashshicheii, Kinyaa'áanii 'éí dashinálí. I am of the Mexican People / Water that Flow Together Clan, born for the Deer Springs People, my maternal grandfather's clan are the Manygoats People, and my paternal grandfather's clan are the Tower House People. My family is from Sand Springs, Arizona, located between Tolani Lake and Coal Mine Mesa on the western side of the Navajo Nation. Our family's customary land base provides a clear view of the Dook'o'oosłííd (San Francisco Peaks), one of the four sacred mountains located west of our home that surrounds Navajo land. When my mother and I would look toward the San Francisco Peaks, she would usually say "The mountain is wearing a hat" after the snow had melted and there was only a snow cap on top of the peaks.

The first time I heard about school was when I was about four or five years old. I recognized at that time I would be at a boarding school based on overhearing my parents' conversations and knowing that my older sister was at a boarding school. The thought of being separated from them made me anxious; yet it was an experience I was looking forward to with reluctance. I recall the day my parents mentioning that we were driving to Tuba City so I could attend Tuba City Boarding School in the early 1970s. It seemed the trip was similar to other trips, with the intention of visiting family or going to the store to buy essential items. Perhaps being in the company of my parents made me feel secure, which assured me that they would not leave me behind. When we arrived at the boarding school, my mother registered me and told me I was going to stay and attend school. That was when I realized she was actually leaving, and I wanted to go home with her. It was a painful moment for myself, as well as my mother. I am the youngest in my circle of siblings. I have one older brother and three older sisters. By the time I was born into the Diné matrilineal society, all of my siblings were at either a U.S. government boarding school or a higher education or trade institution. One experience that stays with me is accompanying my sister and her family to Northern Arizona University to attend summer session courses to complete her degree. Being aware that my sister earned her master's in education set an example for me and my nephews. Weaving my early life and educational journey experience together primarily follows the Navajo philosophical framework of Nitsahakees (thinking), Nahat'á (planning), Iiná (life/living), and Siih Hasin (hope/achievement). These experiences have certainly influenced me in continuing my education beyond high school.

Our homestead sat in a valley between the western portion of Dinnebito Wash and the red sandstone cliffs called Garces Mesa, but we called it by its Navajo name, 'Áłch'i' Deez'áhá' (bluff that's together/toward each other). I was not aware that Garces Mesa was named after a Catholic priest until I did a little research in college. The mesa's cliff is embraced by red sandstone cliffs surrounded by sand dunes, sagebrush, grass, cacti, tumbleweeds, edible wild vegetables, and other plants that thrive in the plateau zone. A scent memory I recollect is the strong, aromatic scent of sand and sage in the air when it rained. When the winds came, the blowing sand grains would sting my exposed legs and arms. During the hot summers, I often looked toward the sky hoping for a cloud that would provide me shade and bring rain for the plants and animals. Being raised in a hooghan (traditional home) with no modern conveniences of electricity and plumbing; helping to care for our sheep, goats, cattle, and horses; and growing our own food are unforgettable, rich memories of living a sustainable, traditional livelihood. Each morning was a ritual of collecting wood for heat and cooking, walking to the well to bring back a couple of gallons of water for daily use, letting the sheep out of their corral for grazing, bringing the horses to feed on hay, feeding our pets, and other chores. When trying to locate sheep or cattle, my parents taught me to see which direction they might have traveled and how long they might have been gone by looking for signs of grazing, hoofs, and droppings. I sometimes assisted my family when they were locating missing livestock and rounding up cattle, not only for taking them to market but also for inventory, branding, and maintenance purposes several times throughout the year.

Having livestock was a form of providing a livelihood for many Navajo families as well as a method of teaching children responsibilities and the value of a relationship with animals. Living a rural, traditional lifestyle was a way for me to gain knowledge that included knowing which plants animals should not be eating, which area is suitable for grazing, which type of plants and animals are in the area, and how the yearly cycle affects the surrounding area. In addition, my father taught me not only to drive but also to "read" unmaintained dirt roads to make sure we did not get stuck in mud or sand. One becomes familiar with the type of dirt composition of the road and recurring road conditions over the years. This has become useful for me while traveling on dirt roads when determining how to best approach various road conditions. As I reflect back, living a rural, traditional lifestyle was a learning process of attaining traditional ecological knowledge through observation, thinking, teachings, or oral traditions within your relationship with the land.

Reflecting on my early years of living a traditional Navajo life on customary lands where family events have taken place, sacred family items are located, and relatives rest within the land, it is clear that these are experiences I value. In my early adult life, I realized and felt the innate connection to land as the foundation of my Navajo personhood. When I was growing up, it was not a concept I thought about. When away from the land, however, one misses the land with an intrinsic sense of the land missing you as well. In my experience with not being present on the land, I noticed I rarely spoke the language and had difficulty accessing medicine people and visiting relatives or significant familial places without having to travel back to Diné Bikéyah (Navajo Land). I have always heard from the elders that we are one with the land. I believe land is our root that is connected to speaking our language and practicing our culture and serves as a source of our identity.

As a young child, I would visit my paternal grandparents at their hooghan with my parents. My father told stories about my paternal grandfather, Dághá Ts'óósí (Slim Whiskers), who lived a very long life of over one hundred years. One story told about Dághá Ts'óósí was of his being born while my great paternal grandparents were returning to Navajo territory after the signing of the Navajo Treaty of 1868 at Hwééldi (Fort Sumner). My mother also told me stories about my maternal grandmother, who was a tough and fierce woman who kept everyone on their toes and made sure everyone completed necessary work. I believe these stories of past generational experiences are embedded within me and are strong motivations toward goal setting, including seeking an undergraduate and graduate degree.

While my family and I were living in Flagstaff, Arizona, I worked at various places until I became self-employed. I operated a clothing design/boutique business emphasizing contemporary Native American fashion and accessories for about eight years. After years of being a small business owner, I found myself engaged in politics and social issues in hopes of impacting the lives of our Native People for a better future. With this in mind, I wanted to complete an unfinished goal of earning a bachelor's degree. I closed up shop and enrolled at the University of Nevada, Las Vegas, majoring in political science. When I met that goal, I felt a sense of accomplishment and a continued motivation to assist Native communities.

In 2008, I began a master's program at Arizona State University's Sandra Day O'Connor College of Law with no real intentions of going further than earning that master's degree. I always hoped to go to law school one day to study federal Indian law. While I was at Arizona State University, I began to do more research on the policy impacts of the 1974 Navajo-Hopi Land Settlement Act, a mandate by the U.S. Congress to relocate both Navajo and Hopi families from their customary land. A professor whom I consider a mentor from the law school suggested that I should apply to a PhD program to continue my research about compulsory relocation of Navajos. At the time of her suggestion, I did not have the full confidence to think about applying to a PhD program. However, the more I thought about it, my confidence grew, and I thought, "Why not?" My research interest centered around second-generation Navajo relocatees, who were children at the time they were relocated with their parent(s) and are now adults. I had questions—with no real answers—about why many children of relocation had no land base to return to and were therefore more unlikely to reestablish their traditional way of life. I knew at the time that having a land base is critically important for the descendants of Navajo relocatees, as it is the foundation for maintaining the essential spectrum of culture and tradition. After graduating with my master's degree, my interest in researching Navajo relocation lingered while I continued to debate whether I should apply to a PhD program.

After graduating with my master's degree, I continued to search for any studies concerning second-generation Navajo relocatees because I was curious about their whereabouts. When I could not find what I was looking for, I decided this could be my dissertation topic. I saw a need to find out more about the second-generation Navajo relocatees and what their perspectives were regarding the loss of their customary lands due to forced relocation. This population base would have been regarded as minors at the time they relocated with their parents according to criteria set by the U.S. federal government, who considered them dependents. The research topic provided me guidance, vision, and motivation to complete the program.

Throughout the years, I was aware that some of my relatives had faced forced relocation and had relocated just like my family did. When I was in my teens, my family relocated in the late 1970s to a one-acre location in the rural area east of Flagstaff, Arizona. I recall my parents imparting that relocating to a confining space of one-acre with a home compared unfavorably to the customary land they relocated from. Life changed from one of activity to one of relative idleness. Attending a new school outside the Navajo Nation presented some challenges, perhaps due to culture shock. I hardly saw any Native students. Growing up as a second-generation Navajo relocatee, I did not discuss or ask anyone about their relocation experience, perhaps due to the memories and stress that came with it.

Prior to coming to terms with being a relocatee, it was stressful to reveal that experience due to potential stigma and feelings of insecurity as a Diné person dislocated from a homeland and lifestyle. I also noticed my contemporaries who experienced relocation did not discuss it either. It made me wonder how others felt about relocation, or whether they were concerned about it. One day, I asked a close Navajo relative of mine about relocation. She indicated she did not discuss it with anyone due to not really knowing who to discuss it with, and when she did discuss it, she felt there was a sense of disgrace in being relocated despite not being at fault. Hearing from my relative inspired me even more to apply to a PhD program to provide awareness about the hardship it imposed on the second-generation Navajo relocatees. One question that was important to examine was where were the Navajo children of relocation who were relocated along with their parent(s) as a result of the Navajo-Hopi Land Settlement Act? They are adults with their own families. I also knew that if I did not do this, questions about relocation impacts would continue to cross my mind, primarily concerning

second-generation Navajo relocatees or children of the first-generation Navajo relocatees.

In applying for a program, I had to have reasons for doing so, and these
reasons had to be meaningful and purposeful. I was aware that undertaking
such an academic pursuit was important in my heart and mind and, most
importantly, for Native Peoples. I understood the time and work commitment the importance of scheduling family time and tightening up the already
restricted budget. Being aware of this undertaking motivated me toward
my journey. I was also aware this was a positive undertaking that overrode
all the statistical American Indian experiences that occurred at some point
throughout my life. During my young educational experience, there was a
lack of teaching about American Indian history prior to college. The lack of
teaching of our history felt like an erasure of who we are in Western society.
It was only when I was in college that I began to learn more about the history
of American Indians. Learning about how colonialism severely impacted
American Indians was distressing; not being taught our own history prior
to higher education disturbed me exponentially, leaving me unsettled and
upset. I felt it was important to fill this gap and educate others about American Indian history and experiences.

I explored other universities but ultimately chose the University of Arizona's (UA) American Indian Studies (AIS) program for several reasons.
First, I wanted to stay in Arizona to be close to my family. Second, I wanted
easier access to potential participants in my study. Third, the AIS program
concentrated on American Indians with an interdisciplinary approach. Prior
to coming into UA's AIS program, I began planning with the purpose of
succeeding by putting my personal and academic concerns in order to allow
me to complete the program within a reasonable time frame. My ideal time
frame plans consisted of being in the program a maximum of four to five
years, including passing my oral examination and dissertation defense. Basically, my universe would revolve around academic commitments. The strategies included calculating when I would conclude with coursework, when
to take the oral examination, when to have a proposal ready, preparing and
completing research, and writing and defending the dissertation. Another
aspect was the financial cost for both tuition and cost of living. On the personal side, to avoid further stress, I began to pay down as much personal
debt as I could. After being admitted into the program, I found that being
in graduate college at this level was a full-time job and required living on

subsistence income and scholarships. In addition, having the support of my sons was encouraging and helpful, especially when it came to maintaining our home and paying for household bills.

While I was waiting to hear from the AIS Department, I visited the department to meet with some of the faculty members for further information about the program. A few months after I applied, I received a telephone call advising me that I was accepted into the program. Receiving notification about being accepted into the program was exciting, and I believed it was meant to be. I recall being anxious and a little fearful, at the beginning, that I might not complete the program at UA. Fear is what partly stoked my determination. One thought that coursed through my mind was "What if I don't make it?" To mitigate this type of negative thinking, I thought about the individuals who took the time to write letters of recommendation on my behalf and believed in me. I certainly did not want to waste their time. I also thought about my parents and all those who came before them, especially my grandparents and great-grandparents. I imagined both of my paternal great-grandparents enduring the Navajo Long Walk as well as my paternal great-grandmother giving birth to my paternal grandfather as she was returning from Hwééldi. Reflecting on my paternal great-grandmother and paternal great-grandfather's difficult journey, I recalled their resiliency and persistence. My family and ancestors are the People who inspired and motivated me to complete my program with a topic that parallels the Navajo Long Walk.

When I entered the program, my peers came from various parts of the country: urban, rural, and Native nations. During my time at UA, the Native graduate colleagues were supportive with everyone's undertakings. The camaraderie that developed with Native student colleagues assisted in motivating us to work hard as we briefly lived the life of graduate students. We would discuss why we were in the program, what our goals were, and perhaps how we might reach those goals, helping one another when needed. One challenge that I struggled with during graduate school was writing, which was nearly remedied with student colleagues, writing tutors, and lots of practice. Some of my colleagues left their families to be in the program. Some moved their families to Tucson. A couple of my colleagues spoke the Navajo language, which allowed us to maintain our proficiency, as well as talk about current events back home or about culture. I had one close student colleague with whom I began the program and with whom I graduated at the same time. We shared office space for a couple of years, helped each other through hard times, cried on each other's shoulders when it became unbearable, and shared some good talks. We were each other's confidants throughout graduate school.

As a nontraditional Navajo woman and an older student, I did not question whether I should be there or not. As a Native woman, I find that we have the strength to move mountains, which translates to being able to proceed beyond the hardships which we most likely have experienced numerous times. When I was going through hard academic times, I would think about where I came from, who my ancestors are, and the hardships I experienced that included poverty, single parenthood, transitioning from a traditional way of life to living in cities or towns, and the emotional crises that come with the territory. In moving forward, I would often recall the Diné concepts of T'áá hwó ájit'éego t'éiya (It's up to you) which I interpret as taking the initiatives to achieve an earned goal. This concept is reiterated in the home and taught in childhood and continues to stay with me. These memories gave me the courage and persistence to continue because I knew where I was, in graduate college, which did not quite compare to past experiences of hardship. In preparation for graduate college, I am grateful for my hardships as they made me stronger.

While I was at UA, the AIS program provided an opportunity for their graduate students to work as graduate teaching assistants (GTAs), providing us valuable teaching experience and ensuring income for living expenses. This is the stage where I began to build my curriculum vitae, as well as develop a teaching portfolio. All of the professors I worked with provided the practical experience to effectively develop syllabi, lesson plans, and lectures; perform administrative duties; and master learning management platforms. As GTAs, we became conversant with our professors' areas of expertise and observed how they presented and lectured to their students. They all had their distinct styles of teaching and course design, as reflected in the syllabus prior to teaching a course. Being able to design your own course reminded me of what artists do. I regarded the work as preparation for the future, whether it was in academia or another profession. Not only were graduate students given an opportunity to assist professors during fall and spring semesters, but some also became instructors during summer sessions, where they were able to design their own courses. Working with professors was motivating, particularly when they shared their early teaching and career experiences. As my role models, they provided direction and support. Even today, as an assistant professor, when I need motivation, I will reminisce about my time as their GTA, what I learned from them, and the support they showed me. Gaining experience as a GTA and instructor helped me to develop skills in course design and teaching. This experience became instrumental when seeking a teaching job in higher education.

While I was a graduate student, I had the honor of teaching my first language course. I became an instructor of a beginning Navajo language course, and a couple of years later, I began teaching the intermediate Navajo language courses. I was not formally taught linguistics but studied it through my work while teaching the Navajo language. During my time as a Navajo language instructor, I found that some of my students had previous Navajo language classes in middle school or high school so they knew what to expect. Not only did they know what to expect, some were informed readers and writers in the Navajo language. One experience I had at a middle school on the Navajo Nation was overhearing other students laughing about traditionally dressed Navajo mothers or grandmothers or students speaking their own language, which led me to discontinue speaking the Navajo language at school. I once read a social media post by one former student who wrote that though she thought her friends were not Navajo speakers at school, they were actually Navajo speakers.

As a Navajo speaker, it is wonderful to see young college students anxious to learn the language. Since I was a speaker and not quite a writer or a reader of the Navajo language, I found it challenging at first. However, recalling my parents' effort to teach me how to read and write in the Navajo language helped to nudge my memory. I recall having to interpret for my parents as a young child who had not yet started school. I grew up speaking the Navajo language since my mother did not speak any other language, and my father spoke mostly Navajo and very little English. My father was more progressive in learning English, and he was able to learn basic phrases. My mother said the English language sounded "warbled" and was difficult to understand and speak. I translated for my parents whenever I accompanied them on shopping trips to border-town communities, such as Winslow or Flagstaff, Arizona, where English was primarily spoken. Both of my parents, fluent in the Navajo language, taught themselves to read and write Navajo despite knowing very little English.

As I reflect, I only wish I had taken the effort to teach my children, who are adults today and understand the Navajo language but are not quite speakers.

As a single parent who spent most of her life working and going to school in hopes of improving our family livelihood, I lost invaluable time for teaching and speaking Navajo to my children. Being busy in contemporary society, it is easy to dismiss the value of a heritage language, especially when the emphasis was on learning English. Perhaps I thought my children would just pick up the language as I had as a child. The Navajo language is richly descriptive and deeply intertwined with knowledge. In hindsight, being on the land allows a higher probability of practicing and maintaining tradition and culture and language.

When I was near completion of my course work for the AIS PhD program, I began to prepare for my written and oral examinations. In reality, examination preparation begins at the start of the program. In hopes of lessening my exam anxieties, I asked a couple of colleagues about their examination experiences but, in the end, everyone has different experiences and outcomes. I found that the accrued courses I completed and my area of interest in relocation set the foundation in preparing me for the examination. The written portion of the exam was tedious, as it was to be completed within a limited time. While writing, I burned the midnight oil doing this part of the exam. When my written exams were completed, I proceeded to taking the oral examination with my committee. The oral exam produced some nervousness, but I was delighted to have passed a challenging oral examination.

Embarking on a dissertation was exciting, tedious, and challenging. I had been preparing to initiate my research to find out more about the second-generation Navajo relocatees for a few years. Prior to working on my dissertation, I was advised that my research might reopen unhealed emotional wounds involving loss of land and home due to relocation. Moreover, I was advised I should do an ethno-autobiography instead. Doing an ethno-autobiography about myself was not a type of research in which I was interested. Instead, I was interested in other second-generation Navajo relocatees' experiences and perspectives rather than my own experiences. To find out about these experiences, it was important for me to do interviews and collect quantitative data for my findings based on experiences and perspectives.

The preparation time for my proposal to the University of Arizona's Institutional Review Board (IRB) was time consuming and a necessary learning experience. Proceeding with an IRB is essential, especially if one is going to do research within a Native community, whether it is off or on a reservation. The IRB process gave me the confidence to move ahead with my fieldwork at various urban communities. I received support from Native leaders and community members through resolutions of support affirming the importance of this study. When I began my fieldwork, I found that having awareness about the community of Navajo relocatees was essential in various urban communities. I also believed that being an insider in the Navajo community was valuable due to an embedded trust factor through experience. During the writing of my dissertation, I was nervous that I might get distracted and not complete it in a reasonable time. The idea of not completing in time was a bit stressful, so I put myself on a strict schedule and treated both dissertation writing and defense like a job, allowing me to complete my program.

After my dissertation defense I remained in academia. My work led me to continue teaching the Navajo language right after graduating from the University of Arizona. To gain further experience, I taught at the University of San Diego in the Department of Ethnic Studies as a visiting assistant professor. While in the San Diego area, I often attended a class at Kumeyaay Community College as a welcomed guest. Being among Native brothers and sisters was grounding for my well-being, as I was away from home and family. I returned to the University of Arizona to continue teaching the Navajo language for the Department of Linguistics and courses in American Indian Studies.

I began my journey with the goal of finding out the experiences and perspectives of the second-generation Navajo relocatees and how compulsory relocation affected them as adults. After completing my study, I presented to interested community members in various urban areas about my findings: removal and loss of a land base impacts relocatees' practice of Diné language, ceremonial cycles, and sacred history, and continuance of traditional livelihood. Despite these effects, the second-generation Navajo relocatees have the hope and intention of one day returning to Diné Bikéyah. Living in an urban area provides access to employment, education, and homes; yet, it can still be a struggle, especially when there is no land base or home on the Navajo Nation to which one can return.

The experience of living on one's customary land base prior to relocation elicits contextualized intergenerational memories of the place where our identity is formed as Diné People, but also provides a catalyst to move forward. Being aware of who I am and where I came from as a Diné woman has led me to study the effects of relocation and motivated me to attend a Western higher educational institution. Choosing to apply to the University of Arizona's department of American Indian Studies was a leap of faith for me. Being accepted into the discipline affirmed the value of studying the experiences of second-generation Navajo relocatees.

Upon reflecting on my research and my own experiences, I find that these are the same issues Native People have struggled with since European contact and continue to struggle with today, but under different circumstances, terms, and time frames. Our past generations have struggled to retain their cultural identity, lifeways, and land. As modern Diné Peoples, we face the same challenges even as we struggle with where our place is in the world, whether we are welcomed in the educational setting, and how we can help our community. Our relatives' persistence under colonialism can provide motivation toward assisting our People and Nations today and into the future. Our connection to land, relatives, lifeways, and community can strongly motivate us to strive, persevere, and accomplish our goals. As I reflect on the landscape of my childhood and think about the landscape of my educational experiences, I am reminded that all experiences have value. Acknowledging the role of the land and our belonging to it is important in remembering who we are as a People and as individuals as we look to the future of our communities.

CHAPTER 4

Who's Watching the Boy?

Creator's Watching Him

MICHAEL LERMA (P'URHÉPECHA)

Introduction

If my journey can ever be summed up in a phrase or quote, it would be "Scratch a Mexican and you'll find yourself an Indian" (Pavlik 1998, ix). This poignant statement is attributed to Robert K. Thomas and reflects a sentiment that mirrors my experience as a young man growing up in Northern Mexico, aka Southern California. It has been a lifelong journey discovering my roots as P'urhépecha in a time and place so far removed from my People's ancestral homeland. However, my voyage into academia created a bridge back to my family's origins and provided a clear path forward for me and my children. The path began with good teachers, such as Thomas. I'm so fortunate "Creator" was watching me.

In the in-between time, who was watching me when I was growing up? Who ensured I didn't get hurt, or worse, in a strange accident or due to my own bad judgment? In the twenty-first century, we obtain a great deal of our information through social media websites. Sometimes Adrian, my wife, will ask me about our son Naabahii. "Where is he? Is he outside?" I recently saw a meme along these same lines. The wife asks the husband about their child playing outside. The husband, distracted with television or some other hobby, remarks, "Who's watching our son outside? Creator is watching him." Living on the campus of Diné College has afforded us a lifestyle enriched by a forest that surrounds our home. The kids run around outside, dodging spiny plants and stray dogs. Sure it can be dangerous, but I pray that Creator is watching our children the way Creator has always been watching me . . . guiding me to good teachers.

Thomas is a man I never had the privilege to meet. Rather, his words were shared with me by the great Tom Holm. Professor Holm is one of many giants that expected a lot of me while I was in grad school. Much of my research was guided by wise men such as the honorable Robert Yazzie, former chief justice of the Navajo Nation, and Diné hataałii (medicine singer), Avery Denny. To this day, their expectations for me remain high, and I pray that I never let them down.

In this personal recollection of my time in graduate school at the University of Arizona, I will share stories about my grandparents whose influence is immense and continuous; my struggles in elementary school that resulted in me rejecting all forms of formal education; to the transformative experience that resulted from my decision to pursue a college education; and the painful and rewarding expedition that resulted in a PhD. Throughout this chapter, readers will see a handful of practical tidbits that, if followed, will make progress and completion all the more attainable. In short,

1. Your elders' knowledge matters, so follow it.
2. Expect to do things twice or three times and only get credit for one success.
3. Be sure that every paper you write in grad school is an attempt to draft a chapter in your dissertation.
4. Comprehensive exams are the worst part of grad school, so be ready.
5. Make your research work for the community.
6. Creator will give you teachers. Shut up and listen to them.
7. Work with faculty that will make you work hard.
8. Defend your dissertation as though you are having a friendly conversation with your friends.
9. Back up your files and NEVER throw away a notebook or paper idea.
10. And, most importantly, eat, sleep, and pray. If you don't make time for your health, illness will knock you on your butt.

I have attempted to highlight those responsible for my success, and to be as brutally honest as I can about what future grad students will face. Above all else, you are your ancestors' prayers, and your success is their resistance to genocide.

A Brief Biography

I was born in 1975 to newlywed parents. The first of three boys, I was fortunate to have early experiences with my mother and father together during the first years of my life. I remember walking hand in hand with my dad through San Francisco and riding on the water boats through the Small World exhibit at Disneyland with both my parents. I don't know the origin of my nickname, Mikey, but everyone called me by that name. It was common to hear my cousins, aunts, and parents exclaim, "Mikey likes it." However, these idyllic memories didn't continue beyond my fourth year. My parents had an imperfect relationship, and my father wasn't doing well. The next set of memories I have are living with my mother and siblings in my grandparent's house. We had a pretty good life during those years, even if my father was often away. I had my grandmother and grandfather to rely upon, a warm home, food on the table, and love. We spent our most stable years living in a small home on a small parcel of land with chickens in the backyard in what would grow into the beach town of Oxnard, California, on the Central Coast. It was a home filled with incomplete projects and rooms connected without hallways, and the smell of food permeated the atmosphere. Sure, sometimes there were mice under the beds, and we did not have any closets, but we had what we needed, and we had each other.

In the early dawn hours, my grandparents would sit at opposite ends of the dining room table under a dim light, smoking cigarettes and sipping coffee. In those quiet hours before the rest of the household rose for the day, they would take that time for themselves. My grandmother did most of the talking, and my grandfather did most of the nodding. When their discussion concluded, my grandfather would rise from the table and go outside to tend to the daily chores. I remember following him around, trying to help out. Sometimes, I'd get in his way, or smash his thumb with a hammer, but he never discouraged me from contributing. To this day, I credit him for instilling in me the work ethic I have because he always kept busy. If something was broken, he fixed it. If something needed to be built, he built it. He was lean and strong, and he taught me how to use tools and create solutions for problems. I often say that my grandfather taught me how to work and my grandmother taught me how to think.

My grandmother was the hub of our family as well as the spiritual guide and mind. She was not heavily keen on forcing me to learn the Spanish language. I can only today surmise that she knew Spanish was not our language. Indians in North America were forced to learn English. She seemed to have little interest in repeating compulsory education practices with me. Besides, she was certain English would be enforced at school as was done with her own children. A great deal of guidance came from her instruction on using my mind to fully develop my ideas and projects. We spoke of the afterlife, the reason we rise early in the morning, and the reason we grow plants in the yard and raise chickens, and we spoke of learning to respect elders and those with knowledge. She taught me about "god," or Creator. She simply explained to me that I had choices to make in this world. She could tell me the correct choices, or she could allow me to understand and make correct choices of my own accord. She would allow me to try and fail, and then she would guide me to a better decision. I think back and recall that my grandmother, Mary, was all knowing and all powerful. She could walk into a car dealer and leave with a brand-new car. She owned a home. She would wave her hand, and her sons and daughters would jump into action. When we spent time together, she remarked about being jealous of my curly hair. She had a nurturing side, but she could also be tough when needed. In this world, she taught me that I better be tough.

At that time, in the late 1970s, my grandparents' house was the best place in the world. Things changed in 1982 when my father passed away unexpectedly. Two years later, my grandfather passed on, as well. This loss was immense, and I began to act out in school. I didn't know if I was grieving or if there was something fundamentally wrong with the educational models imposed upon me, but my earliest memories of school are of my teacher's face red with anger. Mrs. Grego from Kamala Elementary School would clamp down on my arm tight, trying to hurt me. In my mind, it was a meaningless expression of hate, and I would often smirk to let her know she could not harm me. I would tell jokes and ask questions that angered my teachers, and they would react in ways that, today, are considered abusive, which led me to believe that these educators were not to be trusted. When my grandmother would take me aside and tell me how important it was that I listen to my teachers and get good grades, I still held firm to my rejection of authority figures in Western education. I believed then, as I do now, that it was Creator protecting me, telling me to be stern in my position, giving me the courage to stand up to all of the misguided educators.

For the remainder of elementary school and middle school, I did what I needed to do to get by. But in 1992, while in high school, my grandmother walked on, and when she left this Earth, my resistance to the educational system came to a high point, and I walked away from it completely. I was raised to listen, nod, carry out the task, and go home; but after my grandma passed away, I just didn't have the patience or the drive to keep showing up and regurgitating information.

It took a few years for me to return to a classroom, but when I did it was after my first daughter was born in 1995. I was struggling to pay rent and put food on the table. I felt it was a diminutively similar situation to the one my grandfather faced as a young man about my age, but I couldn't stop myself from aligning our struggles. My grandfather, Fred Morales, was born in 1903 or 1908, depending on what document you consult. He left his traditional homeland in what is known today as Aguascalientes, Mexico, sometime in the first half of the last century. As I was trying to navigate this new phase of my life as a father and provider, I often wondered about his life. Did he know he was leaving for good, or did he just never get around to returning home? I wonder if he acknowledged the four directions and fled north knowing he would never return. Or maybe he felt like it was a prison, like many Indigenous Peoples see their reservations today, and could not wait to escape. All I knew was that if he could be brave enough to seek a better life in a different place, then I had nothing to fear. The Creator had guided him, and the Creator would guide me too.

My apprehension connected to higher education was great, but I knew that I needed to do something drastic to shift my circumstances in order to provide for my family. My journey commenced when I enrolled at Allan Hancock Community College in Santa Maria, California. There, I began to find my way and form new ideas about who I was and what I could become. I received an associate's degree in 1998 and then a bachelor's degree in 2000 from the University of California, Los Angeles.

Mikey Goes to Grad School

The secret to surviving grad school is very similar to the secret to surviving life. You better hang on, expect to do everything twice or three times, and you better get used to getting paid just once for the gig.

My journey to a PhD began in 2002 when I decided to apply to the American Indian Studies (AIS) doctoral program at the University of Arizona (UA). A few months later, I was relaxing at my mother's home in Santa Maria, California. I remember watching cartoons, thinking about my future, when something started to bother me. I could not tell what it was at first, but I suddenly felt motivated to pull out a laptop and start searching UA's website for other doctoral programs. It was then that I discovered the Political Science Department and learned that their deadline for applications had not passed. In that moment, I decided I had better submit an application, and it turns out that my intuition was correct because AIS rejected my application for admission. I never asked why that happened, but I suspect that it was Creator, or my grandparents, guiding my fate . . . or perhaps nagging me to develop a backup plan!

In 2004, the UA Political Science Department put me on a plane to visit the main campus in Tucson, Arizona. I had never been outside of California at that time, and I had never been on a plane before. During my visit, I was introduced to all the faculty in the Political Science Department. I also sought out all of the Indigenous scholars within the university. I elected to take at least one class from an AIS affiliate every semester, knowing that in time I would need their support. I accepted my admissions package in the spring of 2004 and began taking courses that fall.

One of my most ardent supporters within the Political Science Department was Professor Brad Jones. One day in 2006, he called me into his office and told me he had accepted a position at the University of California, Davis (UC Davis). He warned me that I was likely not going to receive any more financial support from the other decision makers after his departure from UA because he was my only advocate in the Political Science Department. When he departed, I began the next semester with zero funding from the department. By that time, my family had grown, and I was supporting a family of five. Zero funding was going to be a problem.

When I first accepted admission to UA, I received a financial aid package. Within the package was a graduate minority fellowship put in place by the late Dr. Maria Teresa Velez, who was then serving as associate dean of the Graduate College (Everett-Haynes 2016). When my funding from the Political Science Department ceased, I recall sending Dr. Velez an email seeking guidance. She always encouraged me to reach out to her if I ever ran into problems, so when she learned of my dilemma, she set up a meeting for us to discuss my lack of funding. By the end of our meeting, she had secured a $10,000 fellowship for me. I remember sitting in her office with a poker face, not showing my excitement, when she remarked, "Is that enough?" and I replied, "Oh my god! That is more than enough! I was expecting that maybe you could let me clean the toilets around here! Thank you!" To this day, I credit her for saving my career, because even though the mainstream had decided I was deficient, my work ethic had apparently won over Dr. Velez. She is now considered to be a revolutionary, opening the doors for many people from disadvantaged socioeconomic backgrounds, and I am proud to be one of her benefactors. Before we parted ways, she gave me two pieces of wonderful advice: (1) Look for, and take, any job you can get on campus; and (2) apply to AIS again.

The Clash Between Peoplehood and Political Science

I applied to the AIS doctoral program for the second time in 2008 and was accepted! My plan to take one class per semester resulted in my getting to know many of the faculty and students. The first class I ever wandered into was Tom Holm's seminar on treaties in fall 2004. In many ways that class was a support group for native men. Tom's wealth of knowledge was inspiring, and his healthy skepticism for mainstream explanations reinforced my own disdain for my teachers as a child. His tremendous respect for Indigenous knowledge and for our elders reinforced the teachings my grandparents shared with me as legitimate. I have to admit that there were not too many others that held these beliefs. While this realization was disappointing, I remember feeling that I had, again, been guided to Tom's class.

I was all the more inspired when, during my research on Navajo treaties, I discovered Tom's article on Peoplehood (Holm, Pearson, and Chavis 2003). His model explains Indigenous resiliency, colonization, survival, and even the notion that some child in the future might be able to relearn a song long forgotten by the People. It still boggles my mind why this one article has not transformed Indigenous studies. Regardless, I can see it taking shape in my own work (Lerma 2012) and in the work of my colleagues, professors (Stratton and Washburn 2008), and scholars around the United States (Hannel 2015). I bring this up to cheerlead for Dr. Holm. His article was so disruptive to my previous thinking that it became ingrained in my own career.

For the next few years, I found my thoughts constantly shifting toward Peoplehood. Does it explain colonization's failure? We are still here! Does it explain land appropriation? The land is held in trust by a colonial actor. I would visit Holm in his office to discuss my ideas on how Peoplehood could be further developed. Over time, I began sketching out my dissertation, and I wrote one seminar paper per semester from that point on about Peoplehood. This is the advice that was given to me, and it is the advice that I now give to all graduate students to this day: ensure that every graduate seminar paper is a draft of a chapter for your eventual dissertation.

By spring 2006, I was steamrolling along with Peoplehood, even when the majority of my professors in political science were skeptical of the idea. Perhaps it was unwise of me to heed the skepticism of my political science professors because I did begin to run into problems in the mainstream when Professor Brad Jones left for his new job at UC Davis. He had warned me before he left that others in the department would try to escort me out of the program, and he wished me luck. At first, the backlash was minimal. I received less-than-desirable graduate assistant assignments throughout the next year. The Political Science Department has a practice of pairing its most promising students with the most research-active faculty. I was teamed up with adjunct faculty. There is nothing inherently wrong with working with these individuals, and I learned a great deal from them. But, from the perspective of research institutions, my work with these "teachers" would not advance my academic research. I also recall a time when a prominent international relations scholar visited our campus. The graduate coordinator arranged a dinner at Gentle Ben's, a local bar and grill. When I RSVP'd for the event, I was informed that there "just wasn't room" for me to attend. In these ways, Peoplehood turned into a painful experience that I suspect many Indigenous graduate students are forced to endure in silence.

Comprehensive Exams Are the Worst

In the end, the Political Science Department finally got rid of me during the comprehensive exam process. The comp exam is probably the most stressful period in any person's academic career. The experience is a major buildup to a stressful event followed by an anticlimactic conclusion. When the time came for me to select a committee, I was instructed to select three political science faculty and two AIS faculty. There are two parts: the written exam and the oral exam. The written exam consisted of receiving ten questions on a Monday, with the requirement of answering five of the ten questions the following Friday. On average, students usually produce one hundred pages of content. I submitted my work and then I waited . . . and waited . . . and waited. It was a painfully long experience. I can't remember exactly how long it took to grade the exam, but it felt like forever, and I'm certain that my stomach has some scarring from this experience. In fact, my stomach is churning now as I write about this memory fourteen years later. When I asked if I had passed the exam, the committee chair did not respond with a "yes" or "no." Instead, he said that we would set the oral exam and proceed. Having never been through the process, I figured this was routine.

The oral exam was a three-hour affair with the five members of the Comprehensive Exam Committee. Recall that I selected three political science professors and two AIS professors. Holm was one of my AIS selections. I was very nervous, full of coffee, excited and nauseous. From my perspective, I absolutely could have performed better. At the conclusion, I was asked to step out of the room so the faculty could decide my fate. I was pacing the hallway outside of the classroom for what seemed like an eternity. Again, I have no idea how long I was actually pacing, but it felt like an eternity. When the door finally opened, the chair of the committee informed me that I had not passed the exam. He instructed me to reschedule the oral exam and try again. The committee advised that I meet with committee members individually to seek additional advice in order to do better the next round. I was certainly crushed, but I was not ready to give up.

Later, when I met with Dr. Holm, he told me that when I was out of the room, an argument had ensued among the committee members. He was the only one left standing against the others that wanted to fail me. He said he fought as hard as he could, but there was one individual that was guiding the decision, and the others fell in line. He was angry that no one else in the room had the guts to stand up for me. Had it not been for Holm, maybe I would not be where I am now. Tom's advice was that I retake the oral and be sure to do a better job at citing the "gods of international relations." So, I went back to work.

When the time came to meet with the chair of my committee, he flippantly informed me that I should "just take the whole exam over again." When he said that, my stomach fell into a pit, along with my heart! I really was not sure if I could go through that pain all over again. I kept my poker face and immediately reached out to Dr. Holm. He fired off an angry letter to all members of the committee and to the chairs of both the Political Science Department and AIS. I remember feeling very timid at this point in my life, and I began to consider leaving the doctoral program all together. I thought that maybe I was being greedy with my ambitions. What's more, every time I attempted to reread the articles and my notes on mainstream international relations, I became sick to my stomach. I could not help but wonder if I had let my grandparents and my mother down. Had they survived this genocide so I could try and fail and quit? I felt like a failure. The stress was so intense that I thought I was going bald. There were huge clumps of hair in the shower drain after I would bathe, and I was losing weight because I had no appetite. Herein lies another lesson for grad students: you must always be mindful of your health. Many grad students have found themselves in the hospital for not listening to their bodies in peril. You must decide to make time for your health or your body will decide on your behalf.

Around this time in 2007, I ran into Brad Jones at an academic conference. I gave him the update on things, and he glibly stated, "I told you to watch your back." He has always been a brutally honest man, which I appreciate. It didn't make me feel any better about the situation. I was torn as to what to do next. Due to Dr. Holm's immense advocacy, he was able to get the decision to have me retake the entire exam overturned. Still, I knew that if the mainstream political scientists really wanted to crush me, they could. They could destroy me in an oral exam. The norm of practice is that if a student flunks two comprehensive exams, they're done with graduate school. Would I be tested fairly? Or would I be just another stereotypical "affirmative action" product that really could not handle the real (white man's) world? I expressed my fears to Dr. Holm, and he surmised that I could be correct about the fairness, or unfairness, of the oral exam. I was paralyzed and unsure what to do next.

I decided to reach out to the chair of AIS, expressing that I needed to get my doctorate and would like to integrate fully into AIS. While application submission deadlines had passed, I was still in good standing at the Graduate College. Her solution was to begin taking AIS courses full time and apply for admission for the next term. She hypothesized that by the time I was admitted, I could take the comprehensive exam in AIS. Knowing that AIS was welcoming of my application and supportive of my career helped me decide to abandon political science and switch my focus fully to AIS.

American Indian Studies—A Family

In 2008, I was officially admitted to the AIS doctoral program. A heavy weight was lifted from my shoulders. My nausea went away, my hair stopped falling out, and I gained a little weight. I finally felt home. AIS made a space for me at their fire and granted me a graduate teaching assistantship.

I began working with Tom Holm, Ben Colombi, and Franci Washburn immediately to map out a route for success, and I was seeking out a person within the program to be my dissertation chair. I knew that Manley Begay was a legend in AIS, and I wanted him to sit on my Comprehensive Exam Committee. I was determined to meet him, but every time I dropped by his office, the door was never opened and the light was never on. After months of not being able to connect with him, his legendary status was fully cemented in my mind. He was so mythical. I wondered if he existed at all.

My transition to AIS had me chasing down stray courses other students had taken early on, but it landed me in American Indian Education with Dr. Begay. Taking the higher ed class was going to finally allow me to see if Dr. Begay was actually a person or if he was a legend. During the first day of class I got to see that Dr. Begay was not only a real person but that he deserved his legendary status. He starts the higher ed class with a classroom full of Indigenous graduate students. He shows us a series of statistics involving how we tend to drop out of school at various levels. This system was not made for us to succeed in, and succeeding in the Western educational system may be more of an indictment about our lack of commitment to our communities than to our own intelligence. He would then conclude with the stats on the number of Indigenous People with graduate degrees. He would wave his hand across the room at us and proclaim, "You are the cream of the crop." This did more to boost my esteem because of the focus on my classmates. I was surrounded by the best Indigenous minds in the world! I still think that they are the cream of the crop and that I was lucky enough to be at the party too.

At the conclusion of that first class, I approached Dr. Begay and asked him about where I could find his office. It turned out that the mystery of his empty office in Harvill was that he was never there because he had a second office I did not know about at the Udall Center. So, that first mystery was solved, and I began working on the next mystery: What did I have to do to get Dr. Begay to be my dissertation chair?

Mikey Goes to Diné Bikéyah

I learned that Dr. Begay was a member of the Diné Policy Institute Advisory Circle at Diné College. I had been conducting random Internet searches for the Diné Policy Institute (DPI) since 2003 or 2004. I was intrigued by the idea that Indigenous Peoples could create their own think tank based in their own epistemology. Also around 2003, I attended the Stanford Powwow. I stayed with a friend on campus and, as we walked across campus, we passed by the Hoover Institute building. My friend commented, "That's the Hoover Institute. They figure out ways to kill brown people around the world." My reaction at the time was, "We need an Indigenous think tank!" So, as one can imagine, I was very excited to finally have a link to DPI. The next time I spoke with Dr. Begay, I expressed that I wanted to use the various research methods skills that I had picked up as a political science graduate student and put them to work in Indian Country. Perhaps I could contribute to DPI projects for free, as an intern. That seemed to get his attention.

Manley's legendary status is in the shadow of yet another . . . the Honorable Robert Yazzie. Mr. Yazzie is the former chief justice of the Navajo Nation Supreme Court, and at the time, he was the director of DPI. One day, while at Manley's office, I shared with him that I had the Peoplehood dissertation going, but I did not want to set any agendas for others that serve the community. I said, "I'd rather not disclose my own interests. I'd rather have the community furnish an idea." Manley then said, "Let's get Robert Yazzie on the phone." He started dialing a number. I remember becoming very nervous. How am I going to handle two legendary figures? They spoke and laughed in Navajo for a few minutes before he introduced me to Justice Yazzie. I told him about my yearning to give back to the community. We discussed my research methods skills, and he asked his policy analyst to join us on the phone. Collectively, we decided that I should submit a proposal to DPI. I doubt anyone read my proposal because I got an email from Robert a little later stating, "You can work on the Navajo Constitution project" (Yazzie et al. 2008).

I was stunned by the prospect of working with these gentlemen, but I was also intimidated by the prospect that I might let them down or not work hard enough. Manley and I started to sketch out a new dissertation that I would write in service to the Navajo Nation. I would need to put aside the Peoplehood project for the time being. We exchanged emails and writings but I decided, on my own, that I needed to be on the Navajo Nation to really learn from Justice Yazzie. I applied for, and won, a small grant to work with Diné College in Tsaile, Arizona. I was assigned to work with Dr. Wesley Thomas, but I would regularly sneak away to see the judge. My tasks for Dr. Thomas involved research. I would ask, "When do you need this?" He always responded, "When can you get it back to me?" I knew myself well enough to know how much time I needed, so I'd calculate the time in my head and then double it. So, if I needed three days, I said that I needed six days. Dr. Thomas never objected to my timelines. I worked out of the tallest building on the Navajo Nation. I would work four hours on my assignments on the second floor of the Ned Hatathli Center and then run upstairs to the DPI office for the next four hours.

The first time I went up to DPI, it looked like some kind of party. Music was playing and young people were laughing and working. I asked for Robert Yazzie and someone informed him of my visit then waived me in. I went into his office, shook his hand and let him know that I was the guy on the phone with Dr. Begay from the University of Arizona. I was nervous but figured I had little to lose. He shut his door and we spoke about life and the research and started to joke around. Not since my grandparents had passed on did I feel like I was at home. I think I missed being teased and ordered around by my elders. Robert asked me to look over a draft of a feasibility study (Yazzie et al. 2008), which I did and gave my comments. I did this every few days during that time in Tsaile and was invited to attend an advisory circle meeting and a Navajo Nation Supreme Court proceeding with Chief Justice Herb Yazzie. Once again, I felt like these long-lost relatives were making a space for me at their fire.

A Crash Course in Diné Bibeehaaz'áanii

My time with Justice Yazzie and his team was amazing. They taught me about sacred mountains, the importance of water, where to get a good meal, and the art of navigating the wayward cows and sheep on the rural roads of the Navajo Nation. To this day, I declare myself a refugee in Diné Bikéyah because the People took me in and gave me a purpose. (Since the time of my self-declared refugee status, a medicine man told me that I can't say that anymore, but that's another story. . . .) When I first came to Diné College, I would walk around the campus and see elders that resembled my grandfather or grandmother, and I was taken back to my own childhood. I realized I had not seen my elders in around twenty years. So, because of this, I unintentionally reverted back to being an eight-year-old deferring to their whims. I'd follow them around, trying to help in any way I could. I made coffee and ran errands. I held doors and lifted heavy objects. I read documents and delivered messages. A few weeks in, I called my mom and told her about this, and she got after me, saying that I am a man now and that I should act my age. That made sense, and things were corrected, but I'd often find myself sitting in the dining hall only to be visited by another older male wishing to impart his wisdom to me, and I appreciated it. They told me stories about the creation of the college, the meaning of the logo, the story of the Hero Twins, Changing Woman, and the hogan. I soaked it all up! I loved everything about my experience there in Tsaile.

One day I went for a walk up a hill where a water tower was placed long ago. I was surrounded by a sea of trees, and when the wind whistled through the branches it sounded like ocean waves. When the trees swayed in the wind it looked like a sea of green waves on the shore. I didn't want to leave. There was such a strong pull on my heart. I wondered if I could quit the doctoral program, get a job as an instructor, and move to Tsaile. At the conclusion of the internship, I traveled to Flagstaff and rented a car to go to California. I was driving west when I looked in the rearview and saw Dook'oo'osłiid (the San Francisco Peaks), and I teared up. I wondered if I would ever get a chance to come back again, and I prayed that Creator would make a way.

Guided to Dook'oo'osłiid

Robert Williams is a renowned author and law professor at UA's School of Law. He once advised me to set aside one day a week to write for eight hours. The advice was that the process need not be arduous. You can write for two hours, take a fifteen-minute break, write for two more hours, eat lunch, and in the afternoon repeat the morning routine. With only three or four chapters drafted, I started looking for jobs. I saw a tenure-track position at Northern Arizona University (NAU) in the Political Science Department. They sought a Native American politics specialist. I applied, showcasing my ability to teach staple courses, such as international relations, modern political theory, Native American politics, and tribal government. I made it to the phone interview and then . . . silence.

In 2009, the Arizona state legislature took an ax to public education budgets. This was coupled with the housing crisis that led to a hiring freeze at all Arizona state schools. I contacted the chair of the department at NAU and requested an update on the Native politics position. He informed me that I was about to be invited to an on-campus job talk, but the hiring freeze put an end to that. As I continued to write dissertation chapters, I applied for jobs all over the United States and Canada. I needed a job, but I was also fearful about being taken away from the vicinity of the Navajo Nation.

One day, I received a call from the 928 area code (Flagstaff, Arizona), and I immediately picked up the phone. It was the chair of the Political Science Department at NAU asking if I would be interested in an instructor job. It turned out that the department could not secure the tenure-track job during the hiring freeze, but they could get an instructor line. In my head I wondered at what severely reduced rate this job was being offered to me. I responded in my most convincing nonchalant voice saying that I would entertain the offer.

About a week later NAU offered what turned out to be a year-long job interview in the form of a one-year instructor position. They invited me to the main campus in Flagstaff, Arizona, to see the place. When I arrived on campus, I met with political science faculty, and my gut clinched up because I was reminded of my time within the UA Political Science Department. However, these concerns quickly dissipated when I realized that they seemed to have respect for Indigenous struggles and triumphs.

Afterward, I asked Manley about this job offer. More specifically, I asked him for reasons not to take the job. He seemed thrown but played along for a bit. We ended up deciding that I would be a fool not to take this crazy eight-classes-a-year job that paid well below the poverty line. So, I put it in my prayers and asked Creator to shelter, clothe, and feed me and my family as we moved from the economical, dry, desert town of Tucson to the expensive mountain town of Flagstaff.

As is typical with me, my move was interesting to say the least. When packing the moving truck, I left my work boots on the bumper of the truck. As I was passing through Phoenix, a nice driver honked and pointed at my bumper. I couldn't believe that I drove from Tucson to Phoenix with shoes on my bumper and they did not fall off! In Flagstaff, I found a rental home where the basement was rented as a separate apartment to another tenant. This made the upper house affordable. I was informed shortly after the move that

I had been awarded the Marshall Foundation Dissertation Fellowship from the University of Arizona. This provided an additional amount of money to survive on in Flagstaff. Creator was providing.

I knew I would be okay if only I could follow Professor William's advice. When I first arrived on the NAU campus that fall, I went to the Cline Library with my laptop to draft some syllabi. I must've been sitting there for an hour before it dawned on me that I probably had an office on campus. Talk about a severe case of impostor syndrome!

In the fall of 2009, Wednesdays became my writing day. I took my fifteen-minute breaks outside and would walk around the Castro building to get sun and fresh air. This was especially important because my office didn't have a window; however, I was grateful for it because it was my own, and I did not have to share it with anyone. At a thrift store, I found an espresso machine. To this day I tell people that full cups of espresso every couple of hours kept me employed because that first year was exhausting! There were days when I would go into the office half asleep to make coffee. One time, I became upset because the coffee maker was so slow, and then I realized that I had forgotten to put water in the machine. I told Avery Denny about this, and he said, "That's why you save the leftover from last night and drink it cold first thing in the morning." Wisdom of the elders?

During my first year at NAU I learned from the search committee that I was actually their third choice because I was still writing my dissertation. The first and second choices had tenure-track job offers because they had finished their degrees. I was the default candidate. In the words of Homer Simpson, "De Fault . . . the two most beautiful words in the English language." I was advised by my colleagues to finish my dissertation and keep applying for jobs. They did not want me to leave, and they wanted me to get a tenure-track offer so NAU could match it. So, that is exactly what I did.

Defending a Dissertation Should Be a Friendly Conversation

Finishing the dissertation was an immense endeavor. When it was finally "defendable," I invited my mother out for the public lecture. She was quietly proud; however, she stopped driving long distances a long time ago. I decided to go pick her up in Santa Maria, California, and drive her to Tucson, Arizona. This meant I drove six hundred miles from Flagstaff to Santa Maria. I rested a day or two and drove her back to Flagstaff. We rested another day.

Then we drove from Flagstaff to Tucson. She stayed in one hotel with my brother. I stayed in a different hotel and I prepped for the defense. On the morning of the defense, I wore a white dress shirt with a Diné College T-shirt underneath. I was nervous, my mother was late, and I had spilled coffee on my shirt! As I waited to be called in, some traditional songs that Avery Denny would sing came to mind, and I began humming the tune. At that time, I did not know the words, but I knew that they were coming to me for a reason.

I recall a professor once saying that a dissertation defense is supposed to be a nice, friendly conversation about your work. But, after my first comprehensive exam experience, I felt like I needed all the support I could get. Where was my mom? Was she lost in the parking lot? I didn't have time to think about this fiasco. I had to go and give my lecture. My mom was going to miss everything after all those miles. I was sad and disappointed. I went into the lecture hall and, just like a little one looks out for their mom during recess on the first day of kindergarten, I looked around in hopes of seeing her. She was nowhere to be found.

About twenty minutes into the lecture, I glanced to my left toward the door and saw my mom outside the window teary eyed. I motioned for someone to get the door and I kept talking. My mother is not the kind of person comfortable barging into these kinds of spaces. She may even feel like she isn't deserving of being allowed into the great halls of a university, but as I know and you may know as well, moms are our greatest teachers, and they can go wherever they please. As a woman, and a mother, she is your first teacher and your first leader. When someone opened the door, she walked in looking embarrassed. She made it, and I could see that she was relieved when the door was opened for her. The little scared boy in me delighted to see her. At that moment, Tom Holm stood up, stopping the defense and formally announced the arrival of my mother, loudly exclaiming, "Ladies and gentlemen, Mrs. Linda Lerma." The audience and all of my professors clapped in praise. No other words were needed. Mothers can walk in a room like that and command applause. It was a powerful moment as they gave her a standing ovation, and I clapped for her too! Her smile radiated with pride. We told her with our actions that she was the most important person in that defense meeting room.

I passed my defense that day in 2010. I also earned a tenure-track offer at Evergreen State College, which was matched at NAU. The heavily revised version of my dissertation was published by Oxford University Press in 2017.

It's titled *Guided by the Mountains*. Avery Denny wrote the foreword, and Robert Yazzie wrote the epilogue. My first book, *Indigenous Sovereignty in the 21st Century*, came out in 2014 and was published by Florida Academic Press. The second edition is now currently under review at Oxford University Press.

I still work with Robert Yazzie and Avery Denny on research projects, including books and grants. Thinking back on the last day of grad school, I remember being proud of the fact that I had the biggest "tribe" at graduation. All of my kids, my mom, my brothers, my aunt, and my cousins attended graduation with me. I told my kids that I succeeded because of them and not in spite of them. Put differently, my children served as a causal mechanism by which I was permitted to complete my degree. Robert Yazzie and Manley Begay hooded me that day. And, I believe my grandparents were there too. After the graduation, my mom said she was shocked that my professors were "real" Indians. She said, "With a name like Tom Holm, Manley Begay, and Robert Yazzie, I thought they would be white." I appreciate that I was guided and judged by academics and traditional knowledge holders alike. In fact, I sometimes take their presences in my life for granted and find it shocking when other institutions fail to bring in our elders to lead and guide. Their presence has continually provided a unique and valuable perspective to my work and to my life.

Post-Grad-School Career, Gray Hairs, and Babies Too

I was fortunate to teach at NAU from 2009 to 2016. I had the privilege of guiding several graduate students through the dissertation process by sharing what I went through. Too many are getting run out of mainstream departments. I share my experiences with them and explain that sometimes they will have to do things twice and three times over only to get half of the credit. I tell them it's not fair. I explain that we can't do anything about it now. All we can do is succeed as Indigenous scholars. I tell them to keep doing it because we're not doing it for the credit. And, most assuredly, we can't possibly be doing it for the money because there is no money to be had. We are doing it for our relatives, for the community, and for our elders.

So, you may be wondering, "Whatever happened to Peoplehood?" The answer is I am turning that into a book too! While the manuscript searches for a home, I have to resist the urge to add a new chapter. This is why I urge my students to back up their files, and to never throw anything away, or delete work out of frustration. You do not know when you will need those thoughts and words again. Should you ever visit my office, I'd be happy to show you my notebooks on Indigenous human rights in the international system, or maybe you'd like to see the notebook on social networks and Indigenous economics. I don't know if I'll ever complete these projects, but they are there just in case I find some free time in the next few decades.

In the spring of 2016, I was notified that I had received tenure at NAU. I was elated, but also very tired. After seven years of working at a breakneck speed, I went on sabbatical. I went to concerts, rode my bike along lakes, and took long drives through mountains. During this time, I reflected on everything I had survived. For twelve years, I never once stopped to breathe and enjoy my life. The grad school journey took a toll on my children and their mother. Our kids may not remember me being around a lot growing up because I was always studying and working. But I remember painting up Mikey's first bike, taking Diana on a hike with her classmates, playing guitar for Elizabeth at her school, and attending Michelle's high school graduation. It's impossible to make up for lost time, but I always remind them that it is possible for us to form new memories and use the time we now have together to be together.

Unfortunately, for my children's mom and me, we grew apart and were not in a place to enjoy this next phase of life together. However, I fell in love and married my wife, Adrian, in a traditional Diné basket ceremony on August 5, 2017. I became a father to her two children, Cameron and Alexandra, and we now have our own son, Naabahii. Together, she and I are raising seven children and are expecting our first grandson this year. Avery and the entire Denny family have stepped up to guide us on our path as parents and practitioners of Diné lifeways. Robert Yazzie stepped up to serve as my Zhe'e (father) and spoke on my behalf during the merging of the Bracker/Lerma family. He has stepped up in so many ways, including teaching Adrian how to tie up my hair in a traditional Diné Tsiiyeeł. Most importantly, he stepped up in his capacity as a justice of the peace and facilitated our wedding vows and signed our marriage license.

People, mostly Bilagáanas, now ask me if I am adopted. I say, "No." Rather, I am married into a Navajo family and I am now a community member of the Navajo Nation. In 2018, I accepted a job at Diné College, and since then I have served as founding dean of the School of Business and Social

Science. Adrian also works at the college in the Office of the President as the development and alumni officer. Together we are pursuing our goals to learn more about Diné teachings and practices. We humbly sit on Mother Earth, sing, and pray together through ceremonies. My "refugee" status has been rescinded. Instead, I'm put to work like any other resident of the Navajo Nation. Our family is a reflection of Shimá Nahaadzaan adóó Yadihił Hastiin (Mother Earth and Father Sky). We balance one another out. We each have our own special talents to bring into our home, and we recognize and acknowledge that no one individual is better than the other. Should we ever separate, there would be no life. I'm truly a blessed man to have her as my wife, to have Robert as my father, and to have Avery as my grandfather.

The morning after my eldest daughter, Michelle, informed us that she would make us grandparents, I woke up to stretch and my neck seized with immense pain. I laughed out loud thinking that my training as a grandparent had already commenced. When we announced to our elders that we were expecting a grandchild, they expressed that our true training was about to begin. To be honest, I never imagined that I would see this time of my life come . . . to be a cheii (grandfather) is a true honor that I never knew I would live to see. It feels as though I have been climbing a mountain all my life. On the day Michelle told me I was to be a cheii, I felt like I reached the precipice and could finally stand atop the mountain, see out for miles, and truly gaze upon and take in all of the beauty.

I still believe that Creator and my grandparents are guiding me daily. My grandparents have both walked on to the next life. Still, there are many times when I am moving through my day and I will seek out their guidance in a prayer or wish to share with them great news. For example, when I received the offer from NAU, my gut reaction was to go home and call my grandmother! It was a silly idea because she had passed on, but when I received the news, she was the first person I wanted to tell. I wanted to thank her for instilling in me a work ethic that has made me such a happy person all these decades later. If it wasn't for that I would not have made it through the journey of grad school, and I would not have been allowed to live a privileged life.

In closing, I would like to express my gratitude to the University of Arizona's American Indian Studies Program. It is not the perfect place. Like any family, we fight. I don't know who gets along with me in the whole of academia, but my AIS family has always set aside the nonsense and welcomed me. We are all very fortunate to have learned from, and be trained by, the greatest scholars of all time: Vine Deloria Jr., Robert K. Thomas, and Tom Holm. When I see my AIS relatives at conferences and when I hear of them publishing and receiving jobs, I applaud them on their perseverance and grit. It is great to see us succeeding! It is also great to meet and teach the next generation of scholars. The last thing I'll say is something Tom Holm once said to me. He says this to everyone as a joke: When I was beginning my job search, he said, "Get a haircut and get a job." My response: "Only listen to 50 percent of what Tom Holm says." So, today, I am employed, but I kept my long hair.

References

Everett-Haynes, La Monica. 2016. "Maria Teresa Velez: Farewell to a Revolutionary." *University of Arizona News*, April 18, 2016. https://news.arizona.edu/story/maria-teresa-velez-farewell-revolutionary.

Hannel, Eric. 2015. *Reinterpreting a Native American Identity: Examining the Lumbee Through the Peoplehood Model.* Lanham, Md.: Lexington.

Holm, Tom, J. Diane Pearson, and Ben Chavis. 2003. "Peoplehood: A Model for the Extension of Sovereignty in American Indian Studies." *Wicazo Sa Review* 18 (1): 7–24.

Lerma, Michael. 2012. "Indigeneity and Homeland—Land, History, Ceremony, and Language." *American Indian Culture and Research Journal* 36 (3): 75–98.

Pavlik, Steve, ed. 1998. *A Good Cherokee, a Good Anthropologist: Papers in Honor of Robert K. Thomas, Contemporary American Indian Issues Series.* Los Angeles: American Indian Studies Center, University of California.

Stratton, Billy, and Frances Washburn. 2008. "The Peoplehood Matrix: A New Theory for American Indian Literature." *Wicazo Sa Review* 23 (1): 51–72.

Yazzie, Robert, Moroni Benally, Andrew Curley, Nikke Alex, James Singer, and Amber Crotty. 2008. *Navajo Nation Constitutional Feasibility and Government Reform Project.* Tsaile, Ariz.: Diné Policy Institute.

CHAPTER 5

Warrior

FERLIN CLARK (DINÉ)

"Why is a Navajo with a PhD living in a hogan with no electricity and running water, and why is he not working?" A Navajo man who was curious as to my professional employment status asked me this through one of my nephews. Soon after I heard this, and laughed about it, I was invited to share my experiences and the impact that an American Indian Studies (AIS) degree has had on my career and life for this book.

An academic AIS doctoral degree program was uncommon in the United States during the end of the last century and the beginning of this new century. Universities at that time only offered "ethnic studies" PhD programs or the usual anthropology programs of study that concentrate on American Indians. There were no distance or online education programs. The fact that there was an AIS program with authentic American Indian People who held prestigious academic credentials was impressive, and so I decided that the University of Arizona (UA) was where I wanted and needed to study. I am from Crystal, New Mexico, and I am of the Tabaahi (Water Edge), A'shii'hi (Salt), Ha'na'gha'nii (Those Who Walk Around), and Dził tłahnii (Mountain Cove) Clans.

This story weaves my experience as a doctoral student; professional experience as an education leader of my tribe, including the political battle I encountered; my movement to living off the grid; and what I am doing now as president of Bacone College. I enjoyed a unique professional experience working with Native American tribes beyond the Navajo Nation, including my present work at the original Indian university, Bacone College.

In 2001, I was thirty-five years young and working at Sage Memorial Hospital in Ganada, Arizona, as the director of philanthropy, raising funds while learning about health care when I applied to UA's AIS program. My son was six years old at the time, and he was attending Chinle Primary School. My wife was teaching at Chinle High School. Attaining a doctoral degree by the time I was forty years old was my goal since graduating from Window Rock High School in 1984. We lived in Ganado, and I tended to my duties as parent, husband, son, and employee. Whether it was a random thought or a deliberate plan, I knew that time was running out to pursue this goal. I was happy to receive my acceptance from UA's AIS program but was torn about leaving my homeland. I wanted to be with my family, yet I also wanted to pursue my academic goals, and my self-imposed timeline was closing. Aside from losing a steady income to pay for vehicles, credit cards, and other personal family amenities, we made a decision that I would pursue this goal. I had paid off my student loans acquired while attending Harvard University's Graduate School of Education in the early 1990s, and here I was going further into debt for this last leg of my academic journey. After attending the all-night Azee BeNahagha ceremony at my family's home in Testoh, where I had a chance to pray about my new adventure, even though it was difficult, I drove off to Tucson to find my place at Arizona's finest university.

At one time, one of my colleagues from the Santo Domingo Pueblo asked me on our way to visit a school during my stint with the State of New Mexico, "Why does one pursue an American Indian Studies degree from an education institution? Shouldn't you learn about other disciplines you don't get from home?" Great questions. "Aren't you supposed to learn how to speak your language from your parents, know what to do in particular cultural ceremonies and activities, know how to prepare the proper foods, know the stories, songs, and histories of our tribes from home?" she added. She was absolutely right. I said, "Yes. It's true we can't learn to be an Indian from a university, but we are learning about our collective American Indian experiences so we know and understand how our communities are the way they are, and then we become education warriors with different tools, skills, and 'medicines' to help our people." Being book smart and knowing things about our American Indian histories, philosophies, policies, programs, and even our languages is not being taught at home because of intrusion from American, Mexican, and Spanish people and governments. She then asked if the professors who are teaching at these higher education institutions know their language, culture, and ceremonies to be professors of AIS. Another great question. I think that most of the AIS professors actually know their language and participate in their cultural ceremonies, but as far as living among their own tribe and community, many of them live in the city where they teach. My answers appeared to be inadequate. Simple yet provocative questions that strike at the core of how a person should think about the world but also how to live in the world.

Upon arriving at UA, I was excited to meet the faculty who would guide and share their wealth of knowledge with me. Is an AIS degree program a legitimate academic discipline of study? What will an AIS degree do for graduates? Should institutions of higher learning commit valuable resources for such a program? There was a lot riding on our successful experiences and the application of the knowledge we gained from the program, not just for us personally but also for the AIS program. An AIS degree program needs to be rooted in an epistemology, pedagogy, research method, comprehension, practice, leadership, governance, education, social science, scientific, economical, health, political, and cultural system and frameworks, which may not be published, and should be based on an Indigenous ecological perspective. Students who matriculate through such a program will find relevance, stories, songs, and prayers, as well as deep meaning from such a degree. Such a program does not necessarily fit the timeline of today's academic schedule, but it is an appropriate consideration.

One of the main reasons why I chose UA's AIS program to pursue my doctoral studies was the awesome caliber of American Indian faculty. I had the privilege to study with Luci Tapahonso (Diné), Dr. Mary Jo Tippeconnic Fox (Comanche), Dr. Tsianina Lomawaima (Mvskoke Creek), Dr. Tom Holm (Cherokee), Dr. Jay Stauss (Jamesown S'klallam), Rob Williams (Lumbee), Dr. Manley Begay (Diné), Dr. Nancy Parezo, Dr. Robert Martin (Cherokee), and the late eminent scholar, Vine Deloria Jr. (Standing Rock Sioux). These Native professors, my "dream team" of respected scholars steeped in various disciplines, were the primary reasons students chose UA as the place to pursue their AIS degree. It was an exciting time to be a student there!

I had the honor to meet and study with the late Standing Rock Sioux scholar and prolific writer, thinker, and philosopher Vine Deloria Jr. Before I decided to pursue a PhD in AIS, I was contemplating law school. The great thing about the AIS program at UA was, and still is, having law professor Robert A. Williams as part of the law and AIS programs. One of my areas of focus was federal Indian law, in addition to education and literature. He reminded me of a great professor I had at Harvard, Dr. Charles "Vert" Willie. Two incredible minds.

During my last year to complete my residency requirements for the AIS PhD program, and while rethinking my focus of study, I received word from Diné College that the president, Dr. Cassandra Manuelito-Kerkvliet, announced her resignation and that my name was brought forth as a possible interim president. Prior to her announcement I was consulting with her and Diné College in receiving and installing the R. C. Gorman Library Collection of the late internationally acclaimed Navajo artist R. C. Gorman. This led to the Diné College Board of Regents hiring me as their interim president. Eventually, our relationship with R. C., whose good friend was former New Mexico governor Bill Richardson, led to receiving funds to build the John Pinto Library at the Diné College Shiprock, New Mexico, campus.

Prior to working for the Sage Memorial Hospital-Navajo Health Foundation in Ganado, Arizona, I served as the vice president of development for Diné College under the leadership of Dr. Tommy Lewis Jr. and Dr. Robert "Bob" Roessel, the first president of Navajo Community College, now Diné College. While I was interim president, Bob and I, along with Dr. Lewis and Arizona state senator Dr. Jack C. Jackson Sr., worked tirelessly on establishing a long-term funding stream from the Navajo Nation and the State of Arizona. While securing the Navajo Nation Higher Education Grant Fund Act, which provides $4.2 million per year for twenty years and also included then Crownpoint Institute of Technology (CIT) and grants to the Navajo Nation Scholarship Office, I continued to be enrolled at UA. Diné College spent many years and resources on developing this grant act, but at the end CIT and the Navajo Nation Scholarship Office also benefited. CIT would also benefit from the efforts of Diné College in securing funds from the State of Arizona. I spent several months at the state legislature advocating and securing approval of the Navajo Nation-State of Arizona Transaction Privilege Act, H.B. 2676, which appropriated $1.75 million to Diné College for ten years, and saw its renewal when I was president. These funds helped finance capital and infrastructure projects, including renewing existing structures and building new buildings at the college. Before we secured these important sources of steady funding streams, beyond increasing federal funds from the Navajo Community College Act of 1971 and subsequent federal legislation, Diné College did not have stable and sufficient funds for balancing the annual budget or making long-term plans. Buildings were falling apart, infrastructure was in desperate need of repair, the east entrance road was embarrassing, sidewalks were gravel, and salaries for satellite campus development were unthinkable. Furlough was a common practice to save money. We did not know if layoffs or reduced budgets were going to happen every year. We had to go before the council annually to request funds. That all changed with this historic grant fund act. Consequently, securing this landmark legislation led the Diné College Board of Regents to install me as president of Diné College without conducting a search. By the end of my tenure at the college, we raised and secured long-term funds amounting to over $120 million, including $12 million from the Bureau of Indian Affairs to repave the roads and parking lot at the main campus in Tsaile, Arizona.

As I completed my final year of course work in Tucson, I was working with Dr. Manley Begay as my chair. Manley advised me to align my research question and dissertation proposal with my work at Diné College. Being a doctoral student and having a full-time job as president of a college (including getting ready for a self-study by the accreditation team, developing a strategic plan, implementing shared governance, developing effective institutional mechanisms, exercising de facto leadership, aligning the traditional culture with the academic culture, and tending to other internal and external duties), spending time with my family, and trying to be all things to everyone was not easy. The Nation Building and law courses became essential tools to my position but did not prepare me for the long-standing institutional, cultural, political, spiritual, tribal, and personal politics of the oldest tribal college in the United States.

As I made my way through this multidimensional journey with Diné College, and while achieving historic and long-standing goals, I passed my written and oral exams and then had a trying conversation with my chair— which ultimately proved to be a blessing. I also faced serious challenges at Diné College. My dissertation title, with guidance from my chair, became "In Becoming Sa'ah Naaghai Bik'eh Hozhoon: The Historical Challenges and Triumphs of Diné College." I wanted to discover the critical elements and activities that comprised the cultural history of Diné College. My main research question was "What cultural antecedents contributed to the founding of the first tribally controlled college in the United States?"

I wanted my work to be as authentic as possible to the story that was unfolding through the narratives I was collecting. Further, I started to question my chair about how he and other AIS faculty members were limited in "American Indian" methodology, and how their perspectives and perceived understanding of an American Indian method were not Indigenous enough. We put on our verbal gloves and engaged in a serious dialogue about this and the qualifications of American Indian faculty in the university setting, not just at UA, who claim to be American Indians, but in living, practice, and understanding of their respective tribal culture and language, their "Indianness" was limited or absent. It became apparent to me the requirements for an AIS faculty should not be merely about producing publications, which requires you to cite like thinkers and writers in an academic context, but rather American Indian faculty should know their own language, culture. And live it. Let's be real. Are we Indian when it is convenient and are we Indian because we have federal-tribal documentation (Certificate of Indian Blood)? This leads then to the degree of fluency and competency of our own "Indianness." Sure, we may be fluent speakers of our language, but at the same time we do not participate in or practice our cultural ceremonies. We may practice our cultural ceremonies, but do we know the prayers, songs, and the required plants and procedures of the ceremonies? How often do we do this and to what level do we live it? We may dress like "Indians" but how and where do we live? These are provocative questions that may be offensive to some, but they are direct questions I had to challenge myself to answer.

The "challenges" aspect of my dissertation title was what I experienced when I entered the serious writing stage of my dissertation. Experiencing hardships and challenges are when you find your true self, your true friends, your true family, your true weaknesses, your true strengths, your true enemies. You find what matters most and what does not matter. Hurt finds you, hate finds you, bitterness finds you, falseness finds you, fault finds you, blame finds you, accusations find you, jini and sha'shin find you. You experience financial poverty, taste ridicule and criticism, and experience empty justice. You see your blemishes, cracks, and faults. Then with time you grow stronger, forgiving, smarter, kinder, gentler, and wiser. Being betrayed and hurt by people I trusted and believed would never hurt me has slowly dissolved with time.

Despite all the struggles and battles I experienced as a student and as the president of Diné College, I passed my written and oral dissertation defense and was approved to graduate in May 2009. Although I experienced all the criticisms and negativity, I stayed focused on my goal, and I graduated with my family members in attendance. My grandmother, Glenabah, who was ninety-two years old then, made the trip to Tucson to see me walk across the stage, receive my degree, and then be hooded. One key vision I had about finishing was visualizing my shi ma sani there when I graduated. A couple of months after that she passed on. I had a special relationship with my grandmother.

I thought about how our Diné ancestors were beaten, even killed, on what is known as the Long Walk to Hwééldi, and still they got back up and moved forward. They did not give up. They were strong in many ways. Their prayers and songs, and their courage, helped them persevere. My faith, prayers, and songs were tested, and they became my strength. I heeded that courage, and I had to get back up and move forward.

As president of Diné College I had to make some tough decisions that no one else could make. I admit that I am not perfect; I made some mistakes in my role as president at Diné College. I made some poor decisions. The toughest decisions have to do with people, and as we all know, people are human, and humans are not perfect. However, when people are dishonest about having credentials they do not have in the field of education, there is a toll to pay. My last major personnel decision in this role was to terminate a person who held a critical position, and if I did not make that decision then the faculty would have found me compromised, and that would tarnish my degree and academic integrity. So, I had to do what I did: direct the termination of employment. This led to a trying time for me and my family. Although I had just received an "outstanding" on my performance evaluation and was offered a two-year contract extension, the Diné College board launched an investigation against me. I know a lot of people supported me, and they were hurt too, especially students. I wish them well. Ultimately, I was never provided an opportunity to challenge any allegation or face one accuser, and I eventually departed from Diné College on bad terms. As history tells, I was not the only president to experience this at the college. Bob Roessel wrote about the board's appointment as problematic for the college, and it's part of my dissertation. My dad had told me, and he was the only person who said this to me, not to accept the college presidency because the college always has problems and they always fight with their presidents. He told me to stay in school and finish. He was right, but some of us believe the rhetoric to "come back and help our people once you earn your degree," which is not always advisable. Yes, come back, but be ready to be challenged and criticized.

I believe Diné College has a beautiful philosophy and mission. The cornerstone symbol of the Diné tribal college education philosophical framework, as highlighted through my dissertation work, became the cornstalk. This framework defined the four areas of Nitsahakees (thinking), Nahata (planning), Iina (implementing), and Siihasin (assurance). What I did not explore but has since come into focus, and is probably how an AIS degree has impacted me, is what I define as the corn pollen epistemology. The cornstalk educational philosophy framework that was envisioned and developed by cultural, spiritual, education, and community leaders, and basic grassroots people, belongs to all Diné People and should be understood by Diné educators and parents. Also, I looked more at the Hozhooji (Blessing Way) aspects of the college philosophy rather than the Na'gheiji (Protection Way) elements, though they are interconnected. So, in addition to learning and knowing Hozhoji songs, I also learned Na'gheiji songs to achieve a balance in my life.

After learning that my contract had ended, I found myself unemployed. I was unemployed for almost a year. This period was very difficult for me and my family in many ways with the financial and emotional hardship. At that time, few people would check on me or even give me any money to help us with food or bills. Rex Lee Jim, just then elected as vice president of the Navajo Nation, asked me to help him in his office. I thank him for doing that, and I wish him well.

I had to move forward, as difficult as it was. After a stint with the Navajo Nation President and Vice President's Office as a senior policy advisor, I ended up in Santa Fe with the New Mexico Public Education Department as the assistant secretary for Indian education. I worked with Secretary Hanna Skandera under Governor Susana Martinez's administration. As they were vetting my application, I was thinking that they were not going to hire me because of my Diné College experience, but thankfully that was not the case. I appreciated their understanding and was ready to experience new things in life. The opportunity to work with nineteen unique Pueblos, the Jicarilla and Mescalero Apache Tribes, and the Navajo Nation was an experience to meet and work with an array of culturally astute people. I also worked with twenty-two New Mexico public school districts that enroll American Indian students. A segment of our American Indian community that often gets overlooked, and one that was impressed upon me not to ignore, was the status of urban American Indians. These Indians are from tribes throughout the United States, and they live in places like Albuquerque, Santa Fe, Farmington, and Gallup. Under that federal identification scheme, I became an urban Indian. I enjoyed the different Pueblos and their views of their culture, language, and land in relation to education, as well as their red chili, oven bread, and their many feasts! They treated me well. I advocated for the state's position, and sometimes this conflicted with the tribal/Pueblo position, but through conversations and talking things out, we found paths of consensus. Sometimes our tribal-centric views of the world and how things should be done is not always the best route to take when working with various tribes. I learned a lot through this experience, especially that no matter how many degrees you may have and no matter how big your title and placement within an organization may be, if you have a bad attitude no one wants to work with you. I always thought that I was a nice guy until the ending of my experience at Diné College, which made me somewhat bitter. After being with people who are not threatened by you or who take you as who you are, I rediscovered my sense of humor and started to laugh again. My brother, Dr. Kalvin White, and his family, as well as my parents, conducted ceremonies for me that helped me move beyond my Diné College experience. Time and surrounding yourself with good people can do a heart and mind good. Nonetheless, as I was enjoying living in Santa Fe while meeting and working with the awesome people of our great state of New Mexico, I was drawn back home because of my love for my aging parents.

How could I be so selfish and live my life out there while my parents lived alone, and we (children and grandchildren) come back only for a brief time and then return to our own convenient lives? My dad is diabetic, and my mom's memory is not like it was. My parents were getting older, and I needed to come home. In making the decision to resign from our jobs and return home, which is not easy because you make so many excuses not to do so (kids in school, payment of bills, and other reasons), we moved home. We had no jobs lined up, but we had faith that things would work out. Our parents were our main priorities. Once we made the move home, a new chapter started.

Without a doubt, an AIS degree from UA prepares you to become a college president, a tribal program director, a cultural expert, or an Indigenous cultural ecologist. It is what you make of it and how you apply it in a professional or community setting that it can be helpful to people and communities. However, it is also true that not one faculty or staff member whom

I worked with or studied under at the educational institutions I attended taught me a Diné traditional song, prayer, or ceremony. I had to learn my language on my own, which leads one to learning and knowing the prayers and the ceremonies of our culture. In addition to helping my parents and tending to our agricultural activities, I was able to study, research, and attend many ceremonies. I was able to spend time with cultural and spiritual leaders. But the degrees I earned at these fine institutions legitimated what I learned and spoke about in settings beyond the home. What my father said to me after I returned from my Harvard experience rang true for me in many ways. He said, "Don't get too smart for your own good that you don't know how to build a fire or talk your own language. If you are so smart to learn and then speak English fluently, how come you don't talk our Diné language?" He spoke this to me in Navajo, of course. Basically, he was also saying if you do not have any common sense what good are you out here at home. This became more apparent as I began to attend ceremonies at home. Yeah, I have these degrees, but at a ceremony I just sat there and did not know what to do or did not know the songs. Then, people were thinking, "Yeah, he sure has these nice degrees, but he doesn't know anything." This inspired me to learn Navajo, speak it, sing it, and participate in the ceremonies I was attending. I did not want anyone to ever say, "Gee, he sure looks like a Diné, speaks like a Diné, but does he really live it?" I grew up in it and did not really appreciate it. My parents had ceremonies, my dad went to ceremonies, but they did not really show us or give us the opportunities to "practice" it. We also were not interested, and at some level we were told to learn English and know the white man's ways so we can live a good life, whatever that meant. We were also punished for speaking Navajo and had to eat soap for speaking it at school. While we were growing up, my parents would send us to the Crystal Baptist Church, probably to have them feed us because we ate a lot, and there was little food. Eventually, at Bacone College, this childhood experience came full circle. I understood Navajo but was not fluent until I was thrust back into it.

Fully aware of many things when I began planting corn the spring of 2011, I found myself planting new seeds for future fruits and new opportunities. The whole process of planting corn, tending to each of them, watering them, harvesting corn pollen, making steam corn and kneel-down bread, and all the hard work in this important cultural ritual, I found healing, comfort, guidance, strength, and resiliency. I meditated as I tended to our cornfield, and soon it dawned on me how dynamic and profound the cornstalk education model, which I wrote about in my dissertation, is to a culturally grounded Diné education without the Westernized education influence. I began to understand and appreciate what the original visionaries of the original tribally controlled college had seen and why they identified the cornstalk as the conceptual framework of Diné education. It was not in the many books I read or the faculty and staff from whom I learned, but it was from spending countless hours, days, and nights working and tending to our white, yellow, and blue corn. The stories, songs, and then the prayers all made sense. The twelve ears of corn and the twelve tassels on the top of the corn when it ripens are our Diné education curriculum units tied to the prayers and songs that are sung at ceremonies. It dawned in my mind, body, heart, and spirit that this is authentic Diné education. I discovered ancient truths for a modern world in the field of education. The four directions and the four elements of the cornstalk model on page 208 of my dissertation were not just theory anymore but real. I could feel it, see it, taste it, smell it, hear it, and watch it grow from seed to full ear of corn. This has been the most important impact that my AIS degree has made in my life up to now. I became more in tune with nature and content with my life.

We moved off the grid in more ways than not having electricity or running water. We moved into a hogan atop our Mother Earth and under the immense beauty of clear night skies, stars sparkling all over. I disengaged myself from the rat race, all the media exaggerations about everything, the structured bureaucracies of our government and corporations, and the overcommercialized, immediate satisfactions of our cravings. Taking off the conditional filters of what not to say because you might offend someone and taking off the professional attire for a simple lifestyle is a meaningful experience. I spent time with my parents, albeit a lot of it was driving them to the hospital to tend to my dad's diabetes health status and my mom's hurt hand and diminished memory. I started consulting on education, culture, policy, and other topics with schools, governments, and youth programs. My parents became my primary concern, and with my brothers, sister, nieces, and nephews, the physical health of my dad and mom has steadied and continues to be important to me, though I have reentered the workforce, working the eight-to-five clock and keeping pace with outstanding bills and the latest educational trends. Money, as we all know, cannot buy time, and especially time with parents who raised you and guided you throughout your life and love you unconditionally. I am constantly reminded by people who do not have one or both parents how blessed I am to have my mom and dad, and I do not take them for granted anymore. I was on this sabbatical for nearly four years, and I enjoyed it. I immersed myself back into a Diné world by living in a hogan off the grid and without a temperature-controlled thermostat. I continue to haul our wood and fix our road, which becomes impassable in the winter and muddy during the spring runoff season, though lately that has become challenging. Descriptions about where and how we live do not begin to illustrate the thoughts and feelings of the serenity and peace one finds in such a place. I grew up like this and found peace through this experience. I often think about how tenacious and tough, or resilient as we like to call it, our foremothers and forefathers were long ago. You see the world and life very differently and very simply!

I know why a lot of families on and off the Navajo Nation stop planting and growing corn; it is hard work! The easiest part of working a farm is the planting part, even though it is not that easy, and showing up for a meal of corn stew. Like a person's life, a corn seedling grows, and sometimes you experience obstacles, and you must hoe them away. You must keep them from disturbing your life and taking your needed energy to stay on your right path of growth. That is why it is important to get rid of the weeds that entangle your life. All along this path a person requires love, support, and nutrients, which are the sun, water, and words/songs. Without the sun and without water, either from the rain or from your own sweat and hard work, a seed will not survive and thrive to fulfill its rightful destiny. The weeding, watering, and warmth of the sun occurs while you are dealing with underground assault (prairie dogs and gophers), on-the-ground assault (rabbits, deer, and elk), and air assault (birds, namely crows). When the corn's tassel (A'dzool) grows to maturity, which means you have done a good job in farming (which is a word that wasn't fitting for all that this would engender), then it's time to yield the corn pollen from the tassel.

The Ta'di'diin is important to our Diné prayers. Without it there cannot be a Blessing Way ceremony. There is a prescribed time to make it and there is a prescribed way to make it, either as a female or male, and then there is a process to make it. There are songs that are used when making it. This important process is personal and profound. As I was making Ta'di'diin from our field of education, it occurred to me that without corn pollen we would have no Diné ceremonies, and without knowing and speaking our Diné language we would have no ceremonies and therefore no culture. Our ceremonies and cultural ways of life would cease without our language; corn pollen is the key to it all. Before any plants can be harvested for use (practical, spiritual, cultural, and healing) it is proper to offer corn pollen to those elements for their use. The discussion about the importance of our Diné language and our culture was at its height just recently because someone who was not fluent wanted to be our political leader. At the core of this topic was level of fluency and competency, two areas that never were fully discussed. Westernized legal practitioners, man-made legally trained politicians, and people who believed that speaking Diné is not important to our "Dinéness" created an agreement to allow the voters to decide for themselves who is a fluent Diné speaker, thereby allowing nonspeaking or nonfluent speakers to run for our Diné nation's presidency.

This reminded me of a prophecy that elders talked about throughout my time attending ceremonies, going to meetings all over, and at home, that there's going to be a time when we'll be saying that we don't know our own language. Another prophecy that I heard and has come to pass is the return of the great gambler who promised to return one day after being beaten by the twin warriors. Jack Jackson told this story as one of my research informants. Now, we have Twin Arrows, Fire Rock, Northern Edge, and other casinos on the Navajo Nation taking money from parents, grandparents, and elderly, leading to more social, cultural, and economic poverty—Tee'ii! As a People, we are at a place that prophecy foretold. I do not want to believe it, and I want to do all I can to keep our traditions alive. There is also a story I heard about corn and how there will come a time when Navajos are going to become lazy and cornfields will sit empty. Many fields have surrendered to prairie dogs, gophers, weeds of all kinds, and laziness. There are few cornfields still alive with activity today.

As I was living on the rez, off the grid, John Murray and Tyson Running-Wolf of the Blackeet Tribe of Montana approached me to help organize a capital campaign called the Buffalo Spirit Center. I lived in East Glacier at the time and traveled to Browning, helping organize a fundraising plan to build a cultural museum. I met some great people there and had an interesting experience. That is the time when I received calls to apply for the Bacone College president's position. Not being a Baptist but telling them that I am a contemporary traditionalist—that I am a traditional Navajo who attends Native American Church and Christian churches when invited—they hired me. They said, "Maybe that's what we need." I told them that I pray to the Creator-God all the time, not just on Sundays. The idea of spirituality, faith, and religion, while searching for and remaining Indigenous, would be an exciting challenge as I made my way to Muskogee, Oklahoma.

Now, as president of Bacone College, the AIS PhD gives rise to our vision to transform this historically Christian Indian school into a public, tribal college. This transformation at different historical, political, cultural, spiritual, governmental, and personal perspectives creates varying dichotomies that require understanding, patience, respect, and diplomacy. Aside from being in the eye of the Bible Belt and Tornado Alley, my experience learning about the thirty-nine Oklahoma tribes has been memorable and awesome. Established in 1880 (older than the state of Oklahoma) and known originally as the "Indian University," people would ask me why I chose to take on the job at Bacone College. I was not an alumnus, and I was not from Oklahoma, and on top of that I was Navajo. My son told me I was committing "career suicide" but also said if I could help turn it around it would be a great story to tell. Actually, I do have a tie to Oklahoma—my parents met at Chilocco as part of the Special Navajo Program from 1948 to 1952 during the assimilation campaign to domesticate Indians. As it turns out, I would enter the region of the Five Civilized Tribes. Bacone College sits on Mvskogee (also spelled *Muskogee* and *Muscogee*) Creek land. I have met some kind people here and stand with them for our Native rights.

Bacone College was on the brink of closure when the then nearly all-Native board of trustees hired me as their fourth Native American president in its long-storied mission as a tribal-serving institution. I respect and appreciate the complicated and conflicting versions of Native and non-Native coexistence in this region (Muskogee, Oklahoma) of our country that came to be known as Indian Territory. I have come to interact with the multiple confluences and results of the "Indian Wars" and "Manifest Destiny," including the various treaties with tribes; extermination, termination, and self-determination policies; the 1819 Indian Civilization Act Fund; the 1870 General Appropriations Act; the American Board of Commissioners for Foreign Missions; the Marshall Trilogy cases; the 1887 General Allotment Act (i.e., the Dawes Act); the Meriam Report; the 1924 Indian Civilization Act; the 1975 Self-Determination Act; the 1975-1978 Tribally Controlled Colleges and Universities Assistance Act; and the recent 2020 *McGirt v. Oklahoma* U.S. Supreme Court decision. Understanding our collective histories and our unique status as the original inhabitants of this country—and absolutely knowing how important it is to know our Indigenous culture and language—guides my professional and personal journey of helping our Native People regain our history, language, and culture alongside Western Christian principles. Rather than expect Native leaders and People to come to our campus, I made it a point to go to the leadership of our tribal leaders. This respect for tribal sovereignty led to five tribes—the United Keetoowah Band, the Osage Nation, the Otoe-Missouria Tribe, the Cheyenne and Arapaho Tribes, and the Kiowa Tribe—to charter us as a Tribal College. Living off the grid, or on the Navajo rez, taught me patience and resilience, which has served me well as my team and I, our college family, rebuild and transform this old, historic Christian school into a tribally controlled college. I contracted the coronavirus last year and I recovered with the use of Western medicine and our Native herbs, songs, prayers, and ceremonies. This virus challenges your thinking, identifies your weaknesses, and tests your cultural and spiritual lifeways. I appreciate my life and want to live. I want to continue to be a warrior!

Contending with all the challenges of revamping Bacone College—including working with the Higher Learning Commission, the U.S. Department of Education, the American Indian Higher Education Consortium, and the Bureau of Indian Education; rebuilding our relationships with our tribes; and working with the American Baptist Home Mission Society—we (like all of us in the world) have been managing our college movement through the COVID-19 pandemic. I have visited more than half of the thirty-nine sovereign tribes of Oklahoma. Each of their stories is unique, and I respect and appreciate their continued journeys forward. I must also note the kind relationships I have built with the various tribes of Oklahoma who pray together through the Native American Church. My good Kiowa brothers, Lonnie Emhoolah, Daniel Cozad, and Joe Fish, as well as my Ponca brother, Oliver Littlecook, my naali, Aaron Adson, and our tribal leaders, like Osage leader Archie Mason, Chief Geoffrey Standing Bear, Chairman John Shotton, Chief Joe Bunch, Chairman Matt Komalty, and Governor Reggie Wassana, with all of their families, have helped us bring this old grandma college back to her feet. I want to acknowledge the American Baptist Home Mission Society, the McPherson Baptist Church, the many churches across Oklahoma, proud alumni, the Daughters of the American Revolution, Jerome Steele, the artist and entertainer Ice Cube, and countless others for their prayers and support as Bacone College rises. Throughout this experience, my faith has become stronger and my patience and resolve calm. My family and friends continue to fill my life with love and happiness.

This is what my AIS degree has done for me; I have become an Indigenous cultural ecologist! The sharing of this story has been something my son has been telling me to do, to tell my story, that my story is worth sharing, and I want to thank him for believing in me. I appreciate all the former and present students, former and present faculty and staff, and the good that our education is helping us do for others and ourselves. My story will continue to unfold. A'xe'hee!

CHAPTER 6

Transfer of Knowledge

TARISSA SPOONHUNTER
(ARAPAHO/BLACKFEET)

Oki Nitanikoo Nato Ksiksstaki Aki Amaskapi Pikuni. Hello, my name is Holy Beaver Woman of the South Piegan, Blackfeet daughter of Eagle Thunder Whistle (Arapaho/Oglala) and Many Bundle Holder (Blackfeet/Dakota). I received this name at age nine and at the time I knew it would set the path for my life. I was one of the Minipokaks (groomed children). As a teenager, I realized the status of my name came from the central bundle of the Blackfoot Beaver Bundle. There were times I felt unworthy of such a name among my People. Some of this sentiment was due to Western thinking—a colonization mindset—and the one-quarter pedigree requirement to be enrolled. Most of my young life I wasn't enrolled as a Blackfeet with a 23/100 blood quantum. My family submitted a correction in the 1990s of my grandmother's blood quantum to the Bureau of Indian Affairs that has never been adjusted to this date. Yet, my family has been Beaver Bundle Holders, Thunder Pipe Bundle Holders, Horns Society, and Crazy Dogs through our generational history, but finding that balance in life has always been a journey in pursuing Western education. As a bundle holder, you do not own or cannot claim a bundle—it's the People's/tribe's bundle even though other tribes and societies have personal medicine bundles.

In your tribal community you are often asked, "What is your role in your tribe?" Western education in some ways is selfish—more individually oriented. This was the conflict I endured as Nato Ksiksstaki Aki throughout my life. People would remark that her dad is Arapaho therefore she is not Blackfeet, even though my mother was Blackfeet. I was given a Blackfeet name, attended Blackfeet ceremonies, and grew up immersed in the Blackfeet culture on the Blackfeet Indian Reservation in Montana adjacent to their traditional gathering and hunting area known as Glacier National Park. As a teenager, I was enrolled in the Northern Arapaho Tribe of the Wind River Reservation. My dad—a full-blood Indian of Arapaho and Lakota descent—was not enrolled for over thirty years of his life because his parents, who were in the army, did not enroll their children before the age of two as required by tribal enrollment. They also had limited transportation to get records to the tribal office. The tribal council later passed a resolution to enroll all full-blood Arapahos and soon after began the one-quarter requirement; my siblings and I were now eligible to be enrolled.

Are we tribal even if we are not enrolled? According to our ceremonial People, we are Blackfeet and Arapaho regardless of the one-quarter requirement to be enrolled. I often pose this question to my tribal and non-Native students when it comes to cultural ways of knowing. If an enrolled full-blood has become an alcoholic/addict and has abandoned their children and our culture, are they Blackfeet? Conversely, I am 23/100 Blackfeet—helping my elders, practicing our language and culture, bringing them groceries, giving them rides to their appointments, and making sure they have wood for heat. Who is more Blackfeet? Most would agree from a traditional Blackfeet mindset that I am more Blackfeet than someone who has walked away from their Blackfeet values, even if they are a full-blood according to pedigree. My great-grandfather and his brother were full-blood Oglalas from South Dakota but were working on the railroad in Wyoming years ago. The Indian agents counted all the Indians within the territorial boundaries of the Wind River Indian Reservation and enrolled them as either Shoshone or Arapaho. Even though my papas were Oglala, they were registered as four-fourths Northern Arapaho. The Arapaho Tribe has since acknowledged all tribal blood degree as Arapaho in their records. This was good, as they kept their numbers stable at a time when many were dying of smallpox, foreign diseases, starvation, and exposure within the confines of the reservation. I am Arapaho, Blackfeet, Oglala, and Fort Peck Sioux. Yet, my tribal identification card only lists Arapaho in my blood quantum. My children were enough to be enrolled despite some legal issues of being a single parent. This made them eligible for the Indian Health Service, which was a necessity attending college at the University of Arizona.

I remember very little sharing of Blackfeet ways of life in the K–12 classroom, but my family made sure I knew who I was and carried myself with pride as Blackfeet growing up on the reservation in Montana. We occasionally had the opportunity to practice tribal social dancing and powwow dancing in physical education class about two weeks out of the year. Today, many of my peers recall this as one of the highlights of being in a public school on the Blackfeet Indian Reservation. We also were able to bead in art class starting in about fifth grade at Browning Public School. We had a running club named Antelope Society that ran in the Amateur Athletic Union (AAU) circuit from first grade until middle school. Tribal People are great runners. It is in our bloodline from buffalo runners and footraces to moving camp as hunters and gatherers. I recall my mother making us track suits with tribal designs to represent our People at AAU nationals in California, Texas, Philadelphia, Kansas, and other places.

In high school, I did a science fair project on culture language awareness and preservation. Often the students I saw at ceremonies were the students who were treated differently not only by their peers but also by their teachers. I only had two Native teachers from kindergarten through twelfth grade. In some ways, it was my Blackfeet pride that gave me a sense of who I am and to question things I knew were not true. I began to stand up for our Blackfeet way of life. I stood up for my fellow students who were looked down upon because they didn't have material things like others who were more Western acculturated.

Life on the reservation can be challenging. I grew up in an alcoholic home with dysfunction and many challenges. I made the decision in middle school to excel in academics in order to go to college and show my siblings that we can make our own life and not fall into the cycle of oppression and dysfunction of alcoholism. That same year one of my cousins, Roylene Rides at the Door, was valedictorian and was going to college on a scholarship. I felt that I would also need to have good grades to pay for college because the reality of our tribal People going to college on athletic scholarships at that time was unlikely. In 1991, I was recognized as National Indian High School Student of the Year by the National Indian Education Association in Albuquerque, New Mexico. The late Merle Tendoy of Rocky Boy Indian Reservation was there and spoke on my behalf. His message to me was that I do not just represent my father's and mother's tribes, but I also represent all Indian Country in my educational endeavors. I remember calling my parents to let them know about the award, and they felt bad for not being there when I received it.

By the end of my junior year of high school, I already had enough credits to graduate but was missing two classes necessary for college preparation. The counselor told me that I was in the running for valedictorian. I was surprised to hear this because I had some fellow students who tested higher than me and I felt like I had to work harder to get those good grades. I asked if I could wear my traditional attire, but they said no. I wore it under my gown anyway, and when I stood up to do my valedictorian speech, I took off the gown and danced up to the podium. Today, thirty years later, some schools are still denying Native students the right to wear their traditional regalia at graduation.

After graduation, my mom encouraged me to go see the world, reassuring me that home would always be there if I decided to come back. Our family motto was "They can take away everything from our Native People, but they cannot take away your education." I found myself at Cottey College in Nevada, Missouri, a college no one in my family had ever heard about. Cottey prided itself on having one-quarter international students, and that was my world exposure. It was a private school that introduced me to student loans and student employment to pay for college. I was no longer the top of my class but with ladies who were the top of their classes across the United States. It was stressful, and I failed my first exam there. For me, this was a reality check, and for a minute I doubted I was even cut out for college. I was also experiencing a lot of culture shock—coming from a reservation where my Native demographic made up 95 percent of the population, to being that lone 1 percent minority in a new place. We lived in suites, and each suite had at least one international student. It was a great experience to see the world-views of my suitemates. I recall the women sharing their personal aspirations of wanting to be a CEO, a congresswoman, an engineer, a nonprofit director, and so on. My worldview was so small coming from a reservation. I had never even considered those possibilities because the main employment on the reservation was either being a teacher or working for the tribe. These jobs had little or no education requirements back then. I enjoyed Cottey College, but it was challenging. Ultimately, I decided to transfer to the University of Montana to finish my undergraduate studies.

I started in education at the University of Montana under a teacher training program. The college offered a Native American fee waiver for students from a federally recognized tribe if you were a resident of the state of Montana. We had students from all the seven tribal reservations in Montana, North Dakota, and Idaho as part of the program. Many tribal students need financial assistance and cohort support to be successful because for many, there is still that culture shock going from majority to a minority demographic. We are close-knit families on the reservation, where we know mostly everyone, so at a university you see Native students gravitate toward other Native students to fill that void. I believe there were close to two hundred Native students on campus at the time. My younger brother was there as well, so we helped each other out a lot as he had left a Division II scholarship to come to the University of Montana to try and walk on to the basketball team. I also served as a tutor for a couple of the athletes.

I ended up changing my major to anthropology while at the University of Montana. I was still very concerned about the mostly unknown nature of my People's place in history, education, and larger society. I was leaning toward cultural anthropology around the same time as the passage of the Native American Graves Protection and Repatriation Act (NAGPRA), and tribes were starting to repatriate human remains and items of cultural patrimony. I wrote every paper I could on Blackfeet or Native topics, and in some ways, it kept me from getting too lonesome. My mother facilitated the process for repatriation for the Blackfoot Confederacy. Although it is a U.S. law, many of the bundles, societies, and keepers were from north of the U.S. border that knew the items and protocols of the bundle system. The Blood Tribe sponsored all the museum trips, not the Blackfeet in the United States. They set up a protocol that no bundles would be returned unless they were put back into ceremony with individuals who made vows and protocols for transferring the bundles back to the various bands of the confederacy. I had the chance to tag along to the Cheney Cowles Museum in Spokane. The curators instructed us to bring a U-Haul and take all the Blackfeet stuff that had been acquired by Gonzaga when it was a tribal boarding school. The researchers were scared they were being haunted by these items and wanted nothing more to do with them. As discussion continued, they were told the bundle items were moving around because as Blackfeet, they were kept together and not broken down by scientific categories—this is a rock, this is an animal, this is a plant. You can imagine many bundles end up missing items once in the hands of non-Indians. The Blackfoot Confederacy elders made sure the right people went to these museums depending on the type of bundle and society. In order for this to happen, my mother was given the name Many Bundle Holder with the rites to touch the items of cultural patrimony.

I started to see the importance of my name Holy Beaver Woman and realized that somehow my name brought me to this point in my life. My aunt and her husband had been Beaver Bundle Holders, Thunder Pipe, and Horns Society members for years. I had attended few of their ceremonies, and they began to explain and show me the meaning of their society. I had characteristics of being a caretaker from the role I assumed in my family. Beaver Woman said, "I must love unconditionally and help others even if they may have wronged me or someone I love. Being a Beaver Woman life will be hard, but it is also a good life too." I am human with human traits, but I know that to carry this name requires me to look past those human faults.

I wanted to use my education to help the tribe and decided to intern in the Repatriation Office of the Smithsonian Institution Museum of Natural History. I was pretty good at keeping my life in parallel of two different worldviews: tribal and Western ways of knowing. I was doing well in Western education, moving along in my degree, so I began doing human remains research for the state of Texas for the office of repatriation. The natural history museum had over 33,000 tribal remains at the time, and some were unclear which tribe they belonged to. This research led me to connect with tribes outside of Texas in Oklahoma, Kansas, Nebraska, New Mexico, and Arizona. I became good friends with a physical anthropologist who would call me over to her side when she came upon interesting finds. I will always remember her showing me a toddler-sized skull that had been scalped. I recall the feelings of anger and sadness that overcame me seeing this child's skull. Then one day a tribal employee was retiring and showing his respect to the office and human remains. I was on my side of the office while he was in the collections work area, but I heard him singing and could smell the sage he was burning to say his farewell. At that point, I was awakened, and my heart sank thinking of how many of our ancestors were there and taken from their gravesites or massacre sites. I called home and my mom said that they would be coming there to look at the collections. I told her to ask to visit the warehouse collections, as her agenda only listed the museum. When the Blackfeet came to the museum, they found more items that were not listed in the warehouse and of course the bundles were all taken apart. It was interesting to see that somehow the tribal People would be drawn to a place in the warehouse, pull open a drawer, and find that there was a Blackfeet item not listed on the museum inventory, so our ancestors, the animals, the plants, and nonhuman beings began awakening on these visits.

I started to lean toward working in a museum and applied to intern at the National Museum of the American Indian (NMAI) that was being built but still had most of the collection located in the Bronx at the George Gustav Heye Foundation in New York. I went back to Washington, D.C., and was placed in public affairs for the NMAI under Liz Hill. I was a bit disappointed, hoping I would work in collections, but in hindsight I use more public affairs skills in my career than other skills working with tribes. I did press kits, sat in on interviews, and worked with tribal media for upcoming collections. I also helped with fundraising for the NMAI building and was honored that the architecture for the museum was done by a Blackfeet Indian. The design was very round and difficult for the architects, who worked in lines and squares. I nominated some people to serve on the NMAI board, including one of my professors from the University of Montana, Henrietta Whiteman (Southern Cheyenne). My Aunt Carol and Uncle John Murray eventually served as consultants for the Blackfeet painted lodges for the museum and folklife festival.

During my senior year at the University of Montana, the Native American Studies major was established. I had enough credits to get a minor in Native American Studies, graduating in 1997. I returned to Blackfeet Community College to take Blackfeet studies courses and served as a research assistant on the Baker Massacre project grant from the Bureau of Land Management (BLM) in Blackfeet studies. I also taught a couple Blackfeet studies courses and consulted on a language immersion camp. BLM decided to continue to work with us, and we were able to bring some elders to the Sweet Grass Hills to camp out and share stories. The weather wasn't in our favor, as it rained, and many of the elders' families were worried as we were camping. Family members drove to the Sweet Grass Hills to pick them up. Most elders refused to go with their families, saying that it was one of the best trips of their lives— being able to speak Blackfeet and share oral history. Through this work, we identified some bundle holders that asked if our program could take them to the University of Alberta Museum to visit their bundles. A process of re-patriation was beginning, so we met with the Blackfoot Confederacy elders who assisted us in bringing a Blackfeet elder to visit a bundle her family had kept when she was a child. This bundle was sold before NAGPRA took full effect. I realized then I needed to attend graduate school to be in a better position to help and have a seat at the table with these research institutions.

I visited Brown University, the University of Massachusetts (UMASS), and the University of Providence to get some insight into their graduate programs. I recall waiting two hours at UMASS to identify Native students on campus and thought that I would rather be someplace where there are more tribal students. I was notified of a full-ride scholarship I had received back at the University of Montana but was encouraged by my anthropology professor there to get other perspectives, if possible, at a bigger research institution. I followed his advice and applied to the American Indian Studies (AIS) program at the University of Arizona (UA). I knew that by going to a school in a state like Arizona that had twenty-two federally recognized tribes I was bound to meet more tribal People, as the campus also borders three tribes: the Tohono O'odham, Apache, and Pascua Yaqui.

I had an uncle that lived in Tucson, Arizona, so I contacted him to see if I could rent a room and headed to the "Old Pueblo" in 1999. The city was a lot bigger than I expected, but I was able to figure out the bus route to get to campus with a half-mile walk to the stop. The heat was like nothing I had known in Montana, but there was less humidity than in Washington, D.C., and Missouri. I felt comfortable living among another Blackfeet family and soon found other Blackfeet People living in the Casa Grande and Phoenix areas. I had danced powwow all my life and found powwows go year-round in Arizona and California, seeing many People from up north dancing and singing. I would get so excited to see northern powwow People, and they would ask me what I was doing way down there: "How can you live so far away from home?" I told them I wanted to attend a good graduate school where there were lots of Indians.

At orientation for the American Indian Studies program, I ran into one of my fellow powwow dancers, the late Stephanie Charging Eagle. I knew her not only from powwows but also from her work at Sinte Gleska University, where she had been president for a few years. I was excited to see her as she was pursuing the doctorate program. She stayed for one year, and we would talk about the program and the coursework. We both lived and worked on Indian reservations and started to see the disconnect between academia and the tribal life our families faced. She chose to leave the program before finishing, and I was sad, as she knew what our People were facing at tribal colleges and tribal communities in higher education. I also found it interesting that at orientation, there were thirty-five people, but only three were male students. It was intriguing to see that gender dynamic, but it also was kind of depressing that our Native men were not pursuing graduate school at the same rate as our Native women.

I still had a high interest in cultural preservation and education. The AIS program gave us an exposure to American Indian education, literature, language, law and policy, and sociocultural perspectives. There were some great professors of academia, but I started to miss that direct connection to tribal communities. Being raised Blackfeet, the women are strong and outspoken and have a say in everything. I decided to ask a general question in one of my courses: "All these professors are great academics, but how many have gone back to work in their tribal community?" There were several urban Indians as professors, so I was seeking out those who left the reservation, went back, or found balance in academia. The professor responded that some faculty would take a major pay cut if they went to a tribal community, and others do not have a community to go to. I reflected that as tribal People, we are raised in a communal mindset and are often told to go get educated in order to enrich our communities by coming back and helping others attain an education or opportunity. Yet, Western education is more individually oriented. We see brain drain or lateral violence by our own People who suffered the trauma of boarding schools that broke the connection to our cultural ways of knowing. I know tribal colleges don't pay the same salary as big universities due to lack of funding, but working at the Blackfeet Community College, one student's success is a celebration, and to be part of their journey is an honor. Many have chosen to work at tribal colleges until retirement.

As an AIS student, I struggled in federal Indian policy. I thought it was the most depressing class I have ever taken. The class opened my eyes to how little I knew about federal Indian policy and how my tribal leaders needed to understand and assert self-governance and tribal sovereignty. Despite my struggles, I felt the material was essential to tribal People and communities, so I signed up for two more policy courses. This led me to my thesis topic that focused on Glacier National Park and tribal treaty rights. I finished my coursework in a timely manner, but conducting my thesis research on the Blackfeet Reservation pushed my timeline back. Many of the interviews were done over the phone, and a few were in person. I really tried to bring an understanding of tribal treaty rights and how my People could assert their reserved rights in the 1895 Blackfeet agreement with the United States.

Many tribal directors did not fully understand treaty rights even though they worked in forestry, oil and gas, water, land development, or fish and game, and/or represented the tribe as a leader on the Blackfeet Business Council. In some ways, I wish my tribal council and directors had to take the same courses in tribal governance and the development of federal Indian law and policy. I started leaning toward a policy emphasis in my thesis for my own understanding. As an educated person, I wanted my People to understand what rights they did or did not have in Glacier National Park. My family were hunters and gatherers, so the interest was personal, but then I looked at the treaty and trust relationship between tribes and the U.S. federal government. I tried to continue the educational component of the "transfer of knowledge" like the transfer of bundles among the Blackfoot Confederacy. I completed my interviews the summer of 2001 and finally began to write in the fall semester, completing it five months later. My thesis chair was Dr. Robert Martin, now president at the Institute of American Indian Arts in Santa Fe, New Mexico. Education was always an interest of mine growing up in a highly educated family, and he worked in the tribal colleges—the key to much student success in higher education. My other committee members were Dr. Nancy Parezo and Eileen Luna-Firebaugh. I felt that as an anthropologist, Dr. Parezo could help me keep my emphasis in cultural knowledge and preservation, and law Professor Luna-Firebaugh, who worked with tribes during her summers, could really give me more than academic direction with her applied work in tribal communities. For my thesis defense, my uncle John Bird and his late wife Brenda Olson prepared a traditional Blackfeet meal of wild game, berry soup, and peppermint tea. I felt these traditional foods represented the Blackfeet relationship of the hunting and gathering our People did for generations in Glacier National Park.

I graduated with my master of arts in American Indian Studies in December 2001, pregnant with my first child. I returned to Montana when the state legislature passed the Montana Indian Education for All Act, requiring public schools to include tribal knowledge in all core subjects to help meet the educational needs of the seven reservations in the state. The Blackfeet held a conference during May 2002 and asked me to be the keynote speaker. In some ways, I was a bit surprised in that I had faced lateral violence growing up saying I wasn't Blackfeet since I was not enrolled, but I accepted the invitation. My son Long Time Bear was only two weeks old when I did my first presentation for Indian Education for All. Thanks to my education at the University of Arizona, I was able to share knowledge about blood quantum and federal Indian policy with my maternal People. I spoke about tribal worldview and the Western view as something that really pushed me to pursue higher education. Although I was able to get a degree in a Western educational setting, I never separated from my tribal role to transfer that knowledge to other people.

I promised to present my thesis to the tribal council because at the time there was no institutional review board (IRB) or research committee. Being raised in the country, we always said: "Don't say you are going to do something, walk your talk and let your actions speak for you." So, there I was, presenting my research to the Blackfeet Tribal Business Council. A director I interviewed was now a councilman for the tribe and spoke up on my behalf. The tribal lawyer knew the law, but he lacked the knowledge of Blackfeet oral history and research aspects of my thesis. I gave a copy of my thesis to all those I interviewed and the Tribal Business Council to use as a guidance and reference tool: "Glacier National Park on Blackfoot Territory: The Assertion of Rights on Traditional Lands."

I returned to work at Blackfeet Community College (BCC) as a part-time instructor, where I was able to put my research into action. I was asked by the natural resources program to teach a land issues course and a Blackfeet geography course; they were both short courses, which was ideal for me as a new mom. I also proposed adding a federal Indian law and policy course to Blackfeet studies so that we could meet the needs of our People, helping them understand the tribal and federal government relationship; it was ultimately approved to run at BCC. My students took on the challenge to learn about this relationship and we pushed through the law book together. I was only a part-time instructor during this time, but at the end of the course the students gave such good evaluations that Blackfeet Community College asked if I would teach two more courses, one on treaties and the other on research methodologies.

Despite my positive experiences as an instructor at Blackfeet Community College, I experienced a turning point when I served on an overwhelmingly frustrating consultation panel for the tribe involving the Army Corps of Engineers and outstanding leases to drill oil in the Lewis and Clark National Forest. I decided that I needed to return to UA to pursue a PhD in AIS to build upon my knowledge and experience so that I could better support tribal communities in asserting their rights on traditional ceded lands with reserved rights. The program was interdisciplinary, so I used some of my frustrations to educate myself more on treaty rights and the government-to-government relationship between the United States and tribes. I decided to enroll in a watershed management course since the Army Corps of Engineers seemed to be influencing some decision-making for the Blackfeet Nation. I took another law course that was entitled Anthropologists, American Indians, and the Law. Through the law courses, I was exposed to the joint work that the Indigenous Law and Policy Program was doing with the Native Nations Institute at the University of Arizona.

As first-year doctoral students, we were offered graduate teaching assistantships (GTAs). This was the fun part of being in a two-hundred-student undergraduate lecture course with five other GTAs. It was a lot of work, but well worth it. During this time, I was pregnant with my second child, and the professor planned for me to be moved to a less demanding course, even though my delivery was scheduled by C-section over spring break. In some ways, I was more determined to stay on task but started to feel the concerns of professors who did not have children.

It turned out my watershed management professor, Joe Hiller, had a part-time appointment as director for the AIS program, so I met with him and told him about the great need for a better focus on tribal resource management within the department. I gave him all the reasons on how tribes deal with water, fish and game, oil and gas, forestry, cultural resource access, and so on. Soon after, the program made a new hire by the name of Dr. Ben Colombi, who had done some salmon work with the Nez Perce Tribe in Idaho. A few of us who had an interest in education also convinced Dr. Robert Martin to teach a tribal college course, as he was president of Haskell Nations University and then helped the Tohono O'odham Community College get accredited in four years.

I finished my course work and began preparing for my comprehensive exams with Professor Tom Holm as my chairperson, who still had strong ties back to his tribal community and understood the daily issues our People faced. I continued to work with Professors Luna-Firebaugh, Parezo, and Martin, and added Dr. Colombi to my committee. During this time, I also sought out the opportunity to be a graduate research assistant (GRA) at the Native Nations Institute (NNI) at the University of Arizona, where I was assigned to support the development of the Rebuilding Native Nations distance learning course. I assisted on the readings and questions for the course and was impressed with the huge oral history shared by tribal leaders with the NNI. This was a great fit for my interest in working with tribal communities. I managed to complete my comprehensive exams while being a GRA for NNI but did fail one exam question. There was a bit of concern about being failed on another professor's question, but we addressed it immediately in my exam defense.

I moved forward and began to feel I belonged at NNI and worked there for two years until budget cuts were initiated and I was let go. In 2008, the Blackfeet chairman asked me to review the Montana proposal to the tribe to put off settling their water rights for twenty-five years for $14 million. My initial response was "No! You need to look at tribes here in the southwest where water is scarce and how they are leasing their Winters water rights to the city of Phoenix, Arizona, for $100 million a year." The council was made up of nine individuals, and four had already signed the compact, but they could not get any more signatures. In my opinion, the Blackfeet dodged a bullet in that agreement, but it also showed the lack of knowledge of our tribal leaders having to make million-dollar decisions in tribal resource management.

I started to work full time to support myself and my children, taking the three credits per semester to stay enrolled. I was now the single parent of three children: Long Time Bear, Bluebird Woman, and Red Paint Woman. I recommend not having three kids in graduate school; it will be an adventure. I got into the workforce and just left things on the back burner for my doctoral degree. At one point, my mother said to just come home and be a mom and not worry about that degree. But I felt I made it this far already, and I pressed on. My siblings came and stayed to help with the kids at times, and my mom would come visit often. I worked at a school district on the southside of Tucson as the Indian education coordinator. The district was a feeder school for the Tohono O'odham San Xavier district. The school district received Indian gaming revenue, but none of the funding went to the program I worked for. We had five advisors that served seventeen schools with 17 percent Native students. As much as I thought education was nonpolitical, I was wrong. I lasted a year in this district because I objected to a "scare them straight" behavior-management approach taken upon a Native kindergarten student. I stood up for the student, stating that this type of education was traumatic for our tribal students. I was essentially reminded that I worked for the district and could not voice my concerns or would be fired, so I resigned.

I reached out to Tohono O'odham Community College (TOCC) and began working in institutional research development, which was collecting data for the Higher Learning Commission ten-year report. I would say as an outsider that this was the best working environment I've had, despite the long commute that included a U.S. border patrol checkpoint. The tribal community was very open and structured. They required a Tohono O'odham history class for all employees who worked there for more than a year and a language class for those who stayed for more than three. They had a community garden at TOCC, and employees were able to take some produce home. I started to approach the time limit to graduate with my degree and would be required to retake my comprehensive exams if I did not complete my dissertation on time. The comprehensive exams were the hardest part of my graduate program; I literally cried while writing them and did not want to have to take them again. I called my mother to see if she would come live with me so that I could finish writing my dissertation, which she did. I rented a study carrel at the library and moved in, as I could not write at home with three children and other distractions. My chair was now Dr. Colombi, who was on sabbatical, but we kept in touch over email. Dr. Manley Begay, whom I had worked with at NNI, was also one of my committee members, as was Professor Luna-Firebaugh, who helped with my legal perspective.

My dissertation was entitled "The Blackfoot Confederacy Keepers of the Rocky Mountains," examining the ceded strip of the Blackfeet territory of 1895. The National Park Service had denied Blackfeet reserved rights of the ceded strip, but the forest service recognized treaty rights in the Badger Two Medicine unit. The UA Graduate College deadline for submitting my dissertation and defense was upon me, and I was not quite done writing. I was near completion and was told that if I missed the deadline, I would have to come back in the fall. I packed up my study carrel, thinking that I could either keep writing or take a break. I was sharing the news with my aunt, Dr. Iris Heavy Runner. She suggested I talk to my chair, stating that my department could decide outside of the Graduate College. I called Dr. Colombi, who was out of the country and would not be back until the end of April. He encouraged me to keep writing since I was nearly done; I completed my dissertation during the same week I served as the head dance judge at the 2014 Gathering of Nations powwow in New Mexico. My committee began reading over my dissertation, and my public defense was scheduled for the following week.

I began studying in preparation for my public dissertation defense. This was a big achievement for my family, my People, and my peers as well, who had all faced some struggles in graduate school. My mom once again prepared some traditional food with my uncle and his wife. She sewed all the dresses for my girls, and they were going to be the servers and helpers to provide the traditional meal to all who attended. My uncle provided the prayer and smudge. After the public presentation portion, I faced questions from many people across campus. I felt my dissertation only scratched the surface of the issues the Blackfoot People face with their trust relationship and the stakeholders of the Rocky Mountain region—I passed. Although this was an academic presentation, the end goal was to provide a tool for the Black-foot Confederacy for their rights to help maintain their relationship with the mountains. I was told that my writing should be highly academic, as I was getting a PhD, but I finally found the professors who believed in my endeavor to write for my People, who might not understand legal jargon or highly ac-ademic vocabulary. Rather than use the English names of my interviewees I asked them if I could use their Indian/Blackfoot names. These names not only have a relationship to our People but demonstrate our relationship to the animals, plants, and spiritual beings in the Blackfeet world. My daughter Bluebird Woman, who was nine years old at the time, raised her hand. With the lawyers, professors, and fellow graduate students present, she asked me a question after seeing my presentation on the Blackfoot relationship with the animals, plants, and cultural resources. Then I knew all the years of hardship, wrong turns, doubts, and stress were worth every tear and drop of sweat, as the next generation (my child) was receptive to the "transfer of knowledge" of our relationship as Blackfoot People to the Rocky Mountains.

I graduated that spring thanks to my chair going above and beyond for me to complete my edits. I am so grateful to my mother and family for help-ing me raise my children and coming to live in Tucson, Arizona, so I could complete my degree. I recall one memory in the writing stage: my girls were pretend playing and said, "Let's say we are home since our mom is at the library waiting for our stepdad to come home from work." I had to laugh knowing my kids missed their mom. Even though I was in the same room as them, they only saw me when I sent them off to school every morning during the writing of my three-hundred-page dissertation. I was able to invite my parents and Tucson relatives to the Native student graduation, where most students wore their traditional regalia representing their tribe. Then I walked in the longest, hottest graduation ceremony at the University of Arizona football field, where students were passing out from spirits and being too hot. My kids were troopers and managed to behave through the entire six hours, where four hours were dedicated to watching my cohort entering and exiting the stadium. A local Tohono O'odham woman took me in and helped me with my kids and graduated with a degree as well, so we all pitched in together to have a cookout after graduation.

I was content working for Tohono O'odham Community College (TOCC) and did not really apply to any professorships during this time because I was unsure if I would graduate on schedule. Tucson became home for me and my children. Then I got a call from my sister in Wyoming saying there was a job coming up at Central Wyoming College (CWC) in American Indian Studies that I should apply to since it was a quick hire. I applied for the job and let TOCC know I was considering the job. My supervisor and administrators wanted me to stay at TOCC and were trying to match the salary but couldn't offer anything comparable until the end of the fiscal year depending on a grant. I knew I had student loans that needed to be paid for since I maxed them out to make sure I could cover a good daycare and after-school programs before my mom came to stay for the final year of my program. I looked at student loans as an investment in myself but would recommend that students apply for fellowships to pay for graduate school if possible. CWC offered me the job, and it was inviting because it was located on the Wind River Reservation, even if it was a border town. Ideally, I wanted to continue working with a tribal community in my professional career.

I had become comfortable with the conveniences of the city life, so Wyoming was a drastic change. Yet, I still had that value of giving back and helping my People. I struggled my first year at CWC living in the border town and did not get out in the community since being a community college instructor you are strictly teaching—no research or outreach required. After writing my dissertation, I was okay with not having to do research and writing at the time. I was not sure if I should be at a university and applied to some jobs in Montana and Idaho, thinking it would be good to get closer to home or into a university. To my surprise, my salary at CWC was a lot more competitive than the universities in Montana and Idaho. The community colleges in Wyoming are funded by the state, so I was able to apply for both the Public Service Loan Forgiveness program and the Income-Based Repayment program to start paying back my student loans. I decided as a single mother with three children to stay with CWC, and doors began to open for me to work directly with the tribes on the Wind River Indian Reservation.

As an enrolled member of the Arapaho Tribe here in Wyoming, many eyes were on me to see how I would use my education to give back to my tribal community. While at CWC, I have focused on rebuilding the relationship between the tribes and CWC, along with the University of Wyoming. There have been many researchers that have come into the tribal community to do research who have not been good partners to the tribe. Many times, the research benefited the universities and not the tribe, leading to mistrust of higher education institutions in tribal communities. CWC hired a visionary president who made it a priority to be a better partner to the Wind River Indian Reservation, and he asked me how the college could keep me there. I told him of my desire to work directly with tribes to provide more opportunities and partnerships in the community. Over the years, he has done a lot of outreach to the tribal leaders. Many community members have been impressed with the efforts of the college outreach by the president, American Indian Studies, and the Institute of Tribal Learning at CWC.

I am grateful for the human subjects research process at the University of Arizona and the Collaborative Institutional Training Initiative training module on research in tribal communities that helped guide me in rebuilding a trust relationship between the tribes, CWC, and the University of Wyoming. The tribes in Wyoming are not as far along as the tribes in Arizona in having research protocols or an IRB in place. The University of Arizona is a great resource for providing and sharing tribal research programs that I have used and shared with the local tribes. Currently, we are in the process of helping the tribes in forming an IRB and the process of tribal-specific research protocols. I have currently joined the Cultivating Indigenous Research Communities for Leadership in Education Alliance, made up of six other states with tribal colleges and universities to help expand tribal students into STEM (science, technology, engineering, and mathematics) fields with a focus on traditional ecological knowledge.

Being a graduate of AIS from the University of Arizona has truly been an asset. It not only prepared me to be a professor, but the interdisciplinary program allowed me to tailor my interests in working with tribal communities and the Native Nations Institute. I loved Tucson and the fact that it has three tribes bordering the city, so it was not difficult for me to make friendships/family that kept me in the Southwest for over fourteen years. My children call it home as well, and we do our best to go back and visit at least every two years. I have made efforts to keep in touch with many of my peers as we climb our respective career ladders in various states across the country. Surprisingly, I am finally ready to write again and pick up on expanding my dissertation, along with continuing to help build tribal partnerships in research. I will continue to transfer knowledge to future generations through my courses, outreach, and mentoring. Unya!

CHAPTER 7

"Keep Pluggin'"

New Generations Need Strong Shoulders to Stand On

MICHELLE L. HALE (NAVAJO,
LAGUNA, CHIPPEWA, ODAWA)

My first American Indian Studies (AIS) course at the University of Arizona was with Professor Bob Thomas in 1990. He was a serious intellectual and man of few words who commanded the attention of his students with his enduring presence, vast knowledge, and gift for storytelling. I was impressed by how adeptly this meticulous professor who lectured off of yellowed notepaper could impart such extensive and thought-provoking information on Indian history while barely referencing the writing on his legal pad. Growing up on the Navajo Reservation I had, admittedly, never met a Cherokee before, nor had I taken many university-level classes that were taught by a Native professor. I did not know it at the time, but this AIS professor was a legend. A respected Cherokee anthropologist, Bob Thomas was one of many early AIS scholars who worked to bridge the gap between long-established disciplines in the academy and the newly emerging field of AIS. In his work, Professor Thomas challenged anthropological notions of kinship and community; explored differences in the way Indian People experience nationalism and mainstream ideologies and institutions; and asserted the critical need for an integration of Indian worldview and understanding in the work of cultural anthropology. He, Vine Deloria Jr., and others at the University of Arizona worked to lay the groundwork for AIS as we know it today—a freestanding discipline that honors and values traditional knowledge, asserts and protects space for Indian thinking, and celebrates Indigenous identity and the survival of community languages and culture.

I completed my undergraduate and graduate education at the University of Arizona with a bachelor's degree in cultural anthropology in 1991, a master's degree in AIS in 1996, and a PhD in AIS in 2012. I currently hold a tenure-track position in AIS at Arizona State University (ASU) and will go up for promotion and tenure review in 2022. I am blessed to have the opportunity to work with American Indian students at ASU who are on their own educational journeys, and I do what I can through teaching and mentorship to support them as they gather the knowledge, tools, experience, and inspiration to realize their goals and to make the impact that so many of them aspire to. "Giving back" to tribal communities is a desire that remains unchanged among so many Indigenous youth. I saw that among students I worked with at the University of Arizona and I see it currently among our students at ASU. Students today have countless career options and choices when it comes to colleges and universities, majors and minors, and even modalities for learning. AIS is more relevant than ever as students study science, engineering, business, and other fields to find innovative and sustainable solutions to the challenges we face in Indian Country. AIS helps students Indigenize those solutions and make them practical for tribal communities and culturally appropriate for the societies we are in the process of creating.

My current work is in the area of Indian community and economic development, with a particular interest in community-based planning. I examine decision-making, policy, government, and citizen participation as they pertain to development. At ASU I teach alongside and partner with colleagues from the School of Geographical Sciences and Urban Planning (SGSUP), the Global Institute of Sustainability and Innovation, the Watts College of Public Service and Community Solutions, the Del E. Webb School of Construction, and the Herberger Institute for Design and the Arts. Together, we find ways to tailor knowledge and tools from our fields to equip Indigenous communities to imagine, plan, build, and grow in culturally responsible and thoughtful ways. We help our students to acknowledge and learn from the Indigenous past but also to prepare for and find ways to contribute their ideas and passion to the future. The book I am writing, *Doing for Themselves: Navajo Community Development Through Localized Decision-Making and Planning* (University of Arizona Press), argues that citizen engagement with decision-making and goal setting as it pertains to development places power and accountability on the grassroots level. Who better than local people to think about what they want for their families in the future and to shoulder the responsibility of making it all happen? "Local empowerment" was the slogan of the Navajo Local Governance Act (LGA) when it was introduced in 1998. It is a chance for local chapter communities at Navajo to *do for themselves*. I argue that successfully doing for oneself is contingent on involving the people, the nonelected leaders, because their ideas matter. Involving ordinary citizens may require that they receive a basic education on planning principles, mapping and GIS (geographic information system) technology, and perhaps land-use policy. However, that is a worthwhile investment and one that has the potential to facilitate the scope of local empowerment that was envisioned by the authors of the LGA.

Ordinary citizens on the Navajo Nation are willing to learn new technologies. That was evident at Dilkon Chapter where then doctoral student Jonathan Davis (ASU SGSUP) conducted a series of geodesign workshops that presented Dilkon community members with interactive maps that helped them to see and talk about present land suitability and future land use. Being able to draw on maps, see imagined changes, share ideas, and have those ideas included in a community discussion helped Dilkon Navajos to feel and be part of chapter decisions on land use. It helped them to negotiate plans, work through points of disagreement, build consensus, and work together to set priorities and timetables for implementation. That work is useful for Dilkon or any Navajo chapter that must submit a land-use plan to the Navajo Nation in order to be certified as an LGA community. I joined ASU urban planning professors David Pijawka and Elizabeth A. Wentz on Jonathan's dissertation committee and was able to lend the AIS and Navajo Studies perspective to the work. The Dilkon geodesign workshops are described in our co-authored article in *Landscape and Urban Planning*, "Evaluation of Community-Based Land Use Planning Through Geodesign: Application to American Indian Communities" (Davis et al. 2020). This work across the disciplines underscores the importance of collaborative partnerships and usefulness of such efforts for Indian communities.

As a graduate student at the University of Arizona, I saw multidisciplinary partnerships at work. An example that resonates is the 1992 Poetics and Politics series organized by Larry Evers and Ofelia Zepeda. It featured Indian poets and scholars at the university and brought to campus other renowned poets and authors that included Joy Harjo, Roberta Hill, Daniel Lopez, Nora Marks, Felipe Molina, N. Scott Momaday, Nora Naranjo-Morse, Simon Ortiz, Greg Sarris, Leslie Marmon Silko, Luci Tapahonso, James Welch, and

Ofelia Zepeda. Each gave public readings of their work. Native American Poetics was the graduate seminar linked to the event. It drew students from AIS, education, cultural studies, linguistics, and anthropology, offering students like me a chance to engage with the authors to ask questions, discuss their work, and share our ideas. The exchange helped many of us to find motivation and purpose for our own writing and to explore creative space for our personal contributions to our fields and communities. Central to the seminar was a discussion of ethnopoetics. We explored the poetics unique to each Indigenous community and examined the role of language, identity, history, and culture in the way we write as Indian People. This was my first foray into the power, opportunity, and responsibility that we hold as Indian scholars and writers since our words honor our identity, claim intellectual space, and distinguish the experiences and oral histories of the People we come from.

For me, Poetics and Politics was significant because it introduced me to the work of Luci Tapahonso, Nora Naranjo-Morse, and Leslie Marmon Silko. I am Navajo, Laguna, Chippewa, and Odawa. I grew up on the Navajo reservation strongly influenced by my Diné dad and Pueblo mom who imparted Laguna sensibilities in my way of being, so I was particularly drawn to the Pueblo and Diné women poets. As a Diné person, reading Luci's work was the first time I felt that words on a page reflected my own experience and worldview in a personal and powerful way. The Navajo reservation was my home and, like Luci, I knew homesickness for family and friends, home cooking, and the landscape of familiar places and smells. I laughed, thought, wondered, and felt many of the same things that were powerfully articulated in Luci's poems. Hearing Luci read her poems was mesmerizing. Her poems celebrate the Navajo experience and Navajo English and show us the world through Raisin Eyes. She made lyrical the everyday activities of herding sheep, going to the trading post, riding along dirt roads in Grandpa's truck, and listening to country music on KTNN. Through Luci's work I understood the importance of not just Indian People but Navajo People telling our own stories, in our own words, and in the style, language, and humor of the People, without explanation, apologies, or excuses. Luci's work demonstrated for me the power of our stories, language, and presence, and the importance of being in charge of our own narrative.

I mention these class experiences because we were quite fortunate to be students in Tucson and at the University of Arizona when AIS was blossoming and when so many Indian scholars were present to teach and mentor. I studied literature under Larry Evers, Joy Harjo, N. Scott Momaday, Simon Ortiz, Michelle Taigue, Ofelia Zepeda, and others. Mary Jo Tippeconnic Fox and Jay Stauss were invaluable to my thesis work when I studied Indian higher education. When my focus shifted to policy and government for the doctorate degree, David E. Wilkins, Eileen Luna-Firebaugh, and Stephen Cornell provided the challenge, advice, and support I needed. Most of the professors I studied under are American Indian. As a young and impressionable graduate student, it was, and continues to be, significant to see Indigenous scholars in the academy. With the historic election of Kamala Harris as vice president of the United States in 2020, communities of color felt a moment of triumph because, for once, Black and Brown people could "feel seen" in the highest echelons of this nation's leadership. The presence and success of Indigenous professors at colleges and universities help Indigenous students to "feel seen." It matters that Indigenous scholars earn tenure, write books, teach, and protect that intellectual space carved out by the Indian scholars whose shoulders we stand on. For many of us, the space in which we carry on that endeavor is in AIS.

At ASU, upon the writing of this essay, we are proud to have seven Indigenous scholars full time on our faculty, three Indigenous adjunct professors, three Indigenous emeritus professors, and ten American Indian affiliate or adjunct faculty in English, law, and the Schools of Historical, Philosophical and Religious Studies, Social and Family Dynamics, and Social Transformation. Our students benefit from the breadth of experience and knowledge that our faculty bring to the courses we teach. Book knowledge and research credentials are certainly important, but it is especially meaningful when our students can learn from Indian professors who have worked in tribal communities as community organizers, activists, elected officials, administrators, educators, artists, and health workers. Most of us never disconnected from our home communities through the years of college and work life that take us away from home. Over the years my AIS colleagues actively engaged in helping their communities document oral histories and establish tribal colleges, institutional review board protocols, education policy, and health care practice. Many of us serve on community boards and committees whose work or services directly impact Native People in reservation and urban areas.

It is special to hold a doctorate degree in AIS, especially since the generation of AIS scholars before us often hold PhDs in history, political science, sociology, or education because those were the available degree programs that housed or facilitated work on Native topics. At one point there were three tenure-track Indigenous faculty here at ASU with AIS doctorate degrees from the University of Arizona. In a perfect world, there would be more tenure-track positions available across the country in AIS, especially given the success of the University of Arizona in graduating qualified applicants with this unique degree. AIS programs are often small, with limited resources, but there is hope that, with proven success, these programs will continue to expand and thrive.

Notwithstanding the in-state rivalry between the University of Arizona and ASU—and on the lighter side of things—leaving Wildcat country to become a Sun Devil has been an interesting journey. I find that any rivalry best be left on the football field or basketball court. When it comes to the education of Indian students, and the growth of strong and useful academic programs to support our students, we are all in this together. After all, there remains an undeniable premium placed on education. Many Native students are the first in their family to attend college; that has remained unchanged over the years. Native parents see a college education as their child's key to a better life and greater opportunity and security. This is their chance. As Indian educators we are the teachers, advisors, mentors, and role models who have a critical role in helping students and families to realize those dreams. At each graduation ceremony Native families show up with grandmas and grandpas, kids, and extended family in tow. All are there beaming and so full of love and pride to see their student graduate from college. As faculty we are usually on the stage or part of the formal university procession, but it always makes me proud to see Native families in the audience, the women wearing their best silver and turquoise jewelry and the men wearing the cowboy hats and Wranglers that they save for special occasions. We know that the families sacrifice a great deal to send and keep their student at college, so graduation is truly for the student and everyone who supported him or her along the way. Commencement is always a highlight and motivation to keep doing what we do.

Since teaching, research, and service guide so much of what we do within the academy, I will use those areas to reflect on my AIS experience at the University of Arizona and to comment on how it impacts what I do today as professor, thinker, writer, and citizen of my community.

Teaching

The first time I stepped in front of a university class to teach was in 1994. I was part of the graduate student teaching team that assisted Professors Mary Jo Tippeconnic Fox and Jay Stauss with AIS 100, Introduction to American Indian Studies, a course now called Many Nations of Native America. In 1994, the class had over 150 students, and it was taught in an old-style lecture hall with terraced seating and a large lecture table and blackboards at the bottom center of the room. I mention the particulars of the space because, as a nervous and novice teaching assistant, being at the podium was overwhelming, and the towering rows of students were quite intimidating.

I am indebted to Mary Jo Tippeconnic Fox and Jay Stauss for inviting me to join the teaching team in 1994. I was a brand-new graduate student trying to learn the ropes. I had not articulated an interest in teaching, nor did I feel that I had done anything extraordinary to distinguish myself from my peers as someone who earned one of those coveted teaching positions. Truthfully though, I had always wanted to teach, so the chance to do it at the University of Arizona and for AIS was a pretty big deal. As a kid, I spent many summer vacations playing school with my friends and younger nieces and nephews. Of course, I was always the teacher. I had five nieces and nephews who were usually under my supervision while the adults worked. Playing school was a great way to pass the time, keep the kids busy, and hone the skills that would one day become my "bread and butter." When the kids grew tired of school we would switch gears by playing library, which, for me, was a fun opportunity to teach reading and foster a love of books. I don't recall my nieces and nephews complaining about all the schoolwork.

I applied to the AIS master's program upon a suggestion from Professor Larry Evers. In 1991, after completing a bachelor's degree in cultural anthropology at the University of Arizona, I took Evers's Native Literature class as a way to test the waters in graduate school. After getting my bachelor's degree, I was uncertain about the next steps but not yet ready to return home to the Navajo Nation. I had a good rapport with Professor Evers and shared with him one day that I thought I might want to teach. I enjoyed the Native Literature class and considered a career in writing and literature, although doing that on the university level seemed, at the time, a rather lofty goal. Evers encouraged me to think about teaching at Diné College on the Navajo Nation.

I had the desire and dream to teach; the challenge was figuring out how to get there. Being in front of people and talking terrified me. I was nervous when all eyes were on me and I grew flustered when I could not remember important names, dates, or information at the right moment. My professors were masters at public speaking. They were smart, insightful, funny, confident, poised, inspiring, and good at drawing the audience in and getting them excited about the topic at hand. I could not imagine getting to the point of being just as skillful and effective. As the years went on, I realized that everyone—even the most accomplished speakers—struggles with public speaking and that it is always a work in progress. As a rookie graduate student I needed a great deal of practice, which is why it surprised me when Professors Fox and Stauss invited me to join the teaching team.

The AIS 100 teaching team changed my life. It stoked the enthusiasm and love of the job that endure today. As an AIS professor I have an incredible platform to share all that is strong, beautiful, innovative, and resilient about our Indigenous communities and to use AIS as a vehicle for Native students to feel seen, to be heard, and to figure out how to contribute something positive to their communities. The team dynamic offered valuable lessons in collegiality and camaraderie as we worked together to plan student activities, create assignments, and support each other as we took turns preparing and delivering lectures to the class. Each of us led a weekly small group discussion for twenty-five to thirty students. The small group gave us the chance to tailor the discussion to themes that reflected our own interests and to try our hand at grading exams and essays. It was trial by fire as we learned how to manage the classroom, teach controversial topics, and to handle difficult situations, disagreements among the students, and student challenges to assigned grades or class policies. We learned how to assist when students encountered personal or academic obstacles. Professors Fox and Stauss gave us the leeway to grow, to try new things, and to make mistakes along the way, all while providing steady mentoring and support.

The AIS teaching team experience showed me the potential of AIS and the responsibility that we as Indigenous scholars have as we continue to build and grow the field. I know that I am held to a higher standard being Native and teaching and writing about Native subject matters, or being Diné and teaching and writing about anything Diné. People in our community expect us to get it right. When I write about Diné, people back home expect me to get it right; and they will let me know if I fall short. Representation matters on college or university campuses, where Native students often comprise less than 2 percent of the student body. At ASU we are fortunate to currently be home to more than three thousand graduate and undergraduate students. It is meaningful when Native students see Native scholars, professors, academic professionals, staff, and high-ranking leaders on their college campus. That presence is all the more powerful when those professionals are Indigenous women. A Diné student once told me he was honored to be in my class because I was the first Navajo PhD he had ever met, and he always made a point to address me as Dr. Hale. Another Diné student proudly told his parents that he had a Diné woman professor; they were impressed and always kindly asked about me and my class, offering support from afar, as any good relative would do. Those connections resonate profoundly and remind me of the import of what we do. Students share with me the importance of being able to see themselves in their professor and to work with a professor who understands the Indigenous lived experience and knows the challenges of being reservation educated or juggling family and cultural commitments along with their classes. It means something when we share food, knowledge, humor, and even hardship with our Native students. That connection is even deeper and greater when language is also shared. I was not raised to speak Navajo or Laguna (Keresan) by my parents and sometimes feel that limitation in my work.

The lasting takeaways from the teaching team experience my first year in graduate school are the friendships and the confidence to grow and to do more as a teacher and scholar. I met my good friends Jeneen Wiche and Lori Hansen through the AIS 100 teaching team, and I appreciate that we maintain a connection all these years later. I lectured at Jeneen's AIS class at the University of Louisville in 2017 and again in 2021, and Lori showed up on Zoom this spring to offer moral support when I gave a talk for the University of Illinois at Urbana-Champaign. I learned a great deal from my teaching cohort: some gave impressive lectures that inspired me to be a better researcher and presenter, others amazed me with their public speaking skills or ability to tell a good joke or story, and still others had a knack for coming up with fun activities for class. There was just enough competition among us to challenge us as individuals to be better and to develop expertise but also enough solidarity and friendship for us to support each other. Professors Fox and Stauss did a great job of teaching us to cultivate that camaraderie. Personally, that teaching team was the nudge I needed. If they had not offered me the chance to join the team, and if I had failed to find the courage to do something that terrified me, I might not be doing what I do today. Currently, the exhilaration of a class or lecture well done is what motivates me to continue honing the craft of teaching. Joe Graham is another dear friend whom I met through AIS. We were not on the teaching team together, but he was the only other Laguna person I knew on campus. Being Laguna connected us and fostered a camaraderie and friendship that endures today.

Research

I am an Indigenous policy and governance professor today because of two experiences that changed the way I thought about the federal-Indian relationship and strategies for building strong and resilient Indian nations: the Morris K. Udall Native American Congressional Internship and serving as research assistant with the Native Nations Institute (NNI) at the Udall Center for Studies in Public Policy at the University of Arizona. Both are programs of the Udall Foundation, a Tucson-based agency that honors the legacies of Morris K. and Stewart L. Udall through programmatic work that advances the Udall commitment to the protection of the environment, public lands, and natural resources, and the support of American Indian and Alaskan Native right to self-governance.

I was honored to be selected as Udall intern in 1998 and especially proud to represent AIS among the interns, as most of them were law students. I was assigned to the White House where I worked for Lynn Cutler, deputy assistant for the Office of Intergovernmental Affairs (IGA) and senior advisor to the White House chief of staff on Indian affairs. Holly Cook Macarro, enrolled member of the Red Lake Band of Ojibwe, was Lynn Cutler's right-hand person on Indian policy. Holly was well connected in Washington, D.C., and across Indian Country. As her intern, I saw how adept Holly was at the political calculus of the job, and it was striking to see a fellow Indigenous woman operate among senior staffers with confidence and grit, and push forward an Indian agenda in an environment that was unsparing and among people not always interested in Indian issues.

When Ivan Makil, then president of the Salt River Pima-Maricopa Indian Community, visited, I led the walking tour of the White House grounds for him and his family, and we took photos of them standing at the podium in the press room of the West Wing. Tribal visits were always a momentous occasion, and the better acquainted I became with the people and grounds of the White House and the Eisenhower Executive Office Building, the more fun it was to share that with visitors. I enjoyed any chance to visit the West Wing or walk through the Rose Garden portico, as these are such iconic places. When I attended meetings in the Roosevelt Room in the West Wing, I took photos of the artwork and saved the coaster with the presidential seal for my scrapbook. It was always a bonus to get my hands on the presidential M&M's with Bill Clinton's signature scrawled on the box; those were a real treat when I handed them out to friends and family after my summer in D.C. Other highlights were the annual fireworks display on the South Lawn, the pageantry of the state visit of South Korean president Kim Dae-Jung, and official events where I saw—in person—leaders and lawmakers who were the movers and shakers in our nation's capital. Friends and family back home appreciated the behind-the-scenes photos and the stories that I shared after my summer adventure. Given the historical significance of the nation-to-nation relationship, and the urgency to keep tribes on the radar, it was important for leadership and staffers to see tribal delegations, Holly, and me, the Diné intern, in that space.

The big tribal event that summer was a first-ever interagency tribal economic development conference hosted by the White House. I helped Holly and IGA staffers with planning and logistics. I have group photos of noted tribal leaders with President Bill Clinton, and even a few pictures of interns with the POTUS in the background. Fellow Native interns and I were starstruck. For most of us, that was our first time seeing a sitting president in person. For many of us, that summer was our first time traveling east of the Mississippi. As a rez girl, I recall being in awe of all the green grass, trees, and water; all of that a stark contrast to the desert Southwest. I loved the hustle and bustle of the city, the architecture of the federal buildings and monuments, and riding the D.C. Metro, even though my dorm room at George Washington University was a short walk to the White House.

I was grateful that Lynn and Holly made sure my internship was challenging and substantive, and that I had the chance to be an observer at task force meetings and interagency discussions, and for visits with tribal delegations. Of course, as an intern, I had no role in making policy recommendations at the White House IGA office, but I observed those who did, and I often provided the research for assistants who advised the advisors on the issues. That "fly on the wall" exposure showed me the art of politics, persuasion, and negotiation, and the importance of diplomacy, bipartisanship, and compromise. As a student, one reads about government institutions and the American political process, but being in the room, hearing the conversation, as the process is happening or seeing how decisions truly get made offers a useful reality check. The Udall internship presents an opportunity for Indigenous students to gain firsthand exposure to the inner workings of the government-to-government relationship. The hope is that students come away from the internship experience better informed, inspired, and motivated, and with a growing network of contacts to help them get work done on behalf of their communities.

Networking is critical for most occupations. The 1998 interns were fortunate that Holly and other D.C. Native professionals were so generous and welcoming. They were a family, and they invited us to their table for barbecues and other social events and took many of us under their wings. They mentored Native interns from the Udall program, AISES (American Indian Science and Engineering Society), and WINS (Washington Internships for Native Students, American University). They wanted us to get the most of our summer in D.C., so they introduced us around, showed us the networking ropes, and motivated us to finish our degrees so we could join the fight. Through Udall, I met another dear friend, Gabe Galanda, citizen of the Round Valley Indian Tribes of California, descending from the Nomlaki and Concow Tribes. Gabe was a law student at the University of Arizona in 1998 and a fellow Udall intern. Today he is an Indian law superstar, a managing lawyer at Galanda Broadman, a prolific writer, and a tireless advocate on issues of disenrollment and the protection of Indian-owned business. Holly continues to advocate for Indian nations in D.C. and is a partner at Spirit Rock Consulting. I am indebted to my friend Adrienne King, who recruited me for the Udall internship. As an alum of the program, she was convinced of the many benefits and was correct on all counts.

The second experience that calibrated my interests toward government and policy was a research assistantship with the NNI at the Udall Center for Studies in Public Policy. Stephen Cornell was my dissertation chair. At that point I was an AIS doctoral student at the University of Arizona. The dissertation was an evaluation of the LGA, a 1998 "local empowerment" initiative that intended to kickstart community development in the 110 chapters across the Diné nation by decentralizing powers that historically hampered localized decision-making pertaining to land use, economic development, and governance. The reform effort resonated with the nation building work that emerged from the writings of Stephen Cornell and Joe Kalt, work that was furthered by Manley Begay Jr., Miriam Jorgensen, Stephanie Russo Carroll, and others at NNI and the Harvard Project on American Indian Economic Development. What I observed on the Navajo Nation was grassroots-level nation building, or community building. If successful, the Navajo LGA could dramatically reconfigure the way local communities and the Navajo Nation itself govern and do the work of development. A Navajo chapter, fully certified in all the powers and authorities of the LGA, could assert its self-sufficiency, streamline decision-making, and effectively self-govern with focus and expediency that could improve land use, policymaking, natural resource management, service delivery, and accountability in government. The trick is getting Navajo chapters certified, maintaining that certification over the long term, and putting all the tools and information in place so that chapter officials can utilize all the options and opportunities afforded by decentralization and expanded local control.

Navajo chapters have struggled with certification. Hurdles include the development of an approved land-use plan, updating that plan every five years to maintain certification, training for chapter staff to manage accounting protocols and security measures required by the LGA, and the adoption of a strategic long-term plan to serve as a road map for local leaders and community members. Cornell-Kalt-style nation building, with its call for a governance and development style that matches the community it serves, provides a useful framework for LGA discussion and implementation. As a research assistant for NNI, I helped with nation building workshops and had the chance to travel with Joan Timeche. Through that work I was introduced to elected leaders, program directors, and community leaders across Indian Country who were inspired by the idea of nation building but wrestled with the reality of implementation, particularly when the efforts were thwarted by politics. Even today, the value of the NNI nation building work is in the storytelling, the lessons and advice from people who faced struggle in trying to achieve effectiveness and efficiency in governance but overcame the hardship through tenacity and creative problem-solving.

The NNI research continues to inform my work. My work reflects an interdisciplinary approach to community development and draws from AIS and urban planning and community-based planning. The value of interdisciplinary collaboration is something I learned as a graduate student in

AIS. Today, I co-teach and publish with colleagues who are planning practitioners, GIS specialists, and scholars in planning, sustainability, and community development. The value of our partnership is the practicality of the tools from urban planning, particularly when those tools are Indigenized to match the culture and needs of the Indigenous community that tailors them. With Indigenized tools in hand, that community has the means to tackle the practical work of nation building. Especially useful are the planning approaches that equip a tribal community to communicate and work together to build the society that they want for their future generations.

Most of the students who enroll in my classes are Native. These are young people who are inspired and motivated to do all that they can to protect their community's land and environment, to provide for elders and the youth, and to build something at home so their generation has something to invest in and return to after their education is completed. Many of our students will someday run for council, serve as CEO for tribal enterprises or division directors in tribal government, or raise children on the reservation. My job is to provide them with the knowledge, tool kit, and motivation to realize their personal and professional goals. With every field trip or guest speaker that I invite to class, I try my best to help them to get connected.

Service

I learned service to community from my mom, Rosemary, who did for others constantly, tirelessly, and humbly. When I was a student at St. Michael Indian School, my mom was a reliable volunteer for bake sales, raffles, and the annual school bazaar. She was quick to pitch in for anything that could raise money for the school or somehow benefit the students. A senior trip to London and Paris would have been impossible without the fundraising efforts of our parents. My mom sent donation requests to businesses in Gallup and worked concessions at basketball tournaments and countless bake sales. My dad pitched in as well, but my mom's treats were good moneymakers. She was known for her apple cake, popcorn balls, and Pueblo-style sugar cookies and fruit turnovers. Those treats eventually became favorites of my friends and roommates in Tucson once I went away to college. My mom never expected thank-yous and shied away from the limelight whenever someone tried to recognize her for her contributions. She and my dad, John, were constant companions and were married more than fifty years.

My parents' volunteer work continued even after I left for college at the University of Arizona in 1986. My parents were at every homecoming, family weekend, and annual powwow, and were just as involved and visible as they were in my St. Michael school days. Homecoming was a great chance for my parents to meet my professors and fellow graduate students. I was especially close to Mary Jo Tippeconnic Fox; I was her teaching assistant, and she guided me through the early years of my graduate studies. I called her my "academic mom" because she always looked out for me, and I was glad that she and my mom were acquainted and enjoyed visiting at homecoming or whenever my parents traveled to Tucson. In the 1990s I joined the American Indian Alumni (AIA) and served along with good friends Karen Francis-Begay, Gerald Dawavendewa, Adrienne King, Carl Etsitty, Terry Abrams, Monica Nuvamsa, my niece Veronica Boone, and others. We raised funds for scholarships and hosted an annual reunion breakfast at homecoming; it was a chance to honor the accomplishments of our American Indian alums, highlight the successes of current students—the future generation of alums preparing to make their mark on the world—and give everyone a chance to meet, celebrate, and have a good time. I appreciated that AIA events offered my parents a way to connect with my experience as a graduate student at the University of Arizona and to be part of the Indian community in Tucson, which had become my home away from home. The Indian community in Tucson became my family over the years, and their kindness was graciously extended to my parents.

My mom passed in 2007. I regret that she was not able to see me walk across the stage at McKale Center when I earned my PhD in May 2012. My dad was in the audience, along with my husband, Nathan Pryor—also a former NNI research assistant—and our relatives. My mom always had faith in me. She knew I would someday finish, even though I embarked on a faculty position at ASU before my dissertation was done and defended, which meant a circuitous route to the finish line. She would say "Keep pluggin'!" whenever I felt like giving up and whenever those around me doubted I would finish the PhD. The very idea that I would someday have those three letters after my name is credit to my mom. She was the one who signed me up for piano lessons, ballet classes, and the Navajoland Festival of the Arts when I was a kid because she wanted me to learn discipline and the value of hard work, creative expression, and confidence. My mom signed me up for a library card at the Navajo Nation Library and encouraged me to read beyond what I was assigned at school. It was my mom who sat with me in the principal's office in second grade when Sr. Paulita and Principal Sr. Anne Regina sought parental permission to promote me to the third grade, a harrowing life event for a kid who did not want to leave her friends behind in the second grade. Both my parents taught me to be courageous and resolute, especially when things are unexpected, difficult, and unnerving.

A commitment to service defines my dad as well. Upon the writing of this manuscript he is ninety-seven years old. He fought in the Korean War with the U.S. Army and Air Force, an era when battles were indeed hand to hand, in trenches and on the ground. His frozen knee, shattered eardrums, and beleaguered body attest to the sacrifices made on the battlefield. My dad belonged to a number of Indian veterans' organizations on the Navajo Nation, including the Veterans of Foreign Wars Post 6789, well into his nineties. He enjoyed challenging the leadership of the "young guys" in the veterans' groups: Vietnam-era vets who are probably well into their seventies. In recent years he has become more vocal on veterans' issues at our local chapter meetings in Oak Springs, in front of Navajo Nation leaders, and at gatherings of Diné veterans. His desire is that the Navajo Nation acknowledges the service of our veterans and supports them with adequate housing and access to services.

Service is an expected part of our work as university faculty. As untenured faculty, the expectation is that the bulk of my time and energy is focused on my writing, research, and teaching, but as Indigenous People, service to others, to our community, is simply what we do. In Phoenix, I serve as secretary on the board of directors for Native American Connections (NAC), an organization that works to provide affordable housing and culturally grounded behavioral health services for all people in need. NAC has done incredible work throughout the COVID-19 pandemic to ensure that people in recovery could maintain their treatment, that families had roofs over their heads with Internet for school-aged children who suddenly had to be homeschooled, and that people experiencing homelessness had a safe place to shelter. Through the years I have been honored to serve in support of NAC, Morning Star Leaders youth council, and the Cook Native American Ministries Foundation. Each contributes education, training, resources, or support to help Indigenous People to thrive. I am happy to do my small part. This is the commitment to service that was modeled so profoundly by my parents. Of course, I perform service to my discipline (AIS) and to ASU as well, but it is the service to Indian families in the community that means something extra special.

Conclusion

I wish to acknowledge the AIS faculty who shaped me and my experience over the years. It was Mary Jo Tippeconnic Fox who first inspired me to think about being an academic and pursing a PhD. She was the first Indigenous professor and first Indigenous *woman* academic who took me under her wing and challenged and truly invested in me. I could see myself in Mary Jo. We could relate. Representation mattered then and it matters now more than ever, especially in spaces that have historically excluded or have not been ventured into by Indigenous People. Mary Jo's Indian Education class validated my Catholic Indian school experience and the boarding school experience of my dad. Mary Jo and Jay Stauss made a great team as they provided leadership and a growth opportunity for us all. In an interesting turn of fate, Mary Jo's brother, John Tippeconnic, became our AIS director at ASU in 2010. Like Mary Jo, he was a tremendous mentor, colleague, and friend.

As a University of Arizona AIS alum, I have the dubious distinction of having never taken a class from Tom Holm. Tom is one of those professors who is much loved and fondly remembered by generations of students. Even today, when alums reminisce about their graduate school days in Tucson, there is usually mention of Tom and his classes. Tom was a stalwart member of the faculty who attended every powwow and social event at the graduate center, and students liked to hang out with him as he smoked cigarettes on the breezeway at the Harvill Building. Tom noted that I somehow escaped without taking any of his classes and enjoyed teasing me about that. Though never formally a student of Tom's, I knew that he supported us all equally and wanted us to do well once out in the world with our AIS graduate degrees.

I appreciate David E. Wilkins for challenging me and urging me to find focus in my work. I learned federal Indian policy and case law under David, and I appreciated that he set the bar high for his students. His was not a class to merely skim the readings for. He was a serious scholar and expected the same of his graduate students. Conversations with David about

Navajo government reform inspired subsequent work on the Navajo LGA and a course I'm developing on state-tribal relations. All these years later, I enjoy seeing David at Western Social Science Association meetings and know that I have big shoes to fill since I now teach federal Indian policy to undergraduates.

Professors who connected book learning to what actually happens on the ground include Eileen Luna-Firebaugh, Stephen Cornell, and others at NNI. Eileen's policy and governance classes included field trips to the Pascua Yaqui Tribal Court and to a Legislative Council session on the Tohono O'odham Nation. Those opportunities to meet and talk with elected officials, attend community meetings to get a sense of how the tribal legislative process works, and to see a tribal courthouse and jail facility as you hear a tribal judge explain the process are meaningful and memorable. I mimic Eileen's teaching approach with my own students at ASU. Each spring I take my federal Indian policy students to the capitol to meet state legislators to learn about state-tribal politics and the way that local laws and debates impact what happens in tribal communities. Students have the chance to meet Native legislators who help to connect real issues that students' families deal with to the state legislative process. More often than not, students come away with new interest in voting, running for office, and following the news. I also take my economic development and planning students to see real-world tribal development in action on local Indian nations. Development directors, GIS technicians, and planners from Gila River Indian Community, Salt River Pima-Maricopa Indian Community, and Ak-Chin Indian Community have been gracious hosts to our students over the years and have inspired ASU students to connect their classroom learning to the work in the community that must get done to provide positive quality of life in urban and reservation areas.

From Stephen Cornell, Manley Begay, Joan Timeche, and the rest of the team at NNI, I learned the power of the people. The NNI executive education program is about people sharing their stories and learning by doing and the NNI youth camps are about bringing along the next generation. There is no better way to connect book knowledge and classroom learning than by working alongside community leaders and citizens as they debate and revise constitutions, address mismanagement or corruption in tribal government, or figure out how to stabilize and strengthen reservation economies. These are real issues, and although the academic community can document stories, record history, analyze case law, theorize strategy, and even inspire, it is the community itself that must act. The community members, the citizens, are the ones with the ownership and solutions.

I also wish to acknowledge my new AIS family at ASU. When there was opportunity to grow the AIS faculty with the hire of two assistant professors, it was Myla Vicenti Carpio and James Riding In who encouraged and supported my application. Carol Lujan, Rebecca Tsosie, and David Martinez helped me to get my bearings at ASU. Peter Iverson became a treasured colleague and friend. Upon his retirement, he gave me several of his favorite books on Navajo history and government. I remember him seated in the front row, beaming, when I gave a talk on Navajo campaigns for the Labriola Center at the ASU Hayden Library. I felt that Peter, a respected historian who wrote a number of books and articles on Navajo history and government, was passing the baton as he supported my just-blossoming career. Nathan and I were fortunate to have the honor and pleasure of sharing dinner and conversation with Peter and his wife, Kaaren, before he passed.

It is a blessing to work with students. It is a gift that I do not take for granted. In them are the extraordinary optimism and steadfastness that will sustain our Indigenous communities for generations to come. They carry the stories and strength of their families and their nations. As AIS professors we have an obligation to impart the knowledge, tools, and support to sustain that optimism and aspiration so they might someday provide the leadership, innovation, and action that will help their communities to flourish. Through my own journey and experience, I know that opportunities, accomplishments, and good things happened because someone took the time to offer words of encouragement, write a letter of support, or simply believe in my potential. We must do the same for the generations coming up behind us. It means something when we encourage a student to apply for an internship that will someday help them get into medical or law school or when we celebrate their graduation, first job, new baby, or admission to graduate school. Students need for us to be in their corner, consummate cheerleaders through thick and thin. That support will help them to face the compelling new challenges and obstacles in the world today. There is new attention on issues of race and inequity, and the importance of representation and inclusion. Black Lives Matter and Missing and Murdered Indigenous Women and Girls have prompted the examination of social justice for Indigenous People. AIS is more relevant than ever as it provides an Indigenous platform to speak to our history and resilience and to craft new directions for the future.

References

Davis, Jonathan, David Pijawka, Elizabeth A. Wentz, and Michelle Hale. 2020. "Evaluation of Community-Based Land Use Planning Through Geodesign: Application to American Indian Communities." *Landscape and Urban Planning* 203:103880. https://doi.org/10.1016/j.landurbplan.2020.103880.

CHAPTER 8

No Madness for a Nomad

GREGORY I. REDHOUSE (DINÉ)

Abstract

This manuscript reveals manifold forms of support that shaped and influenced a Navajo father to persist and graduate with a PhD in American Indian Studies (AIS) while enduring court hearings for a divorce and legal custody of his children. In retrospect, it is an assessment that explores how a Native American student veteran endured and navigated the collegiate environment by balancing his veteran and Indigenous identities within the context of higher education. Through the individual voice of this Native American student veteran, the results of this manuscript illustrate decision-making processes, weighing of options, and reasons for sacrifice. This individual had unique experiences, situations, and circumstances to consider while committing and transitioning into the PhD program in AIS. The confluences of situations and circumstances often determine the ability of a Native American student veteran to engage, persist, and complete academic endeavors; therefore, support systems are vital in helping a person navigate and overcome obstacles. Respectfully, the Native American student veteran experience has the power to influence future generations and to help clarify their options when transitioning from one environment to another environment. Moreover, the findings from this narrative can inform colleges and universities to strategically respond and develop support systems specifically designed to recruit, retain, and graduate its students.

Introduction: An Indigenous Vignette

Ya'at'eeh. Shi ei Gregory Ivan Redhouse yinishye.
Deego-hootsoi-dee' naasha.
Todich'iinii nishli.
Bitahnii bashishchiin.
Tsenjikini ei da shicheii.
Kinlichii'nii ei da shinali.
Ahwot'ao Diné nishli.

Greetings. I am called Gregory Ivan Redhouse.
I am from where "it becomes greener in an upward sloping motion" [Denne-
hotso, Arizona].
I am of the Bitter Water People.
I am born for the Folded Arms People.
My maternal grandfathers are the Cliff Dweller People.
My paternal grandfathers are the Redhouse People.
This is who I am as a man.

Navajo parents who choose to maintain their cultural identity will often influence their children from an early age. Navajo infants that are raised on
the Navajo reservation are in a social context of being surrounded by other
Navajos. When they are old enough to begin speaking, Navajo parents may
instruct their children to recite a set of Navajo words and phrases. Navajo
parents often train their children to formally introduce themselves through
clanship identity. Navajo identity is fourfold, meaning Navajos will identify
themselves as members of the mother's clan, the father's clan, the maternal
grandfather's clan, and the paternal grandfather's clan. This was, and still is,
the cultural protocol of K'e (kinship), in which Navajo speakers introduce
themselves to other Navajos. This Navajo introduction sets the parameters
and rules that dictate how one speaks and conducts oneself around particular relatives.

The Warrior Identity

To elucidate upon the way a Native American student veteran transitions
and traverses the university environment, I provide several transitioning ex-

periences. In these narratives, I reflect and examine the intricate layers that constitute the cultural identity of a Native American student veteran. My diverse experiences provide insight to an Indigenous perspective, influential dynamics of identity, and multiple identities. By exploring my experiences as a Native American student veteran, the multiple experiences collectively come together and share visions and academic interests that come through the narratives of transitional experiences. These experiences demonstrate an unexplored Indigenous identity that helped me to respond to different cultural environments, resolve sociopolitical conflicts, and negotiate unfamiliar realities. We must remember that cultural identities are composed of multiple dynamics of history, politics, and education.

In the year 1868, the Navajo People entered into a treaty with the U.S. government. Within this treaty document, under Article VI, Navajo leaders agreed to a Euro-American form of education for their People provided by the U.S. government. This treaty agreement was not condoned by all members of Navajo society, but over time, education came to be seen as a strategy for succeeding generations to endure into the future (Begay 2014). Naat'aanii (Navajo headman) Chief Manuelito became an outspoken advocate of Western education and encouraged Navajo society to pursue it. These words continue to echo through many Navajo families from one generation to the next, from the late nineteenth century, throughout the twentieth century, and into the early twenty-first century. My parents reiterated the words of Manuelito as I was growing up. My motivation to pursue Western education was also taken to another level when I was a child. At the age of four, I witnessed my father graduate with a bachelor's degree from the University of Arizona (UA). A few years later, my mother pursued a master's degree at Northern Arizona University, and during the summers I would tag along. Simply being on a university campus and exploring the environment permeated my mind and the experiences made quite an impression upon me. For the most part, I grew up with the feeling that this was what adults do—they continue going to school and never stop learning. To this very day I continue to pursue online professional development courses when the opportunity presents itself. As an educator, the constant goal of learning is part of my ongoing identity, and I continue this trend by permeating my children's minds with the importance of higher education.

According to neuroscientists, identity is not fixed but is constantly changing due to different environments and circumstances. The environment initially shapes the brain in children, but a person's identity is an ongoing narrative because life experiences continue to shape the brain; therefore, identity changes over time. We must understand that identities are always changing (Eagleman 2015). A Navajo may have always considered himself or herself to be a warrior. A Navajo may have been given a warrior name by his or her culturally inclined parents when he or she was born; this is customary in Navajo culture. Navajo children, both male and female, are identified as warriors through their names. For Navajo males, the first half of their names are hashke and, depending on context, translated to mean *stern* or *forceful*. For Navajo females, the second half of their names are baa and translated to mean *war*. These warrior names are only spoken during Navajo prayers and ceremonies in order to identify oneself to the Diiyin Dine'é (the Holy People). Native American scholar Dr. N. Scott Momaday (Kiowa) states: "Names in the Indian world are very important. As important or more important, I think, than any other society that I know. Naming is, it coexists with meaning. It is indivisible with being" (Burns 1996).

When I was a young boy attending Dennehotso Boarding School, I was introduced to a couple of elderly Navajo men that served in the U.S. Army, participated in the European theater, and survived the Normandy invasion. I was immediately captivated by their experiences and continued to research World War II in my spare time. As I perused black-and-white images from a book, my mother noticed my enthusiasm and stated to me: "You know . . . your grandfather was a Marine during the war." In time I would also learn that one of my grandmother's older brothers and one of her cousins were Marines; they were trained as Navajo Code Talkers. They became my heroes; as a result, military service would also become one of my goals.

When entering Marine boot camp, the first things to notice are the similar environments between the federally operated Indian boarding school and the Marine Corps Recruit Depot. The military barracks mimic the boarding school dormitories and the Marine Corps drill instructors are reminders of boarding school teachers, dorm attendants, and cafeteria workers that supervise the boarding school students. Another familiarity is the early morning physical training. The similarity between Navajo warrior culture and the Marine warrior culture is obvious. Culturally inclined Navajo parents regularly wake up their children early in the morning and encourage them to run. As Navajos run to the east, they are encouraged to sing Navajo blessing or protection songs. In the military, Marines are trained to run in the early mornings and to sing military cadences in unison. Participating in the military provides several benefits: physical fitness, mental discipline, camaraderie, and the G.I. Bill. The military can shape part of one's identity and how he or she perceives himself or herself as a Navajo, a warrior, and a Marine. These identities can compel a person to strive for success—to improvise, adapt, and overcome obstacles. It is this warrior mentality that aids a student veteran to pursue advanced degrees and a relentless drive to succeed in higher education. In retrospect, Navajo elders often stress a common phrase: T'áá hó ájit'éego t'éiya (Only you can take the initiative). Both Navajo and military concepts complement each another and can develop into motivational concepts to achieve personal goals.

Improvise, Adapt, and Overcome

During my collegiate career, I often found myself struggling with producing academic scholarship, but my desire to seek higher learning outweighed the negative comments I received at the postsecondary level. In fact, moments like this only motivated me to pursue avenues of acquiring the skills and expertise I needed to improve my writing. So instead of succumbing to failure, I purposely sought the advice and guidance of my most demanding professors because I knew they would push my intellectual capacity to work harder. Ultimately, I accepted the challenge to prove not only to myself, but to all my professors, that I belong in higher education. My philosophy of improvising, adapting, and overcoming obstacles goes back to my cultural and military experiences. Born and raised on the Navajo reservation, my upbringing demanded discipline, perseverance, and time to reflect upon my accomplishments. This process would repeat itself when I entered the military and pursued higher education.

In August 2007, I resigned from Diné College to pursue my studies at UA. As soon as I garnered eighteen graduate hours and solidified my credentials in the discipline of history, I pivoted in order to focus upon administrative leadership and postsecondary educational issues. I pursued and earned my second master of arts degree in higher education (HED); this program increased my competency to articulate issues of diversity, socioeconomic status, access, finance, organization, and student development theories. But I also felt it was necessary to pursue the PhD program in AIS with a focus in Native Nation building. I was certain that a professional degree in AIS would also provide me with increasing opportunities to establish new relations and to apply my research capabilities. It most certainly has, and it simultaneously provided me with additional opportunities to return home, to pursue credentials in a new discipline, to collaborate with fellow faculty in order to develop new program curricula to consult and provide feedback for tribal officials, and to participate in multiple committees and research teams at a tribally controlled college.

In retrospect, my strategic plan was to take what was gained from HED and to merge current student and cognitive development theories with Indigenous educational pedagogies. My goal was not only to highlight my negative experiences in higher education but also to develop a new model of cognitive development that would transform collegiate environments to become more inclusive atmospheres for Native American students and to further develop innovative curricula and teaching methods that would be effective in motivating Indigenous students. My cultural background would contribute to the ongoing process of diverse learning by sharing the traditional concepts, philosophy, and teachings of Navajo culture, including other Native American cultures.

I feel that the Navajo worldview is a unified one; everything is connected. Navajo People have a desire and a need to stay together, to work together, to share together, and to care together. I adopted this concept into my profession so that Native American students could learn within the context of their traditional values and philosophies. My perspective on education has always been grounded in Navajo philosophy, but it was also influenced by Western concepts of learning. I am very conscious of my teaching methods and what I share with others because I want people to get as much as possible out of what I tell them. Aside from my ability to motivate and facilitate, I prefer to place much of the learning responsibility on my listeners.

Based upon my teaching experience, students often come into my classroom with a certain set of ideas on how the world has been shaped. Should these ideas be overlooked, I risk students building their studies upon incorrect information and developing faulty cognitive structures; in the future, this could encumber their success in learning. As a Native American educator, I believe my duty has always been to assist students in clarifying their ideas, correcting those ideas if necessary, and facilitating the integration of Navajo and Native American ways of understanding to enhance their academic skills. In contrast, education in many non-Indian educational institutions is fractured and compartmentalized; therefore, the learning may become irrelevant to the needs and experiences of tribal students. In short, I try to model an approach to Western academic subjects that will admit Navajo and other non-Western interpretations. The success of collegiate institutions to recruit, retain, and graduate Native American students is directly linked to the fact that tribal students thrive when their learning is purposeful and relevant to their lives.

Oral Narratives and Life Lessons

On November 14, 2013, the Veterans Education and Transition Services (VETS) office at UA hosted an event that honored a Navajo Code Talker who served in the Marines during World War II, Mr. Thomas Begay. The event was well attended by university students, university officials, political dignitaries, and even Pentagon officials. At the beginning of the event, the VETS director asked me to provide a synopsis of Indigenous warrior traditions and a brief overview of Native American historical participation in the U.S. military. Following my presentation, I was compelled to share an abbreviated traditional narrative about the Navajo Twin Warriors. At a time when monsters roamed the earth and threatened humanity, the Twin Warriors, Tobajishchini (Born-for-water) and Naayeeneezghani (Monster-slayer), journeyed to their father, Johoonaa-ei (the Sun), to ask for his help. The Sun bestowed upon his sons a bow and lightning arrows to slay the monsters. Upon their return home, the Twin Warriors became disoriented. I then explained to the audience how a particular chant, the Dzil Biyiin (Mountain Prayer), was utilized by these warriors to get reoriented to their environments when necessary. This chant is sung as a means to regain focus, stability, and one's equilibrium in any environment. I proceeded to sing the chant for Mr. Begay and all the veterans and student veterans in attendance. I sang this chant for those who served as warriors and were still transitioning.

The oral tradition is a powerful tool of transformation in order to teach life lessons in one setting to another and to inform younger generations of their roles within a society and of their options or resources they can pursue. The Twin Warriors are examples of people asking for assistance and resorting to tools/resources they will need to be successful. Many times, we hear that veterans are reluctant to ask for help or guidance. Mainstream institutions and organizations have responded by soliciting the message that it is okay to ask for help. The Wounded Warrior Project has labeled a number of their products with a message: "It takes a Warrior's strength to ask for help" or "Asking for help is not weakness" (Wounded Warrior Project n.d.). When Native American student veterans seek help and are willing to share their experiences, this is an ongoing process of life lessons being learned through an ancient practice—the oral tradition. In other words, "Every traditional American Indian social event presents a context for story, sharing, and experience (Cajete 1994, 193).

Optimizing My Academic Aim

Looking further back, the morning of September 11, 2001, started out routinely for me—a cup of coffee and turning on the television to catch the morning news. Suddenly I realized a peculiar scene as the images on the television screen revealed smoke emanating from one of the Twin Towers in New York City. Moments later, I saw a passenger jet slam into the adjacent tower; it all seemed surreal. A number of questions and ideas filtered through my mind. I wondered what these tragic events would mean for my formal release from the U.S. military. I was still attached to the Marine Corps Reserve and was scheduled to be discharged on September 17; however, the events that unfolded that morning placed everything on hold. After the dust settled, I was honorably discharged, and I pursued my teaching career at Diné College (formerly Navajo Community College). Over the next few years, I noticed a number of Navajo veterans returning from Iraq and Afghanistan and enrolling at the tribal college. As their numbers increased, it soon became apparent that the tribal college was not prepared for the volume of concerns and grievances coming from these Navajo warriors.

Initially, only a single counselor was available to process the G.I. Bill benefits for these student veterans. Soon after, the counselor become overwhelmed with the growing needs and requests from the student veterans suffering from post-traumatic stress disorder (PTSD). Tribal college employees who were Vietnam veterans formed an ad-hoc committee to advise the student veterans. The tribal college also responded by accommodating the student veterans in various ways: a dormitory was set aside exclusively for student veterans, alternative or Indigenous counseling was provided, a combination of Navajo and Native American Church ceremonies was periodically conducted on campus, and a student veterans club was reestablished. These efforts were carried out to help Native American student veterans transition to their new collegiate environment. From what I recollect, the Navajo veterans that I came to know on a personal level successfully completed their course of study at the tribal college, earned their associate degrees, and then transferred to a mainstream four-year university. Since then, I have often wondered about the choices those post-9/11 Native American student veterans made while transitioning into a larger mainstream institution.

As fate would have it, I gained an opportunity to explore the university experiences of post-9/11 Native American student veterans while pursuing a PhD in AIS. As I became familiar with the Veterans Education and Transitioning Services (VETS) office at UA, the VETS director and VETS counselor approached me in the fall of 2014 and asked if I would consider researching the topic of post-9/11 Native American student veterans. Their concern was the lack of information and the gap in academic research on this topic. They explained that in previous years of attending and presenting at student veteran conferences across the country, presenters and attendees at these events had no information on Native American student veterans.

The VETS director and VETS counselor were adamant about the prospects of gaining feedback from Native American student veterans attending UA. They were confident that I had the insight and academic background to take on this mission. I held a couple of master's degrees, one in AIS and the other in higher education. Auspiciously, I was a Native American veteran pursuing a PhD in AIS and previously benefited from the G.I. Bill. Needless to say, the topic of post-9/11 Native American student veterans became my research project following the approval from my dissertation committee. My intentions were to ignite a conversation about Native Americans within the context of post-9/11 student veterans and to start filling the gap we found in the academic literature. The fact that I was focusing my research within the disciplines and fields of study that were familiar to me, I was extremely motivated to continue developing my dissertation project.

Naabaahii: The Warrior Culture

Historically, the bow and arrow are ubiquitous with warrior cultures. Nearly every society around the globe, from the time of antiquity to the present, developed some form of the warrior culture. From a Native American perspective, Dr. Tom Holm (Cherokee-Creek) elucidates upon the warrior culture as an important component of religious and political organization. The warrior culture was the driving force of spiritual power during times of war. Warrior societies kept order, planned logistics, held hunting expeditions, strategically relocated the general population, and distributed resources. Warrior societies punished the guilty and sacrificed their own lives in order for the general population to escape from danger.

The warriors also led reconnaissance missions for buffalo, conducted particular ceremonies, and shared what they had hunted with the entire community (Holm 1996, 38–39). Over time, the concept and meaning of being a warrior have transcended from traditional Native American cultures over to the Euro-American military institutions and organizations. For example, years ago when I was training to become an intercollegiate archer, my coach consistently expressed to the team, "Respect your equipment!" Our coach explained from a Navajo point of view that the bow and arrow were sacred tools. Sacred because the bow and arrow had the power to give life and take life. He meant that the bow and arrow sustained the livelihood of Navajo ancestors: to hunt for food, to engage the enemy, and to defend families.

In fact, the bow and arrow are still utilized in particular Navajo ceremonies and can be seen hanging above the entrance of Navajo homes. Reinforcing this message of respect reminded the collegiate archers to be cognizant that we were benefiting from an archery scholarship that covered tuition, books, room, and board. Our archery coach even recommended that archers needed to identify a Hatathlii (a Navajo medicine person), a spiritual advisor who could provide the archer and archery equipment with blessings and protection prayers. The archery coach instilled this mindset into his archers—a strong sense of respect for their equipment. This training of respect echoed again as I entered the U.S. military. When Marine Corps drill instructors issued me a conventional weapon (M16), they indoctrinated me to respect, clean, and care for my equipment.

In the modern era, the mission of a conventional military organization is to prepare for war and to engage in war. Generally speaking, the modern military is regarded as a combat profession and is structured around combat activities; therefore, warriors are organized and trained for combat (Dunivin 1994). Combat notwithstanding, the teachings derived from the military are also many and depend upon the purpose, type of society, organization, and institution that is training its warriors. The military can also bring warriors together in a particular space, where values are instilled, traditions are practiced, and the concept of unity reinforces shared experiences and strengthens the resilient bond between individuals and organizations. Moreover, the military has the influence to enhance the lives of warriors because it can serve as a pathway for warriors to enter higher education. The military benefits gained by warriors can be applied toward gaining a university education and a rewarding career.

Metaphorical Bow and Arrows

In these changing and challenging times, Native American student veterans have become neoteric warriors and hunters. They have experienced conflict, are seeking new opportunities, and regularly come across challenges. Historically, warriors and hunters have harnessed the bow and arrow to defend the community, to battle the enemy, and to hunt for food. The bow and arrow(s) can be utilized as a metaphorical lens for understanding what systems of support (opportunities) work on and off the university campus. The bow represents education and the arrows represent the students. The bow produces the power that will thrust arrows forward. In a similar fashion, education has the power to enable students to move forward. Just as arrows are dependent upon the bow (potential energy) in order to accelerate (kinetic energy) for speed and distance, students are dependent upon education (stored knowledge) to move progressively forward and to reach their academic goals.

Influenced by the natural elements, each arrow will land in a different location. The multiple dynamic forces in life will take each student through a particular path and will result in variegated experiences and outcomes during their collegiate career. When shooting an arrow from a bow, an archer will need to consider factors such as wind, terrain, distance, and the quality of the equipment. Each factor provides a different challenge, and the archer must be strategic in order to compensate for these dynamics. Metaphorically, the same can be said for students who need to strategically assess their academic situation (wind) and circumstances (terrain) and to know their options (compensate for challenges): "For archers, the ultimate goal is to land in the sweet spot [the target]. . . . Archers must have an awareness of their own form and their surroundings. . . . In field archery especially, the variability of the trails causes changes in the archers' angles" (Robbins 2016). In order to optimize one's ability to hit the intended target, an archer must have a solid foundation: stance, form, and follow-through. In other words, the preparation and training to handle the elements (natural weather/terrain) and equipment (bow, arrows, and apertures). In a similar fashion, students striving for a collegiate degree must have strong foundations of support and guidance, including an understanding of options and resources available to them in order to deal with variegated situations and circumstances.

Situations and Circumstances

January 7, 2013, would be a life-changing moment. After meeting with my lead AIS professor at UA to discuss my graduate teaching assistant (GTA) responsibilities, I returned home to discover that my wife of fifteen years had decided to leave me and took our children with her. To give up, pack my belongings, and return home to the Navajo reservation crossed my mind, but as I sat in my living room staring at the portraits of my late mother and my late father, I wondered what they would say to me. Of course, I knew exactly what they would tell me because they instilled into me a sense of Navajo identity and the oral traditions so that I could deal with hardships and challenges. I could hear the voices of my late parents in my mind; I remembered their expectations of me. They had raised me in a manner that involved Navajo cultural values. It is important to note that researchers have demonstrated that Native American students who encounter cognitive dissonance tend to return to their traditional teachings to reevaluate and reaffirm tribal identity (Garrod and Larrimore 1997). The premise is that a strong cultural identity forges an emotional and cultural anchor for Native American students. I even went to the extent of allowing my hair to grow long again. This return to cultural roots carried over to periodic meetings with AIS professors, who I saw as Indigenous elders who could proxy for my late parents. In retrospect, the networking capabilities of a Native American student are crucial because it influences the way individuals will respond to multiple situations and circumstances. This is important when analyzing student support services since it has been determined that college students learn more and complete their degree programs when they perceive faculty and staff as supportive of their academic endeavors (Lundberg and Schreiner 2004). This support provides a strong positive influence for academic achievement and cognitive development (Cejda and Rhoades 2004).

On-Campus Resources

Although I could feel the pressure of having my back up against a wall, I knew that I had the option and the power to reach out for help. I then took advantage of all the readily available sources at UA: professors, administrators, counselors, and free legal services. As I returned to the UA campus to inform my AIS professors of my sudden predicament, I was very grateful when the AIS family came to my aid and referred me to other important and useful resources located across the UA campus. This was a pivotal moment in my life, a time where the AIS faculty came to my aid by sitting me down, taking the time to listen to my dilemma, and then providing me with constructive feedback. My AIS family made the effort to advise me, to guide me, to coach me, and ultimately to reinforce me with the emotional support I once received in the past from my late parents. My AIS professors were elders I could rely upon; they told me where I needed to go and what I needed to do in order to figure out where I stood in my predicament.

I then proceeded to meet with UA counselors, advisors, and professors from multiple disciplines to explain my extenuating circumstances and gained quite a bit of feedback. This included the Graduate College, Financial Aid Office, VETS, Counseling and Psych Services, Student Legal Services, and the UA Law Clinic. Many of these on-campus support systems allowed me the opportunity to navigate my way through a pending divorce as I worked to maintain my academic responsibilities. On one occasion, I was asked about my academic training and about my mental/emotional progression and coming to terms with the divorce. I explained to the counselor that my graduate program in higher education covered student development theories and cognitive development theories, so I had a very good understanding about the meaning of cognitive dissonance and what I was feeling during the divorce. Simultaneously, much of my time would be spent in the VETS office where I connected with other student veterans and they became my surrogate family. As it turned out, many of the student veterans had also gone through a divorce, so they were willing to listen and share their own experiences. And it was there that I spent so much time in a particular area of the VETS office that fellow veterans began renaming my corner space "the Dissertation Station."

In terms of motivation, camaraderie was essential because I was looking for an environment where I could relate to other people. This is reminiscent of what has been assessed by researchers examining Native American college students. Academic persistence and motivation among Native American students in higher education were linked to a space where group cohesion and support was maintained and reciprocal to other members in the group. This space provided them with a strong sense of self-confidence, self-efficacy, and positive interactions with university officials (Minthorn, Wagner, and Shotten 2013). Although I was a member of the Native American community, I could not always relate to younger generations of Native American students, whose habits and interests differed from mine. Instead, I found a sense of home, comfort, and understanding when hanging out with fellow veterans on campus. In this setting, my sense of altruism was achieved by participating in conversation, social activities, and community projects with other veterans. As a Native American student veteran, I participated in veteran-led community functions that benefited humanity.

Overall, the on-campus resources were very useful and empowered me with insight on how to respond to legal procedures on grounds for divorce, court jurisdiction, and child custody. I would not see my children for a total of seventy-one days. I hired a lawyer, attended court hearings, and patiently waited before being reunited with my children. Realizing I had ample amounts of time on my hands because my children were no longer with me, I decided to make use of the UA Recreation Center on a daily basis and any time I felt overwhelmed. In the past, I would often return home to participate in a sweat lodge ceremony with my father. The sweat lodge ceremony provided a space for consultation, counseling, meditation, singing, and praying. But there was no sweat lodge on the UA campus, so the student recreation weight room became my sanctuary. I consistently trained in the weight room nearly three times a day. There, I could release all my negative thoughts and negative energy by lifting weights, doing cardio exercises, and breaking a sweat to the point of fatigue. In the process, I also made new friends at the Recreation Center and established a solid workout schedule with a fellow Native American student veteran. My comrade would join me in the early morning hours to stretch, run, and lift weights. In less than a year, the physical intensity resulted in dropping eighty pounds of body weight. I had a new routine, a new diet, a new enthusiasm for life, and a yearning to continue improving myself, learning about new things, and reaching new goals.

Off-Campus Resources

A colleague, a non-Native who previously graduated from the AIS program, made sure I did not become a hermit. He made the effort to check on me, got me out of the house, and encouraged me to engage in a number of social activities. My aunts and uncles took the time to share their experiences about marriage, divorce, and what they observed over the years. My relatives also took the time to listen and provided much helpful feedback and advice. Last but not least, one of my older cousin-sisters advised me to develop a list of questions and goals on a sheet of paper and to post this statement on the bathroom mirror; she insisted that I read it each and every morning when I woke up. This morning routine was to remind myself of my daily priorities. I share this in hopes that it can become a template for others to help themselves.

A Native Father's Contemporary Challenges in the Twenty-First Century

What did I do wrong?
No time to ponder the less important things; I must stay busy with school,
   work, and exercise.
Why must I focus?
I must challenge the negative stereotyping of Indigenous men: stupid, drunk,
   and lazy.
What do I have to gain?
I need the PhD in order to seize new opportunities for myself and my children.
What are the other dynamics?
Serving in the U.S. Marines can equate to more stereotyping: combative,
   PTSD, and suicidal.
What must I do?
I need to be a positive role model, work through my emotions; sing, pray, and
   exercise.
How am I doing?
Cognitive development: emotions are a part of learning and internalizing new
   information.
What do I mean?

Dissonance is not a bad thing; intellectualizing my emotions puts things into perspective.

What do I have to look forward to?

Opportunities to raise my children with Navajo culture; we play, communicate, sing, and pray.

What do my children see?

They see their father lecturing in the subjects of American Indian Studies and world history.

What do my children think?

Their father is a strong, intellectual, and cultural warrior who is committed to his children.

Hozho-nahasdlii', hozho-nahasdlii', hozho-nahasdlii', hozho-nahasdlii'

[Harmony is restored, harmony is restored, harmony is restored, harmony is restored].

In addition to these daily positive affirmations, I need to point out that singing, chanting, and praying in my Navajo language are vital to maintaining my mental faculties. Within the chants, prayers, and rituals, there is meaning within the Navajo words, terms, phrases, and lyrics. The application and utilization of the Navajo language in a ceremonial process is imperative. Otherwise, the significance of these traditional practices will be in vain, meaningless to the patient, and without merit or value. It must be understood that there is a certain element in which hearing one's native tongue gives and provides added meaning in the traditional manner. For those fortunate people who understand their native language and have experienced traditional ceremonies, they will agree that there is a certain level of understanding and meaning that simply cannot be replicated in another language. Applying traditional/cultural knowledge is a survival technique that can be modified and applied to different settings. The meaning of the oral tradition possesses elements of truth, morals, teachings, and lessons learned by the listener. It is more abstract than concrete, but it symbolizes strength, courage, harmony, and protection.

Allowing tribal methods of teaching and learning allows Indigenous survival skills to transcend beyond Indigenous environments and into mainstream environments. This means the application of cultural knowledge and an Indigenous lens helps a Native American student become reoriented, refocused, and confident: "what we as Native people feel about being balanced emotionally, mentally, physically, and socially" (Ali-Christie 2013). In essence, an Indigenous person must know himself or herself through a quest of knowledge that he or she comprehends. In other words, it is about tradition, history, culture, and language that cannot be found in books, but the sort of knowledge that exists in the minds and hearts of a people. The oral traditions and customs of Native American societies is an example of how a people perceive themselves (Cajete 1994). Dr. Amanda Tachine (Navajo) describes the oral tradition this way: "A powerful way Indigenous peoples have skillfully passed on methodology is through storytelling. . . . The fluidity of storytelling and stories within Native societies have been vital and a legitimate source of understanding and navigating through the multifaceted dimensions of life including solving problems" (2015, 74). In addition, Dr. Gregory Cajete (Tewa) explains that "it is the oral history that presents how a people see themselves in their journey as a people" (1994, 193).

Whenever time and resources were in my favor, I actively sought out Navajo spiritual advisors. I was fortunate to consult with Navajo ceremonial practitioners that took the time to travel to the UA campus in order to provide encouragement and blessings for Navajo students and Navajo employees. Navajo relatives and Navajo colleagues in Tucson also provided me with other social networks and helped me to get protection ceremonies performed for me and my children. According to Elizabeth Tisdell (2006), individuals can develop an emotional or spiritual drive to work in social and political movements, reinforced by cultural practices (i.e., praying, meditating, celebrating, etc.). As people become increasingly cognizant of how systems of oppression and privilege impact their lives, this is an emotional or spiritual process. From another angle, spirituality can also be described as a search for meaning (Parks 2000; Love 2001). As people participate in "social, volunteer, leadership, and community service, these activities may be a manifestation of their spiritual development and quest for meaning" (Love 2001). Moreover, "spiritual development, like student development, can either be fostered or inhibited by the environmental context in which students live, grow, and develop" (Love and Talbot 1999).

After seventy-one days of waiting, I firmly held my children (Haylei, Bradley, and Octavia) in my arms and cried. This overwhelming and emotional feeling of reunification fueled my motivation to succeed in my PhD program. At that moment, I was inspired to demonstrate to my children that despite life's challenges and setbacks, we must forge ahead and accomplish what we set out to do. This mindset of perseverance also carried over from the military training I received years earlier. For example, the Marines often promote the following mottos: Pain is a sign of weakness leaving the body. Failure is not an option. Improvise, adapt, and overcome. This mental fortitude and way of thinking gave me the ability to focus upon my PhD program in AIS, to engage my peers each day, and to seek additional opportunities. In addition to being a graduate teaching assistant at UA, I secured additional courses I could teach for Pima Community College (PCC). Fortunately, I also garnered graduate credits in the discipline of history while pursuing my second master's degree. At PCC, I was certified in three different disciplines: American Indian Studies, history, and political science. Other times I instructed online courses for Navajo Technical University and Diné College. These extra employment opportunities were vital because they provided me with additional income to help cover my attorney fees and court fees during the divorce proceedings, including the high cost of living in a metropolitan city.

Conclusion

Higher educational structures of recruitment, retention, and graduation are not always conducive to student veterans or Native Americans, but the ability to adapt to changing situations allows for Native American student veterans to alter their pattern of survival. My views and perceptions as a PhD student in AIS included both positive and negative experiences and certain people who were instrumental in helping me pursue different goals at different points in my life; this included Navajo relatives, military officials, and university officials. My story provides insight to the particular support services and systems that have an impact on the ability of a Native American student veteran to persist and complete a PhD program. The ability of Native American student veterans to adapt to changing situations and circumstances allows them to alter patterns of survival from one environment (reservation/military) to another environment (university) and simultaneously transplant Indigenous culture, military skills, knowledge, and behavior.

Huffman's transculturation theory (2011) provides a model to explore how a Native American student veteran traverses and internalizes three different cultural environments: Indigenous, military, and university. Transculturation theory emphasizes that Native Americans are able to function and learn within the dominant culture because they concurrently rely on their Indigenous heritage for a strong sense of identity and purpose. This means Native Americans who possess a strong sense of cultural identity are confident, resilient, and willing to explore new experiences. In retrospect, I recognize that my cultural, collegiate, and military experiences exposed me to many concepts, peoples, and cultures. I learned how to negotiate different circles I found myself in and frequently transitioned between the military environment and the university environment. In the past I was a weekend warrior serving in the Marine Corps Reserve, training one weekend a month and two consecutive weeks during the summer. I was not alone in this experience, as there were several other university students serving in the reserve unit, and we would network, informing each other about our academic pursuits and identifying on- and off-campus resources from which we could benefit.

As I see it now, the military was a positive experience because I met people that influenced me with new ways of looking at the world and developed new friendships in the process. Simultaneously, I learned that transculturation is a socialization process that allows an individual to learn how to effectively participate in more than one cultural setting. There is no cultural loss but a progression that builds upon preexisting cultural knowledge (Huffman 2011; Huffman 2013). Keep in mind that this argument can also be applied to student veterans in higher education. My PhD experience in the AIS program illustrated that my increased persistence was not caused by simple networking. Rather, it was produced by a series of individual decision(s) and by significant others in my academic and surrogate family environments—social capital, cultural capital, and habitus: an environment where people from the same social class share common attributes (Walpole 2003; Dowd, Cheslock, and Melguizo 2008). I contend that the ability of a Native American student veteran to harness a variety of support systems, inside and outside the university, leads to a degree of persistence and success. Social capital and cultural capital were significant factors to encourage me to be persistent even when faced with obstacles and challenges, situations, and circumstances. Before pursuing any form of support, a Native American student veteran will first reflect upon his or her own sense of identity, thereby attempting to establish a link between one's identity and a support system. If post-9/11 Native American student veterans are able to relate their identities to a support system, designed to serve those identities, then post-9/11 Native American student veterans will pursue it.

I realized that my academic success was mostly owed to my ability and willingness to listen to elders, to take advantage of existing resources, to make sound academic choices, and to allow for an inherent cognitive ability to recognize and cultivate a family model that mirrors a tribal community (Heavy-Runner and Decelles 2002). Military camaraderie, veteran cohesion, and a Native American sense of belonging to a particular group created a safe place and a contact zone with the mainstream—a space for understanding and sharing common goals, resulting in what resembles "a well-functioning American Indian community" (Ali-Christie 2013, 332). In this sense, the university officials mimic Native elders and military leaders, and the student veterans center became a proxy for a home or family community. From this perspective, I was reinforced with a sense of self, space, and security. Today I have come full circle by returning home with my children to rebuild our communities, to help our people, and to improve our nation. I have managed to successfully secure employment on my tribal reservation so that I can continue supporting my children; as a family, we plan to renew our farming and ranching lifestyles.

References

Ali-Christie, A. 2013. "American Indian Collegiate Athletes: Accessing Education Through Sport." PhD diss., University of Arizona.

Begay, C. 2014. "Guest Essay: Chief Manuelito's Words Are Still True Today." *Navajo Times*, December 4, 2014. https://navajotimes.com/opinion/essay/guest-essay -chief-manuelitos-words-still-true-today/.

Burns, Ken, prod. 1996. *Ken Burns Presents* The West: *A Film by Stephen Ives*. Premiered September 15, 1996, on PBS. 537 min. https://www.pbs.org/kenburns/the-west/.

Cajete, G. 1994. *Look to the Mountain: An Ecology of Indigenous Education*. Durango, Colo.: Kivakí.

Cejda, B. D., and J. H. Rhoades. 2004. "Through the Pipeline: The Role of Faculty in Promoting Associate Degree Completion Among Hispanic Students." *Community College Journal* 28 (3): 249–62.

Dowd, A. C., J. J. Cheslock, and T. Melguizo. 2008. "Transfer Access from Community Colleges and the Distribution of Elite Higher Education." *Journal of Higher Education* 79 (4): 442–72.

Dunivin, K. O. 1994. "Military Culture: Change and Continuity." *Armed Forces and Society* 20 (4): 531–47.

Eagleman, D. 2015. *The Brain with David Eagleman*. Documentary series. https://www.pbs.org/show/brain-david-eagleman/.

Garrod, A., and C. Larrimore. 1997. *First Person First Peoples: Native American College Graduates Tell Their Life Stories*. Ithaca, N.Y.: Cornell University Press.

Heavy-Runner, I., and R. Decelles. 2002. "Family Education Model: Meeting the Student." *Journal of American Indian Education* 41 (2): 29–37.

Holm, T. 1996. *Strong Hearts, Wounded Souls: Native American Veterans of the Vietnam War*. Austin: University of Texas Press.

Huffman, T. 2011. "Plans to Live on a Reservation Following College Among American Indian Students: An Examination of Transculturation Theory." *Journal of Research in Rural Education* 26 (3): 1–13.

Huffman, Terry. 2013. *American Indian Educators*. Reno: University of Nevada Press.

Love, P. 2001. "Spirituality and Student Development: Theoretical Connections." In "Implications of Student Spirituality for Student Affairs Practice," edited by Margaret A. Jablonski, special issue, *New Directions for Student Services* 2001 (95): 7–16, https://doi.org/10.1002/ss.18.

Love, P., and D. Talbot. 1999. "Defining Spiritual Development: A Missing Consideration for Student Affairs." *NASPA Journal* 37 (1): 361–75.

Lundberg, C. A., and L. A. Schreiner. 2004. "Quality and Frequency of Faculty-Student Interaction as Predictors of Learning: An Analysis by Student Race/Ethnicity." *Journal of College Student Development* 45 (5): 549–65.

Minthorn, R. S., S. P. Wagner, and H. J. Shotten. 2013. "Developing Native Student Leadership Skills: The Success of the Oklahoma Native American Students in Higher Education (ONASHE) Conference." *American Indian Culture and Research Journal* 37 (3): 59–74.

Parks, S. 2000. *Big Questions, Worthy Dreams: Mentoring Young Adults in Their Search for Meaning, Purpose, and Faith*. San Francisco, Calif.: Jossey-Bass.

Robbins, N. 2016. "Wildcat Archery Hits the Bullseye with Math and Physics." *Daily Wildcat*, February 3, 2016. https://www.wildcat.arizona.edu/article/2016/02/wildcat-archery-hits-the-bullseye-with-math-and-physics.

Tachine, A. 2015. "Monsters and Weapons: Navajo Students' Stories on Their Journeys Toward College." PhD diss., University of Arizona.

Tisdell, E. 2006. "Spirituality, Cultural Identity, and Epistemology in Culturally Responsive Teaching in Higher Education." *Multicultural Perspectives* 8 (3): 19–25.

Walpole, M. 2003. "Socioeconomic Status and College: How SES Affects College Experiences and Outcomes." *Review of Higher Education* 27 (1): 45–74.

Wounded Warrior Project. n.d. Accessed August 6, 2021. https://www.woundedwarriorproject.org.

CHAPTER 9

THINKING BIG

"The Goddamn White Man Took Everything,
but He Can't Take Away Your Education"

LOUELLYN WHITE (KANIEN'KEHÁ:KA
[MOHAWK]/AKWESASNE)

THINK BIG read the large white block letters on a black chalkboard. I was moving through an old school building guided by a stranger. I could learn whatever I wanted, whenever I wanted and could come and go to classes when I pleased. My guide asked me what the message meant. I held my hands close together in front of my face and said, "This is to think small." And then I held my arms out as wide I could and cried, "This is to THINK BIG!" And then I woke up.

The dream happened sometime in the late 1990s when I lived in Denver, Colorado, and has stuck with me over the years as a message that there is so much life has to give if we think beyond our wildest dreams. Think big and dream big. I've experienced quite a lot in my life, despite a turbulent childhood, unhealthy choices, and harmful habits. I share some of my story here in hopes it might inspire others.

"MOMMMMMM, I DON'T WANNA BE INDIAN ANYMORE!!!!" I cried as I ran from the school bus and down the crushed stone driveway into the house. My white mother didn't understand what the fuss was about. I wore my new red-fringed poncho to school for show and tell that day. My father, who was Kanien'kehá:ka (the People of the Flint, aka Mohawk), bought it for me at the Bear's Den Trading Post on the reservation—St. Regis, as many called it back then. Or he just said, "Up north." Every summer we drove from where we lived in the Mohawk Valley in central New York to visit relatives in Akwesasne (Land Where the Partridge Drums). My dad wanted to make sure I knew my family. We stopped to buy fresh bread from the Amish in rural New York for Aunt Bea, some jam for Aunt Mildred, and some booze for the guys. I came to realize later in life that this generous spirit was a cultural value passed on to me from my father. My dad loved to fish and brought his boat and fishing gear to the St. Regis River. Some of my favorite memories are being out on the boat on a hot summer day, eating liverwurst and mustard sandwiches and drinking icy cold Coca-Cola.

When we first arrived in Akwesasne we'd spend our time visiting, stopping in unannounced, the way people used to do. We'd hop around and say hello and do the same thing on the last day to say goodbye. The value of kinship was one of the first things my dad taught me about being Kanien'kehá:ka. I loved jigging around the kitchen at cousin Darlene Sunday's house with her kids Jennifer and Julie and swimming in the river behind Aunt Mildred's. The rez was always a part of my childhood, and I never thought it was anything out of the ordinary, even when my father yelled while pounding his fists on the kitchen table: "It's like another country. It's SOVEREIGN!"

The red poncho I wore so proudly symbolized my connection to my family in Akwesasne. When I wore it to school though, other kids made fun of me, doing a war whoop that I'm sure they saw in a John Wayne movie. They teased me to the point where I didn't want to be Indian anymore. I tried to hide it, and I could get away with it with my light skin and eyes that I inherited from my mother.

I was my father's only child, while my mother had birthed eleven children. My parents never married but my mother married four times. Twice after I was born. Our home was often filled with alcoholism, abuse, and poverty. I don't have many memories of husband number three, except the time he gave my mother a black eye. That scene is forever burned in my mind.

My mother was the opposite of my dad. She relied on men to support herself and her children, and she repeated the same cycles as her own mother and was abused by men her whole life. She never talked about her own childhood or her abusive father. Because of her own upbringing, she made unhealthy choices for herself and her children. I was surrounded by pedophiles, be it a brother, cousin, stepfather, stepbrother, and family "friends." There are some painful memories, but it's important to talk about it because it's all too common, and I rose above and through it and changed the course of my mother's family legacy to break the cycles. I decided a long time ago not to keep shameful secrets. All of this has informed who I am and why I've made the choices I have. My educational journey, why I chose to study American Indian Studies, and how it has impacted my life cannot be compartmentalized into simply a story of schooling because my life story and my identity as a whole human being has informed my educational journey.

My mom made a lot of sacrifices for her children, like when she gave us the change she dug out of the bottom of her purse. She made me homemade lemonade in the middle of a hot summer night when I couldn't sleep. Most of the time she didn't have a bed of her own to sleep in. I was the youngest, and my mom always made me feel special. She told me, "You can do anything you want in life if you just put your mind to it."

I survived that time because I was young, protected by my older siblings, and was always off climbing a tree, playing in the creek, or digging for worms. When I was a kid, it was the 1970s and life was simple. We watched Elvis concerts on our console TV and waited for *The Wizard of Oz* to come on once a year. I also had a father who came around regularly, unlike my siblings, who either never knew their father or whose only memories were of drunken violence.

My dad never married and never had any other children. He pounded it into my head to be independent and not become a pregnant teenage dropout. He was a World War II vet who grew up during the Depression and only went to school until fifth grade because he worked to help his family. He was a harsh disciplinarian, and I never felt like I could do anything right. He yelled when I was a kid because I didn't sweep the floor properly. He told me I was ugly. When I was nine, he gave me back the birthday card I gave him because it was a day late. In my early twenties, he disowned me and refused to speak to me for two years because he thought I lied and stole money. I kept trying to see him and sent cards, letters, and flowers. He finally gave in and opened the door, hugged me, and apologized. It was the second time I ever saw him shed tears. The first was when his mother died.

I can't blame my father for the bad stuff without crediting him for the good stuff he taught me, like tenacity, a work ethic, and to have thick skin. He told me I had "zip," "pep," and "gumption." I get that from him, along with his quick wit and wacky sense of humor. Sometimes he took his false teeth out and danced around in his red-and-white-striped pajamas. He would do anything for a laugh. He gave neighborhood kids Indian names. He called one of them Ota. He never told him it meant "shit" in Kanien'kéha. He affectionately called my boyfriend Soniskatsia, not telling him it meant "gotta take a shit." He made that one up and remained convinced it was in Kanien'kéha, and no one could tell him otherwise.

In many ways, I owe my survival to my father. It wasn't easy being his daughter even though I learned what it meant to be Onkwehon:we (Original People) from him. I learned about valuing family, responsibility, and generosity. My dad hunted wild turkey and white-tailed deer. He fished and gardened and respected all life and thanked the animals for giving up their lives. He rubbed dirt from the worm bucket on his hands before putting the worm on the fishhook so he wouldn't scare fish with his scent. He picked puffballs out in the fields and had a tremendous green thumb. My dad also collected coins and fed birds and squirrels in his backyard. My dad was always reading about politics, history, World War II, and esoteric subjects like the lost city of Atlantis and Carl Sagan's books on philosophy. I always loved to read anything I could get my hands on. Thankfully, my dad paid for the Scholastic book club so I could get lost in Judy Blume novels. I was so proud of my encyclopedia set my dad got with stamps from the grocery store.

My paternal grandfather, Mitchell Arionhawakon White, went to the Carlisle Indian Industrial School and thus was raised by an institution designed to eradicate his Native identity (White 2016). My dad didn't see it that way, and my father always talked about Carlisle with a sense of pride. He thought of it as a prestigious school, where his father learned to play clarinet, marched in the band, attended classes alongside people like Jim Thorpe, and made a better life for himself. My grandfather was able to rise above impoverishment on the reservation, but it came at the expense of losing some of his identity as Kanien'kehá:ka. I now teach about assimilation efforts of boarding and residential schools. In part, I owe my own pursuit of education to Carlisle. My father saw Carlisle as a means out of poverty, and while pounding his fists on the table (he did that a lot), he shouted: "THE GODDAMN WHITE MAN TOOK EVERYTHING, BUT HE CAN'T TAKE AWAY YOUR EDUCATION!!!"

Well, appreciating school didn't exactly rub off on me in my early years. I didn't like school and skipped a lot. I failed second grade because I missed so many days. I was tired of being poor. I didn't want to eat commodity cheese or carry my garbage bag full of laundry across town anymore. I didn't want blisters on my hands from washing clothes in the bathtub when we couldn't afford the laundromat. I didn't want to eat potato chips for supper and live in a dirty house. I didn't want to be embarrassed when friends came over and we had nothing to eat but stale bread. I wanted to have a full package of Double Stuf Oreos in the cupboard just like my friend Missy. We never had groceries in our house, so every night one of us went to the corner store with our food stamps to buy milk, bread, Hamburger Helper, or sometimes just a can of potted meat and potato chips. Potted meat wasn't bad though if you put it on bread with mustard. We had government cheese and powdered milk too. I grew up a poor white Indian eating commodity cheese. I was resentful and angry and jealous of my friends who lived in nice houses, ate good food, and had a car to drive them to track and field practice. I was embarrassed in grade school because I had head lice, I peed the bed, and our house was ugly.

I was tired of moving around, and I wanted out of cycles of abuse, alcoholism, and poverty. But I didn't know how. I was angry and jealous, so I became a bully. Once, when I was twelve, I punched my friend Leslie in the eye because she crushed my pack of cigarettes. She had a shiner through the whole summer. I gained a reputation as a fighter, which meant older kids left me alone once I got to junior high. Then, at about thirteen, I started drinking and using drugs.

Anger, fueled by drugs and alcohol, took over the freedom of my youth. There weren't many things for kids to do in the city except hang out at the pool hall and play Pac-Man. Those seemingly innocent pastimes led to bored teenagers congregating on Main Street, which led to keg parties on back roads. I'd sneak out the window, party all night long, and sneak back in the morning. I became disconnected from my identity as an Onkwehon:we and no longer went to the rez with my dad. It was easier to try and blend in with everyone else. After moving to the city, we moved from apartment to apartment to find cheaper rent—ten times before I finished high school.

My negative attitude toward school was summed up in my sixth-grade yearbook: "I, Louellyn White, leave this school and hope never to return." I wanted desperately to feel a sense of freedom. It took me a long time to realize freedom wasn't smoking cigarettes and sneaking off to smoke pot by the apple tree when I was in high school. Nor was it hopping on a bus and running away to the big city at thirteen years old with twelve dollars in my pocket or staying out all night drinking.

I found freedom as a young kid, swimming in the river and climbing trees. I found freedom hiking with my brother, exploring wide-open fields, rolling hills, and apple orchards. I found freedom riding my bike, trying to catch up with my brothers as the neighbor's German shepherd nipped at our heels. I also found freedom walking down the path to my uncle's house, eating wild strawberries along the way. My sense of adventure and connection to nature were nurtured during those formative years when we lived in the country. The disconnection from the natural world affected me profoundly during my teenage years.

I loathed high school and skipped a lot of classes. I had a lot of friends but always felt different from everyone else. I started to turn things around in my senior year. I guess I was feeling a midlife teenage crisis and realized I needed to think about my future more seriously. I started coming to school on Mondays and even took a night course in psychology. That was at Herkimer County Community College, or Harvard on the Hill, as we called it. I thought if I studied psychology, I could figure out my own problems and understand my dysfunctional family. And maybe I could fix things. I didn't have many positive role models to follow. No one else in my immediate family went to college, and only four of us eleven kids graduated from high school. Even though my high school guidance counselors discouraged me from going to college because they didn't think I was serious enough, I wanted to prove them wrong. So, I got my associate's degree in human services. I got by in high school as a B student without doing much of anything, so I started applying myself a little more and managed to do pretty well. I received a few scholarships for Native students, which always puzzled the registrar's office because I was the only Native student there.

I started working at sixteen and moved out on my own I was eighteen. I sometimes worked three jobs at a time and went on to earn my BA in psychology. I kept going to school because I didn't know what else to do and thought I could make more money with a graduate degree. I received an MA in counseling psychology from Marist College in Poughkeepsie, New York. I chose Marist because I wanted to get out of Little Falls, and it was just three hours away. I did well in the program but realized psychology just wasn't it for me. I was too impatient to sit and listen to other people's problems. After doing an internship with severely abused and emotionally disturbed kids, I was burned out. I had drive to do something more active, to get out of my head.

I wasn't able to find a decent paying job and was drowning in student loans and racked up a lot of credit card debt in the process. I went from job to job, never feeling satisfied or fully committed. One of the last jobs I had in New York was helping a disabled girl in her home. I was there for almost a year, and her parents were kind to me, sometimes inviting me for supper, until I said something about going to the reservation. Then they didn't want me there anymore. I could get away with being white, but after my rebellious teenage years I came to realize this was not my reality. I wasn't ashamed, but I learned to discern who I could tell and who I couldn't.

In 1995, I left the East for a job in Denver, Colorado. I was hired for a one-year assignment with AmeriCorps. I went home to tell my mother and spent a whole day hiking and driving through the Adirondack Mountains in central New York. I knew it would be a long time before I saw those mountains again. It turns out I was gone from my homeland for fifteen years. My adventures started with a road trip across the country with my teddy bear in the passenger seat. I could easily pick up and leave any place I lived. I have moved at least twenty-five times in my life. It can be both lonely and thrilling at the same time. On my drive to Colorado the whole world opened to me as soon as I saw the Rocky Mountains. In the five years I lived in Denver, I worked on environmental projects, backpacked and rock climbed around the whole region, worked with Colorado Outward Bound and Native youth programs, job hopped some more, and then landed a job at the University of Colorado National Center for American Indian and Alaskan Native Mental Health Research. I traveled to Pine Ridge and the Navajo reservation every month, where I opened up field offices for a research project. I met so many wonderful friends and colleagues along the way. I thrived on being immersed in Native communities and learning about how other Native People lived. I went to my first sweat lodge on the Cheyenne River Reservation and to ceremonies at Pine Ridge that were life changing.

I took a Native women's course at the University of Colorado in Boulder. I cried after reading about the Sand Creek massacre and children in boarding schools. The anger and sadness I felt growing up came bubbling up and hit me hard. After the grant ended at the University of Colorado, I didn't want to be stuck in the office. I couldn't sit still in one place for long, whether it was a town, home, or job. So my boyfriend and I ventured south and spent two years in Taos, New Mexico. I worked at a youth program, lived in the sagebrush, and raised chickens.

Before starting the PhD, I traveled the world with my boyfriend. Volunteering at an orphanage in India and hanging out with street kids in South Africa opened my eyes to global poverty and diverse cultures. I rode a bus full of chickens through southern Thailand, hiked through jungles, swam through caves, and went on safari in Kenya. I spent time at an Athabascan fish camp in Alaska and backpacked through Denali. I thrived on travel. It helped me reconnect with the earth and to who I was.

My boyfriend encouraged me to explore a doctoral program because I had been so passionate when I took the Native women's course. I thought about my dream, and a PhD certainly seemed to scream "THINK BIG!" I started the PhD program in American Indian Studies (AIS) at the University of Arizona in 2001 and found myself living in the Sonoran Desert surrounded by saguaro cactus and coyotes. I was welcomed to the desert by a huge black tarantula waiting in our empty adobe house that was tucked into the desert landscape. I almost sat on a scorpion in my living room. I found rattlesnakes and javelinas in the carport, black widow spiders in the Arizona room, geckos everywhere, and pack rats in the ceiling vents. The desert was so alive and vibrant, unlike anything I had imagined it to be. I loved all of our little visitors.

Like many grad student couples, my boyfriend and I split up after living there for a couple of years together. I finished my comprehensive exams and moved into an apartment in town. I made some lasting friendships, but there was always a lingering sense of loneliness and feeling out of place. I don't think I had the same sense of homesickness experienced by younger students who had left their reservations to pursue an education, but it still wasn't always an easy place for me to be. Sure, it was helpful to have so many educated Native faculty members as mentors and role models, but the contrast of the dry desert compared to the lush greenery of the east made me homesick. I missed the east, rain, soft green grass, trees, and the change in seasons. I missed the connection to land and sense of place. As much as I loved the desert, I felt like I was on Mars. And the heat. Oh. My. God. The HEAT! I got bloody noses because the air was so dry, and my skin must have aged decades.

I didn't have much background in Native studies, so I felt like there was so much I needed to catch up on. And boy, did I feel dumb. During my first year another student asked me who my tribal chairman was. How the hell do I know?! I felt like I knew nothing about Native history or even my own community. Even though I did well academically and won a ton of scholarships, I was still insecure. I didn't have a clear path in mind when I started, but I was interested in Native education. I thought it was a way to reconnect with my community and find ways to contribute. I was angry for so long, and I wanted to use my education as a tool rather than stay stuck in a place of anger. While going through the program did help me reconnect with my own community in ways I couldn't have imagined, divisions among students and sometimes faculty were distracting.

I quickly learned about identity politics and dysfunction created by colonialism, even though I couldn't name it at first. Sometimes students bickered among each other and directed their anger toward faculty for not being Native or not being Native *enough*. I was also from an eastern Native nation and didn't have dark eyes and skin like some students. I didn't look like them. I didn't grow up on the rez and, my mother was white. It was most hurtful when politics between students escalated to "full bloods" and "mixed-bloods." Some students couldn't understand why mixed-blood Native People struggle with identity issues: "Either you are or you aren't Native, what's the big deal?" Identity issues continued to arise in a variety of situations throughout my time in AIS. Like the time someone said "Well, if you were just a little bit darker, you'd look Native." These interactions made me question everything I felt about who I was. It wasn't the first time I heard such things though. My own sister used to call me "Indian nose," and other people said "Gee, you don't look it" and called me "whitey." I was always caught in the middle and felt like I didn't fit in with Native People because I wasn't Native enough. With non-Native People, I was constantly faced with stereotyping. I started realizing the layers and complexity of identity and the myriad of backgrounds and stories Native students came to the program with.

I possessed what I came to realize was white privilege. I didn't face as much overt racism as some of my peers because of the way I looked. Like the time my car went into a ditch late one night when I was driving on a dirt road toward Pine Ridge. A white farmer pulled me out after ranting "You're lucky one of those Natives didn't find you. Who knows what they would do?" I kept my mouth shut and was anxious for him to get my car out and leave. I often think of that night and how it might have turned out if my skin were darker. Unlike many other Native People, who may not have been so lucky in that situation, I could hide my Native identity. I usually couldn't hide my identity for long because people eventually found out, especially when they asked what I was studying in grad school. There were times when I dreaded the barrage of questions that inevitably followed. I didn't want to have to continually explain who I was, what I was doing, and why. I didn't want to have to prove that I was Native or talk about my blood quantum.

It helped to remember what my family from Akwesasne told me. My cousin Dan Jacobs told me people like me were important in our history. We acted as a bridge between Native and non-Native worlds. My cousin Connie Thompson said, "Don't ever let anyone tell you that you are not Onkwehon:we." Those words from my own family have stuck with me over the years and have been so important to me in finding my place with my feet planted firmly on the ground.

Despite my lack of confidence and dealing with student politics, I made lasting friendships. I absolutely loved the education courses with Mary Jo Tippeconnic Fox and K. Tsianina Lomawaima, and Federal Indian Law with Rob Williams. Luci Tapahonso's class, Poetics and Politics, was a highlight. Her poetry and prose were like listening to ceremony. I was a teaching assistant, went to academic conferences, and met all kinds of well-known Native academics, activists, and celebrities. I still draw on the invaluable experiences gained during those years.

I loved the University of Arizona and all it offered. Yet, I still questioned my place in academia and wondered if it was for me. Why was I getting my PhD? What was I going to do with it? In my carefree, wandering nature, I was always interested in the journey not the destination. While I was still trying to please my dad, I finally connected to the idea of becoming formally educated, particularly because AIS allowed me the freedom to explore who I was in ways no other discipline could.

Part of my journey into self-discovery was during the process of completing my dissertation. I focused my research on the Akwesasne Freedom School, an independent community-run language immersion school. I was excited to start data collection and interviewing parents, students, alumni, and community members about how the school impacted its students in terms of linguistic and cultural identity. I planned to spend the entire summer living at my Aunt Mildred Bero's house. I grocery shopped and set up a post office box while Aunt Mildred set up my bedroom and wondered what the heck soy milk and almond butter were doing in her cupboard. I spent one night with her and then things drastically changed.

June 14, 2004, the day I was to start interviews, my father had a massive hemorrhagic stroke. After brain surgery he was left with poststroke dementia and short-term memory loss. He was in several different hospitals and rehab centers and spent the winter in Akwesasne's nursing home, Iakisohta. Even though it was a monumental task to take care of his needs, finances, appointments, and household, it was my responsibility as his daughter and only child. Slowly, my dad became confused and depressed and grew to hate me, convinced I stole his money and his house. So, I was getting depressed, filled with anxiety and burned out. I put my entire life on hold for someone I barely recognized anymore and who hated me.

Things took another turn for the worse in May 2007. My friend and I were on a week-long canoe trip down the Green River in Utah when a park ranger tracked us down. First, we were worried we were in trouble for drinking and towing a raft full of beer behind our canoe. They put all our stuff in their patrol boat, beer and all, and brought us back to shore. Then the ranger told me my mother was dead. I couldn't believe it and thought he was mistaken because my mom didn't have any known health problems. She died in the operating room after a heart attack. I hadn't seen her in two years, and the guilt was unbearable.

When I thought things couldn't get worse, two months after my mom passed, my dad was dying from pneumonia. He hung on for five long, miserable months in the hospital, had a tracheostomy, so he couldn't talk, and had his toe amputated. Once, when he was lucid, he smiled at me, held my hand, and mouthed "I love you." I don't know if it was the drugs or what, but I was so thankful to have those final moments with him. I lay in the bed next to him, hugged him, and told him I forgave him. He died eleven months after my mother.

I developed what my therapist called "complicated grief." It took several years of therapy to have some of the grief lifted. My dream world was confusing. I dreamed my father was in a torture chamber and I was crippled with guilt for not being there for him more. Dark shadows came into my room, I was awakened by a presence above my bed, and I felt intense vibrations throughout my entire body and woke up terrified. I became obsessed with death and what happens to us after we die. I suffered from chronic fatigue, burnout, aches and pains, depression, and anxiety, all of which made it feel like I was swimming through molasses. Some days I couldn't get out of bed, and some days I just wept all day long.

I've always been sensitive and intuitive, absorbing other people's emotions, so growing up amid chaos and dysfunction compounded feelings of despair and anxiousness. I was a dramatic kid and wanted to name my feelings, but communication didn't come easily in our family. I thought I came out of my childhood free from physical and sexual trauma, unlike my sister. I thought I was a perfectly well-adjusted adult until everything came crashing down, I hit bottom, and couldn't get up. I didn't make it out of my childhood free of emotional and sexual trauma. It wasn't until I was in my midthirties that I was officially diagnosed with depression and anxiety.

A Navajo medicine man and other healers worked on me. I was seeing a therapist, and through ceremony, dreaming, and taking one day at a time, I got through that dark time. My dreams got better over time and were a gauge of how I was doing in my waking life. Out of the blue I would have an upsetting dream, and I knew the grief was still there, lurking just under the surface. Once, I dreamed my sister and I saw our mother. My sister asked her if she missed us and my mom replied, "It's not like that here." My mom wasn't sad or happy. She just was. That dream comforted me and let me know she was finally at peace.

As long as I could remember I have been a dreamer. Dreams have always been an important part of Haudenosaunee culture and were to be honored and shared, sometimes acted out to avoid illness or death. Powerful dreamers could receive messages and guidance from spirits that might impact the entire community. I'm grateful to have this insight and know that if I ignore my dreams, they will cease to exist. A most profound dream came to me about a year after my mother passed. A circle of Indigenous women were singing. I was floating above them, and when their singing became so faint I could hardly hear it, I started slowly falling to the ground. I pleaded with them to keep singing, and as long as they sang loud and strong, I rose up and soared higher above the earth. That dream gave me hope and reminded me to stay close to ceremony and the earth.

Slowly, my grief became more bearable. I was able to get back to dissertation writing. I kept a journal most of my adult life, and writing helped me to process all of the confusing emotions. Because I was so connected to my father and to my identity as an Onkwehon:we through him, I once again questioned my place now that he was gone. Journaling melded into writing about identity and helped me find my way back to my dissertation. I realized that I was a part of the research and needed to write about my own experiences with language and identity.

It took me nine years to complete my PhD. I never wanted to quit, in part because I could hear my father's wrath pushing me to "get an education." Yet, there was a sense of intrinsic motivation and cultural responsibility to contribute to Native issues. I knew I would finish my PhD because I dreamed of my graduation. I held on to the idea that if you can dream it, you can make it happen. It helped to have understanding faculty in AIS who understood family comes first, always. My advisor, Tsianina Lomawaima, understood I needed to take care of my father and put my writing on hold for however long it took. I chose her as my advisor because she was brilliant and no-nonsense. I knew she would push me to do the best job possible. And she didn't fail me in my worst moments. She was gentle when I needed it and pushed when I was ready. She believed in me, and I will be forever grateful.

I graduated with my PhD in 2009 and moved to Champaign-Urbana, Illinois, for a Chancellor's Postdoctoral Fellowship in AIS. I was more than ready to leave the desert and start my next chapter in life. I cried when I first arrived and drove through lush greenery while rain drizzled on my face. I was still grieving, went to therapy, and spent a lot of time working things out in my dreams and in revising my dissertation, which was finally published in 2015 (White 2015). I was thankful to have freedom and flexibility without teaching obligations. Yet, I felt much like a baby bird kicked out the nest, trying to find my courage and the strength to fly on my own. I have never felt so lonely in my life living in conservative Middle America. I was in limbo between grad school and a job and was panicking because there were so few faculty positions and I still had underlying doubts about being an academic.

At the last minute I landed my current job in a newly created First Peoples Studies program at Concordia University in Montreal, Quebec. I was over the moon with excitement at starting a new life in a new place closer to home. It was a little over an hour away from Akwesasne. After fifteen years in the Southwest, I was going home. I knew it would happen since I dreamed Winona LaDuke, Anishinaabe activist, told me, "Now is the time. Go be with your people."

Montreal wasn't what I imagined. I didn't expect such an intense culture shock and difficulty adjusting to big-city living. The first year on the tenure track in a new program surrounded by French-speaking people everywhere was a bit unnerving. I thought I could just easily learn French. I thought it would be fun. It wasn't. I struggled with my self-confidence at first, especially in teaching. Impostor syndrome got the better of me, and I was afraid people would think I got my PhD out of a Cracker Jack box. Fitting into academia felt like putting a square peg into a round hole. I couldn't find my way even though I learned to think critically in my PhD program and could build courses from an Indigenous perspective. I was taught by some of the best faculty in the field and was lucky to have been in the company of Vine Deloria Jr., N. Scott Momaday, and Robert Williams.

I was happy to be closer to family. The smell of sweet grass, the taste of strawberry drink, the sound of my Aunt Bea speaking Kanien'kéha and having Kanien'kehá:ka students made me feel more at home. I have students going through the same emotions I did so many years ago. I tell them it's okay to feel whatever comes up and to use their energy to educate themselves and make a positive impact in their own lives and communities. They experience similar identity issues as I did. I developed a stronger sense of self and talk to students about identity politics so they will feel less isolated. Being honest and making genuine connections with students helped me find a more comfortable place as an academic. I learned through AIS to think and teach critically, always striving for uplifting Indigenous Peoples, perspectives, and ways of knowing while affirming Indigenous sovereignty and respecting the diversity of Indigenous cultures. AIS gave me this solid foundation and a framework for how I approach teaching and research, and how I engage with the academy. I continuously advocate for a greater understanding of Indigenous studies. I still use teaching skills I learned as a teaching assistant in AIS, scholarly works, and learning activities. My favorite go-to for teaching about ethical dilemmas is still a set of scenarios Nancy Parezo generously shared with me.

My research has continued in education. I dug into the archives of the Carlisle Indian School, piecing together family histories. Another dream helped steer me in continuing this work. After spending weeks transcribing documents and thinking about my grandfather and what he must have endured at Carlisle, my grandfather came to me one night. I asked, "Grandpa, what do you want them to know?" He answered, "Tell them we didn't have a choice." I have since published book chapters and journal articles on my family at Carlisle and became an activist, saving one of Carlisle Indian School's buildings, and am working on creating a heritage center dedicated to Carlisle's legacy (White 2015, 2018). I have searched through cemeteries looking for children who died while on outing from Carlisle Indian School. I have received funding from the Quebec provincial government for this work, have helped plan conferences for the National Native American Boarding School Healing Coalition, Carlisle Journeys biannual symposia, and have presented at numerous academic conferences and panels.

At Concordia, I have been a part of the Indigenous Directions Leadership Council since its inception, co-created the university's territorial acknowledgment, and have served on numerous hiring and student committees. I teach a series of proseminar courses that I have created that are foundational in Indigenous ways of knowing, involving elders, and getting students out on the land. Another interesting project that I'm involved in is called Decolonizing Light, with physics and engineering colleagues. I'm helping bridge the gap between Western science and Indigenous epistemologies, and while elevating and amplifying Indigenous voices in the field of physics sounds way out of my league, it's really about opening up ways of thinking on something that is as universal as light, its origins, and the numerous Indigenous stories surrounding light sources like the sun and celestial bodies. A background in AIS has helped support me as I engage in interdisciplinary relationships. I have also continued my relationship over the years with AIS and have been invited to give guest lectures both in person and virtually.

The most important event of my life happened in 2012 when my son, Skye Louis White, was born. I dreamed of a son years before he was born, and when it was the right time, he came to me again, ready for this world. Motherhood filled me with more love than I've ever known and at the same time filled me with absolute terror. When I see my dad in my son's eyes, I know he was meant to be in this world and his purpose will be grand. I have a responsibility to pass on cultural values so he has a stronger sense of identity than I did. I know I'm doing something right when he asks for the story of Skywoman at bedtime and wants to visit Tota (grandparent) and his cousins. I am lucky and grateful for my cousin Connie who has become his Tota. It means he is accepted and will always have a place.

Even though I received tenure and promotion and do fairly well in the academic realm, I sometimes still struggle with my place in the world. And I still struggle with depression and anxiety. Being an Indigenous academic can be exhausting work, especially in a place where there are so few. Both my successes and struggles come from a lingering sense of inadequacy. I never felt good enough so always pushed harder. All the years in school, all the degrees, a book, tenure, motherhood, none of it felt like enough. I'm working on embracing an internal striving for excellence rather than being a perfectionist and trying to please others. I'm also working on changing my internal dialogue to be more kind to myself and focus on seeking guidance from within and from my ancestors. I've learned that keeping things in can make you sick, so I'm learning to let go of shame, anger, and resentment. Dreaming, ceremony, remembering our traditional teachings, and connecting to the earth help me remember to be a good human being and give me hope for the future. Gratitude is a central tenet in Haudenosaunee culture, which we call the Ohen:ton Kariwahtekwen or the Thanksgiving Address. I teach my son to give thanks for all that Shonkwaia'tison has created in the universe and to remember that we are related to all living things.

There is one more dream I want to share. It happened sometime when I was working on my doctorate. It started as a disturbing one, in which my father drowned. I sobbed as I watched his body slowly sink beneath the river's surface. In a nearby field, yellow lights from the inside of a little cabin glowed against the night sky. I could hear faint voices talking. Suddenly, my cousin, Dan Jacobs, appeared in front of me and said, "Don't feel sorry for yourself. You must help her heal. You must return to your Mother Earth. To your homeland." Suddenly my tears stopped flowing and I knew what I had to do. I needed to go home. I eventually fulfilled that dream by reconnecting with my family, and to this place, my homeland.

References

White, L. 2015. *Free to Be Mohawk: Indigenous Education at the Akwesasne Freedom School*, Norman: University of Oklahoma Press.

White, L. 2016. "White Power and the Performance of Assimilation: Lincoln Institute and Carlisle Indian School." In *Carlisle Indian School: Indigenous History, Memories and Reclamations*, edited by J. Fear-Segal and S. Rose, 106–23. Lincoln: University of Nebraska Press.

White, L. 2018. "Who Gets to Tell the Stories? Carlisle Indian School: Imagining a Place of Memory Through Descendant Voices." *Journal of American Indian Education* 57 (1): 122–44.

Conclusion

MARK L. M. BLAIR

(ANISHINAABE)

"Through the Stories We Hear Who We Are"

This powerful quote is from Laguna Pueblo author and former affiliate faculty member for the American Indian Studies Program at the University of Arizona, Leslie Marmon Silko (1996). Stories are a gift and often hold the community's core values, providing a road map for future generations. These stories offer insights into the educational journey of the graduates who shared them. In the foreword, my colleague Sheilah E. Nicholas mentions how she is "deeply humbled" to be part of this collective journey. I am proud of each graduate. Likewise, I am extremely humbled and grateful to be able to share parts of my story along with theirs. Through these stories, we hear who they are. We can hear a voice that is often lacking in academia: the Native Voice.

There is a lack of data concerning Native Americans in higher education, especially from an Indigenous point of view. Improving Native American success in higher education begins by addressing the lack of data that exists for graduate students. This project hopes to fill the void and shed light on the unique factors and experiences that Native American PhD students face in obtaining a doctorate degree, the highest attainable degree in academia. We are able to witness the incredible stories and journeys that our Native American students experience in pursuit of their PhD in American Indian Studies (AIS).

Most of the research available concerning Native American higher education centers on the tribal college and university (TCU) movement (Warner and Gipp 2009). There is only a handful of literature that examines Native American graduate students in higher education (see Carney 2017; Brayboy et al. 2012; Shotton, Lowe, and Waterman 2013; Fox, Lowe, and McClellan 2005). While I was working on my dissertation, "Taking the Next Step: Promoting Native American Student Success in American Indian/Native American Studies Graduate Programs," I found that there were only "eight dissertations, two essays, and six articles, four of which were based on empirical studies" (Brayboy et al. 2012, 73) pertaining to Native American graduate studies in higher education. Of these, "eight were qualitative and three were quantitative" (Brayboy et al. 2012, 73), and all contained small sample sizes.

This book project was an aspiration of mine dating back to 2015 as a newly minted PhD in AIS. During my dissertation journey, I was motivated by the nagging question presented in "Why So Few American Indians Earn Ph.D.'s, and What Colleges Can Do About It" (Patel 2014). It was a compelling question that my colleagues and I had debated ad nauseum. I had discussed the very topic with several of the contributors to this volume—during class, in office hours, in the hallway, during events that AIS would sponsor. Without the help and direction of my mentor, Dr. Fox, and the tireless efforts of my colleague Dr. Smith, this work may never have come to fruition.

The American Indian Studies graduate program at the University of Arizona is responsible for most of the doctorates conferred in the field nationwide, with over fifty and counting—the majority of which identify as Native American—and demonstrates the unique role American Indian Studies programs have in the retention and success of Native students. The PhD program in AIS at the University of Arizona, the first and largest such program in the country, played a pivotal role in the journey of our participants. The following table echoes these achievements.

The number of AIS PhD graduates is amplified by these numbers and illustrated by Michelle Hale's story that she was the first Native American PhD that her students had seen. Arizona State University, Dr. Hale's current employer, now leads this chart, graduating the most Native American PhDs in the country, in large part due to the creation of programs specifically designed to recruit Native American PhD students (Terrill 2016). The student highlighted here was a graduate of Dartmouth College and a classmate of mine.

TABLE C.1 Institutions awarding the most doctorates to American Indians, 2008–12

Rank	Institution	Doctorate Recipients
1	Univ. of Arizona	28
2	Oklahoma State Univ.	25
3	Cal-Berkeley	17
3	Univ. of Minnesota	17
5	Arizona State Univ.	16
5	Univ. of Oklahoma	16
7	Univ. of Kansas	12
7	Univ. of New Mexico	12
7	Univ. of Wisconsin	12
10	Univ. of Texas	11
10	Univ. of Washington	11

Sources: Patel 2014; Blair 2015.

I graduated from Dartmouth in 1994 and was a classmate to several of the students profiled in the *First Person, First Peoples* book from Colleen Larimore and Andrew Garrod (1997). I was heavily influenced by this groundbreaking text providing a space for Native American students who graduated from Dartmouth to tell their own stories pertaining to higher education and their journey navigating the path. The stories are powerful and deeply relatable to an entire generation of Native American students seeking higher education. I chose to attend school there due to the Native American Program and their strong commitment to Native students. Without the help of Colleen Larimore, who was the Native American Program director at the time, and the relationships I forged with fellow Native American students on campus, I might not have completed my journey during this time.

I am Anishinaabe from Detroit, Michigan. In many ways, I was the quintessential "urban Indian." Urban Indians typically grow up off the reservation and make up over 70 percent of all Native Americans in the United States: "Today, 78% of Native Americans live off-reservation, and 72% live in urban or suburban environments" (Whittle 2017). Although I attended meetings and events at the Southeastern Michigan Indian Center, I was always left questioning my identity with no clear ties to the tribe—much like some of the contributors here. From what I am told from other relatives, my father was very proud of his Native heritage, but like so many of our relatives, he suffered from debilitating addictions. My mother left my father on the day I was born. He showed up at the hospital with flowers, and my mother chased him away. I have a vague recollection of meeting him once when I was very young, but my mother otherwise tried to erase him from my life.

To her credit, my mother never denied my heritage. She would tell me I was Native and take me to powwows and local events; but I was often left with the same void some of the graduates of our program identified. Like several of them, my American Indian Studies story was a journey of self-discovery. I have spent my career trying to find myself and find ways that I can give back and help Native communities. In a sense, this is me "returning home," as Louellyn White eloquently stated in her chapter.

"A Space at the Fire"

For me and many others, "home" was the AIS program. Writers identified AIS as a safe place where they could embrace their identity and feel a sense of belonging. As Michael Lerma states, "I finally felt home. AIS made a space for me at their fire." Students felt supported and embraced by faculty and staff, where AIS became a surrogate community.

Native American communities want their students to succeed in post-secondary education. Many tribal governments have developed education offices that help finance and support students while they are away at school. The Navajo Nation, for example, has a long history of involvement in higher education dating back to the 1960s. At Dartmouth, many students would joke that the acronym NAD (Native Americans at Dartmouth) could instead mean "Navajos at Dartmouth" due to the large number of students with Diné heritage.

Arizona has one of the largest Native populations in the country, including two of the largest reservations in the nation at Navajo and Tohono O'odham. The nations provide such services as scholarship and liaison officers that regularly visit and meet with students on campus. It is no small wonder that students from these communities constitute a large proportion of the Native American students on the UArizona campus.

When Native students are away at school they often feel "isolation from other students, family, and community [that] can lead to feelings of loneliness and self-doubt and, in more severe cases, to depression and dropping out" (Brayboy et al. 2012, 78). This is perhaps why many Native students choose to go to graduate school close to home or to a program with a Native American focus. If any public university system would be sympathetic to Native American student success, one could presume it would be in Arizona.

TABLE C.2 AIS PhD graduation information for UArizona

PhD Degrees	UArizona AIS
2020–21	3
2019–20	0
2018–19	1
2017–18	2
2016–17	4
2015–16	4
2014–15	7
2013–14	5
2012–13	5
2011–12	3
2010–11	3
2009–10	3
2008–9	2
2007–8	6
2006–7	4
2005–6	1

Sources: University Analytics and Institutional Research, n.d.; Blair 2015.
Note: 2020–21 numbers shared by AIS Department.

The primary responsibility for Native American graduate student retention falls to the program in which the student is enrolled. Institutionally, this is often relegated to Native-centered programs such as American Indian Studies. As pointed out in the introduction, 40 percent of all doctorates conferred to Native American students at the University of Arizona are from the American Indian Studies PhD program.

I am extremely proud to be a member of the largest graduating class in 2015. Much like my undergraduate journey, I cannot stress enough what a large part my classmates and the AIS faculty played in my success. Despite waning resources and support, the AIS graduate program is conferring more doctoral degrees than most.

Due to budget cuts, resource reallocations, attrition, and restructuring throughout the university, the AIS program is once again housed as a department in the College of Social and Behavioral Sciences (SBS)—the same department it had fought to leave for many years. Coupled with the Academic Program Review conducted in 2013, revealing some deep-seated issues, there has been a great deal of transition and change within AIS.

Joining SBS has opened the ability to offer an undergraduate degree. After many years of lobbying, the AIS Department now offers a bachelor of arts (2015) in AIS and is one of the few programs in the country that offers BA, MA, and PhD degrees in AIS. In part due to past misgivings with SBS, the graduate program decided to remain a Graduate Interdisciplinary Program under the umbrella of the Graduate College. However, there have been significant changes including tenure operating budgets now falling under

SBS. Some of the effects can be seen in waning PhD enrollment and graduation numbers in the previous table. However, fall 2021 admissions numbers look strong.

Native American graduate students have access to student support programs on campus; however, most of these programs are geared toward undergraduates and often do not meet the needs of graduate students. In addition, services are chronically understaffed and underfunded. Graduate programs are expected to provide the needed support for their own students with some assistance from the Graduate College. Native American graduate students are dependent on the AIS program to provide resources and any other support needed to achieve success. AIS graduate programs are doing the best that they can under very difficult circumstances despite microaggressions and societal ills.

Recent events involving higher education and civil unrest have illustrated that racism and discrimination are still issues in this country. There is "both blatant and covert racism directed at Indigenous graduate and professional students" (Brayboy et al. 2012, 82). Sadly, most of America is badly misinformed and perpetuates stereotypes about Native Peoples that carry over to institutions of higher education. From silencing the Native voice to outright racist chants and actions to institutionalized microaggressions, racism exists in higher education.

The stories shared here provide a forum for the Native voice. They are powerful, full of meaning, and as Sheilah E. Nicholas states in her foreword, "relational." Although the writers and their journeys are connected in so many ways, three overarching and interconnected themes emerged:

- Family and Kinship
- Mentorship
- Service and Giving Back

We divided the authors among these three themes, but they could easily fit under all three. They often overlap with shared experiences, challenges, and triumphs. Not so surprisingly, these themes mirror the most significant factors that promote Native American graduate student success: "individual determination and resiliency, supportive relationships, including mentoring, and the desire to give back to one's tribe and support Native communities" (Brayboy et al. 2012, 87).

Family and Kinship

The role of family, and in particular loss of loved ones, plays a major factor for Native American students seeking doctoral degrees. The statistics bear this out. The average age of Native American doctoral recipients is thirty-eight, while the national average for all groups is thirty-two (Brayboy et al. 2012). Many of our contributors discussed this in their pieces as they tried to balance family responsibilities against the realities of trying to become an academic. I was thirty-five when I finished my PhD, and frankly it could have taken much longer without the support and accommodation of my family. Like Georgina Badoni, I was caring for a toddler with another on the way when I started the AIS PhD program.

Devastating loss of family also shaped the journeys of many of our students. It took me six years from start to finish to complete my doctoral studies. One small reason for this was the shuttling back and forth to Michigan for funerals. In a three-year span, I lost my mother, grandmother, and father. Although I had not been that close to them in recent years, I had family obligations to tend to and needed to be there. This parallels the tragic losses that my colleagues and many Native communities continuously face. These losses take their toll on students and have a cumulative effect. It is one factor among many in longer completion rates. The time to doctoral completion for Native American students averages 9.9 years, with students averaging 6.1 years to complete a doctorate in the sciences and 11.7 years for a doctorate in education (Brayboy et al. 2012).

Mentorship

All our authors mentioned working with world-class faculty as a draw and a contributing factor to their success at UArizona. Students seek out role models who "look like me" or have shared experiences and background. AIS programs are a natural fit. Native student success at the graduate and professional level depends on access to Indigenous faculty and on a "relationship with one's mentor/advisor that starts early and requires consistent interaction" (Pavel, quoted in Shotton, Lowe, and Waterman 2013, 133). Indigenous faculty offer strength, mentoring, and supportive relationships for Native American students and is often a service requirement.

Historically, "American Indian faculty and staff share a community responsibility to advise, mentor, and nurture Indian undergraduate and graduate students from across the university, regardless of their majors" (Champagne and Stauss 2002, 11). This is added pressure to faculty who are already overcommitted, serving on committees and constantly fighting the stereotypes and preconceived notions of what AIS is as an academic discipline (Kidwell 2005). The role of faculty in advising, mentoring, and motivating students cannot be understated.

Perhaps no one was more beloved, controversial, and intrinsically tied to AIS than Vine Deloria Jr., whose legendary status in the field is well known across the discipline. His work laid a foundation for the application of decolonization and critical race theories to Native American education (Deloria and Wildcat 2001; Deloria et al. 1999). Deloria argued that the problem with Western worldviews was that they failed "to produce a coherent worldview encompassing the process of the world and how we humans find meaning in those processes" (Deloria and Wildcat 2001, 7). His teachings influenced the likes of Robert Williams and David Wilkins among others, who, although they have their own institutional issues and stressors to deal with, continue to guide Native American doctoral students today.

As noted previously, Native American graduate students are often nontraditional age and are often responsible for providing for a family in addition to their studies. Financial support is "essential to successfully complete a professional or graduate degree program" (Pavel, quoted in Shotton, Lowe, and Waterman 2013, 133). The AIS program at UArizona currently guarantees a graduate teaching assistantship for all incoming PhD students. Unfortunately, this can only be guaranteed for the first year of the program, and students are limited to certain classes depending on enrollment. This often means that student must be graduate teaching assistants for classes outside of AIS.

With over three hundred alumni, UArizona AIS graduate programs boast the largest network of any of the graduate programs in AIS. This could be an invaluable resource for mentoring, collaboration, and growth. A 2009 survey of AIS alumni showed that most want to be involved in some way with the program, but no formal outreach, other than asking for donations, had been conducted. A small, but very vocal, group of alumni have expressed extreme dissatisfaction with the program. This bad publicity and ill will has never been adequately addressed by AIS or, most recently, by SBS.

Service and Giving Back

One of the overwhelming reasons for Native Americans to pursue graduate study is to help their families and to give back to their community. Many of the writers expressed a need to connect or reconnect with and give back to their community. This is often in the face of daunting sacrifice. Native students "willingly make personal sacrifices on behalf of their families and communities" to give back in some way (Pavel, quoted in Shotton, Lowe, and Waterman 2013, 130). Many students may suffer a personal cost by going to school because they feel they cannot include their family or seek advice about their graduate school experience. For many students, AIS programs become the community from which students draw strength and support. Most AIS programs were started with the mandate to support and promote Native American recruitment and retention.

The pressure of school may "leave students feeling like they have to distance themselves from family and culture" (Brayboy et al. 2012, 80) and negotiate two distinct realities or worlds. There is a need to reconnect to the community if the student feels that connection was severed. Negotiating and balancing "two worlds" is a comment made by many students in higher education. I remember a profound discussion that I had with Manley Begay concerning this in class. He stated that he does not believe that there are two worlds. It is a misnomer in that there are not two distinct worlds at all, it is the reality of the current world where students must simultaneously embrace their culture yet distance themselves from it in academic pursuits.

He also shared with the class how higher education is a way for students to connect to their Indigeneity or an opportunity to seek knowledge and identity. Talk to professors, talk to other students, learn native languages— take advantage of the resources available to you in higher education. I remember asking him, "So, you mean think outside the box?" He responded, "No, throw out the box!" We need to get rid of the notion that there is a balancing act where students feel they have to "manage" their cultural integrity as an Indigenous person in ways that conform to the norms of graduate school (Brayboy et al. 2012, 79). I took his advice to heart and have been trying to support Native student success at the University of Arizona ever since.

Native American Graduate Student Success

There are many factors contributing to the lack of American Indian success in higher education: (1) inadequate academic preparation, (2) vague educational goals, (3) financial aid or lack thereof, (4) new environments, (5) prejudice, and (6) social isolation (Larimore and McClellan 2005 in Fox, Lowe, and McClellan 2005). Key factors in student persistence are "support from family, supportive staff and faculty, institutional commitment, personal commitment, and connection to homeland and culture" (Fox, Lowe, and McClellan 2005, 19). American Indian Studies programs are inherently constructed to address some of these issues, many of which are amplified at the graduate and doctoral level. A successful undergraduate record is often a great determinant for a successful graduate career since many Native American students have already faced myriad issues to get to this point in higher education, having developed the ability to "survive" the academy during their undergraduate studies (Brayboy et al. 2012).

The defining characteristic of successful students is the will to succeed and overcome challenges. The single greatest indication of Native American graduate student success is individual self-determination and resiliency. This is expertly illustrated in all the chapters of this text. Ultimately, it is the individual's drive that compels the student forward. Many times, the best thing that the university can do is get out of its own way, get out of the students' way, and listen to the students share the gift of their stories!

References

Blair, M. 2015. "Taking the Next Step: Promoting Native American Student Success in American Indian/Native American Studies Graduate Programs." PhD diss., University of Arizona. http://hdl.handle.net/10150/556961.

Brayboy, Bryan McKinley Jones, Amy J. Fann, Angelina E. Castagno, and Jessica A. Solyom. 2012. *Postsecondary Education of American Indian and Alaska Natives: Higher Education for Nation Building and Self-Determination*. ASHE Higher Education Report, vol. 37, no. 5. San Francisco, Calif.: Jossey-Bass.

Carney, Cary. 2017. *Native American Higher Education in the United States*. New York: Routledge.

Champagne, Duane, and Jay Stauss, eds. 2002. *Native American Studies in Higher Education*. Walnut Creek, Calif.: AltaMira.

Deloria, Vine, Barbara Deloria, Kristen Foehner, and Samuel Scinta. 1999. *Spirit and Reason: The Vine Deloria, Jr., Reader*. Golden, Colo.: Fulcrum.

Deloria, Vine, Jr., and Daniel Wildcat. 2001. *Power and Place: Indian Education in America*. Golden, Colo.: Fulcrum.

Fox, Mary Jo Tippeconnic, Shelly Lowe, and George McClellan, eds. 2005. *Serving Native American Students*. New Directions for Student Services, no. 109. San Francisco, Calif.: Jossey-Bass.

Kidwell, Clara Sue, and Alan Velie. 2005. *Native American Studies*. Edinburgh: Edinburgh University Press.

Larimore, Colleen, and Andrew Garrod, eds. 1997. *First Person, First Peoples: Native American College Graduates Tell Their Life Stories*. Ithaca, N.Y.: Cornell University Press.

Patel, Vimal. 2014. "Why So Few American Indians Earn Ph.D.'s, and What Colleges Can Do About It." *Chronicle of Higher Education*, May 27, 2014. http://chronicle.com/article/Why-So-Few-American-Indians/146715/.

Shotton, Heather J., Shelly C. Lowe, and Stephanie J. Waterman. 2013. *Beyond the Asterisk: Understanding Native Students in Higher Education*. Sterling, Va.: Stylus.

Silko, Leslie Marmon. 1996. *Yellow Woman and a Beauty of the Spirit: Essays on Native American Life Today*. New York: Simon and Schuster.

Terill, Marshall. 2016. "A Force to Be Reckoned With." https://inclusion.asu.edu/content/force-be-reckoned. Accessed May 23, 2021.

University Analytics and Institutional Research. n.d. University of Arizona (website). Accessed May 17, 2021. https://uair.arizona.edu/.

Warner, Linda Sue, and Gerald Gipp, eds. 2009. *Tradition and Culture in the Millennium: Tribal Colleges and Universities*. Charlotte, N.C.: Information Age.

Whittle, Joe. 2017. "Most Native Americans Live in Cities, Not Reservations. Here Are Their Stories." *Guardian* (US edition), September 4, 2017. https://www.theguardian.com/us-news/2017/sep/04/native-americans-stories-california#:~:text=Today%2C%2078%25%20of%20Native%20Americans,in%20urban%20or%20suburban%20environments.

CONTRIBUTORS

Alisse Ali-Joseph, PhD (Oklahoma Choctaw), joined the Applied Indigenous Studies family at Northern Arizona University in 2013 and specializes
in the importance of sports and physical activity as a vehicle for empowerment, cultural identity, health, and educational attainment for Indigenous
People. She also focuses on Indigenous health and wellness, with an emphasis on child and maternal health. Dr. Ali-Joseph was appointed by the president of Northern Arizona University as the faculty athletics representative
in fall 2015. In this role, Dr. Ali-Joseph works with the athletic department to
ensure institutional control and to maintain academic integrity with student-
athletes and faculty and support the overall well-being of student-athletes.
Dr. Ali-Joseph also serves on the National Collegiate Athletics Association's
Minority Opportunities and Interests Committee, where she ensures the
importance of minority student-athlete voice, access, and opportunity.

Georgina Badoni, PhD (Diné), is a University of Arizona alumna; she graduated in 2017 with a PhD in American Indian Studies. Currently, she is an
assistant professor of Native American Studies at New Mexico State University. Her research focuses on Native American visual culture, Native American education, and Native American women's issues. She has served as a
Native American consulting teacher for Seattle Public Schools; her collaborative work includes professional development for teachers to strengthen
culturally responsive teaching. She has taught K–12 for twelve years in tribal
communities and urban education settings. She currently is working with

charter and public schools in southern New Mexico as an Equity Council member and teaching Native American Studies undergraduate courses and upper-division graduate courses.

Mark L. M. Blair, PhD/JD (Anishinaabe), is currently a Professor of Practice and associate director of the master in legal studies and the BA law programs at the James E. Rogers College of Law at the University of Arizona. He has over twenty-five years of experience in the field of student services, much of which was working directly with Native American students. Dr. Blair previously served as a lecturer and director of graduate studies with the American Indian Studies Department at UArizona. His dissertation, completed in 2015, is titled "Taking the Next Step: Promoting Native American Student Success in American Indian/Native American Studies Graduate Programs." Originally from Detroit, Michigan, by way of Alaska, he now calls Tucson, Arizona, home.

Ferlin Clark, PhD (Diné), is originally from Crystal, New Mexico. He is the fourth Native American president of the Indian University (now known as Bacone College). He is entering his third year as president of Bacone College, located in Muskogee, Oklahoma, one of the oldest operating colleges in the United States established to educate American Indians. He is a professional educator, cultural ecologist, and philosopher, and serves as consultant to tribes in the area of higher education, culture, Indian history, and philanthropy. His recent professional experiences include serving as campaign director for the Blackfeet Tribe's Buffalo Spirit Center, assistant secretary for Indian education for the State of New Mexico, senior policy advisor to the Navajo Nation president and vice president, development director of Sage Memorial Hospital, and president of Diné College. Dr. Clark earned a bachelor's degree in English and communications from Fort Lewis College, a master's degree in education administration, planning, and social policy from Harvard University, and a doctoral degree in American Indian Studies from the University of Arizona.

Mary Jo Tippeconnic Fox, PhD (Comanche/Cherokee), is an enrolled citizen of the Comanche Nation of Oklahoma, research professor of American Indian Studies (AIS), and an affiliated faculty in gender and women studies at the University of Arizona (UArizona). At UArizona, she previously served as head of AIS, associate director of AIS, assistant vice president for Minority Student Affairs, and associate to the president for Indian Affairs. Dr. Fox's scholarly activities are focused on American Indian education, particularly higher education and AIS, and American Indian women's issues. She has numerous publications and over thirty-five years of experience working in higher education and with Native organizations, communities, and tribes.

Michelle L. Hale, PhD (Laguna, Chippewa, Odawa, and a citizen of the Navajo Nation), is from Oak Springs, Arizona. As assistant professor of American Indian Studies at Arizona State University (ASU), Dr. Hale's work focuses on issues of community and economic development, planning, and public policy. At ASU Dr. Hale teaches courses in reservation economic development, tribal community planning, and federal Indian policy. In the community she serves as board secretary for Native American Connections, a nonprofit that provides affordable housing and culturally centered behavioral health services for clients in the Phoenix, Arizona, area. She previously served in board leadership positions for Morning Star Leaders youth council and the Cook Native American Ministries Foundation.

Michael Lerma, PhD (P'urhépecha), was born and raised on the Central Coast of California. He is dean of the School of Business and Social Science at Diné College. His recent research explores the efficacy of traditional Diné institutions of governance. His current projects involve the launch of a virtual business incubator and the creation of a database to locate missing and murdered Diné relatives within Diné Bikéyah. Lerma received a bachelor of arts in history from the University of California, Los Angeles, and a master of arts in political science and a doctorate in American Indian Studies from the University of Arizona. His background in American Indian Studies and international relations has benefited his work within academic institutions, where his research advocates for future Native Nation building via consolidation of Indigenous interests and the expansion of Native Nation control of norms within the international political economy. He is author of *Indigenous Sovereignty in the 21st Century* and *Guided by the Mountains*.

Sheilah E. Nicholas, PhD (Hopisino), Sunforehead Clan, is from Songoopavi Village on Second Mesa, a Hopi community located in the Black Mesa region of Arizona. A professor in the Department of Teaching, Learning, and Sociocultural Studies at the University of Arizona, she teaches courses in Indigenous culture-based education, language and culture, oral traditions, and teacher research. Also a faculty instructor for the American Indian Language Development Institute, she teaches courses in Indigenous language revitalization and reclamation. Her scholarship and research centers on Indigenous/Hopi language maintenance and reclamation; Indigenous language ideologies and epistemologies; the intersection of language, culture, and identity; and Indigenous language teacher education. She is the UArizona co-principal investigator of a Spencer-funded, multi-university national study, Indigenous-Language Immersion and Native American Student Achievement, investigating Indigenous immersion as an innovative education practice. An instructor consultant for the Indigenous Language Institute in Santa Fe, New Mexico, she assists tribal communities in their language revitalization and reclamation efforts.

Gregory I. Redhouse, PhD (Diné), is a culturally inclined member of the Navajo Nation and currently serves as an assistant professor of economics at Diné College's School of Business and Social Science. Dr. Redhouse has taught at two public mainstream institutions (the University of Arizona and Pima Community College) and multiple tribal colleges and universities (Diné College, Tohono O'odham Community College, and Navajo Technical University). From 1999 to 2007, he also served as an intercollegiate archery coach at Diné College. During the summers, Dr. Redhouse volunteers as a guest lecturer for the Warrior Scholarship Project, based out of Washington, D.C., a seminar hosted through the University of Arizona's Veterans Education and Transition Services to assist military members and veterans transitioning from the military environment to the university environment. Last, but not least, Dr. Redhouse is a proud Marine veteran who benefited from the G.I. Bill.

Kestrel A. Smith, PhD, is the department chair of the American Indian Indigenous Studies (AIIS) program at Wenatchee Valley College at Omak. Much of her work has focused on how to place Indigenous epistemologies and education within broader historical and cultural contexts in order to better understand the contemporary Indigenous experience. In 2014 she completed her MA in American Indian Studies at UArizona with a thesis examining the social impacts of tribal colleges and universities. In 2018 she received her PhD in American Indian Studies with a minor in higher education from UArizona, completing her doctoral dissertation on American Indian student access to college-preparatory resources. In the summer of 2018, Dr. Smith moved to Washington State to begin building a new AIIS program at Wenatchee Valley College, the first full AIIS program at a community college in the state.

Tarissa Spoonhunter, PhD (Arapaho/Blackfeet), has a PhD in American Indian Studies and is an enrolled member of the Northern Arapaho Tribe who was raised on the Blackfeet Indian Reservation in Montana. Her research has been focused on treaty rights on ceded territory and traditional ecological knowledge. She is a current professor at Central Wyoming College (CWC) and has established partnerships on the Wind River Reservation with CWC and the University of Wyoming through student mentoring and liaison initiatives. Her work has allowed her to utilize her education as a tool for her tribal community and colleagues. In 2018, she was recognized as an upcoming diversity scholar in higher education. She is culturally inclined to the traditional way of life and finding balance between her life as an academic and role in her tribal nations. Currently, she directs a mentor and internship program in partnership with Wyoming EPSCoR, CWC, and the Wind River Reservation.

Aresta Tsosie-Paddock, PhD (Diné), is an assistant professor in the Department of American Indian Studies and the Department of Linguistics at the University of Arizona. She is a citizen of the Navajo Nation from Sand Springs, Arizona, affiliated with the Leupp Chapter. Dr. Tsosie-Paddock earned a PhD in American Indian Studies from the University of Arizona and a master of legal studies with an emphasis on federal Indian law and policy from Arizona State University's Sandra Day O'Connor College of Law. Her study is in the area of displacement and dispossession of cultural heritage, Navajo language, language revitalization, Navajo history and philosophy, Native Nation Building, American Indian urban studies, tribal government, and federal Indian law and policy. She is a proficient speaker of the Navajo language, which is her first language. She is currently doing research with Native language transmission.

Louellyn White, PhD (Kanien'kehá:ka [Mohawk]/Akwesasne), grew up in the traditional homelands in the Mohawk Valley of central New York. She completed her PhD in American Indian Studies at the University of Arizona in 2009, where she focused on Indigenous education and language revitalization. Dr. White was a postdoctoral fellow at the University of Illinois. Her book *Free to Be Mohawk: Indigenous Education at the Akwesasne Freedom School* was published in 2015. Her most recent research includes Indian boarding and residential schooling with a focus on Carlisle Indian Industrial School. In 2011 she cofounded the Carlisle Indian School Farmhouse Coalition, a historic preservation initiative at the site of the former Indian school. She joined Concordia University in Montreal as a founding faculty member in the First Peoples Studies program in 2010.

INDEX

AIS, as academic field, 5–7

AIS program at ASU, 108, 112, 165

AIS program at UArizona, xv; 20th anniversary celebration of, 3–4; Ali-Joseph on, 21, 22; Clark on, 76–77; graduating from, 10–12; Hale on, 107, 109–11; history of, xvi–xvii, 7–10; Lerma on, 63, 72; off-campus resources of, 141; on-campus resources of, 139–40, 169; overview on graduates of, 165, 167–72; Spoonhunter on, 97, 106; Tsosie-Paddock on, 46, 48; White on, 155–56, 157, 159–60. *See also* dissertations; examination experiences; graduation day experiences; *names of specific students and teachers*

Akwesasne Freedom School, 157

'Ałch'i' Deez'áhá' (Garces Mesa), 42

alcoholism, 24, 91, 92, 149, 150, 152

Ali, Albert, 16, 17, 22

Ali-Joseph, Alisse, 13, 16–28, 175

American Board of Commissioners for Foreign Missions, 87

American Indian Alumni (AIA), 121

"American Indian Collegiate Athletes: Accessing Education Through Sport" (Ali-Joseph), 23

American Indian Studies. *See under* AIS

Anaya, James, x

anger, 152, 155, 162

anxiety, 158, 159, 162

Applied Indigenous Studies program at NAU, 17, 25, 26–27

Arapaho Tribe, 88, 91

archery, 136–37

Archibald, Jo-ann, xii

Arizona State University (ASU). *See* AIS program at ASU

Army Corps of Engineers, 100

athletics, 16–26, 92

athletic scholarships, 18, 19, 20, 22, 24

Bacone College, 74, 83, 86–89

Badoni, Georgina, 13, 29–40, 175–76

Begay, Manley: as AIS faculty, xvii, 76; Blair and, 172; Clark and, 78; Lerma and, 63–64, 70; NNI work by, 103, 124; Spoonhunter and, 103

Begay, Manley, Jr., 119

Begay, Thomas, 133

belonging, 21, 52, 146, 167

Black Elk Speaks (Black Elk and Neihardt), 5

Blackfeet, 90–92, 94, 95–99. See also
names of specific persons
Blackfeet Community College (BCC), 96,
98, 100
Blackfeet Indian Reservation, 92
Blackfoot Confederacy, 90, 94, 96, 99,
103–4
"The Blackfoot Confederacy Keepers of
the Rocky Mountains" (Spoonhunter),
103
Blair, Mark L. M., xv, 10, 164–73, 176
A Blessing (Tapahonso), 3
BLM (Bureau of Land Management), 96
blood quantum, 90–91, 99, 156
boarding schools: Badoni on, 30–32;
military camps and, 130; trauma of, 27,
98; Tsosie-Paddock on, 41–42; White
on, 151, 161. See also education; forced
removal
bow and arrows, 133, 135–37, 138
Brewer, Nanabah, 22
bullying, 31–33, 149, 152. See also physical
abuse; racism
bundle system, 90, 94–95, 96, 99
Bury My Heart at Wounded Knee
(Brown), 5

Cajete, Gregory, 143
cancer, 38
Carlisle Indian Industrial School, 151,
161
Central Wyoming College (CWC), 105–6
Chana, Leonard, xi
Charging Eagle, Stephanie, 97
Cheney Cowles Museum, 94
Cheyenne River Reservation, 154
Cheyenne Tribe, 88
Choctaw People, 18–19, 21–22, 27. See
also names of specific persons
Clark, Ferlin, xii, 13, 74–89, 176
Clinton, Bill, 117
cognitive dissonance, 138, 139, 142
Colombi, Ben, 63, 101, 103

community service. See service and giving
back
Concordia University, 160, 161–62
Cornell, Stephen, 111, 118, 119, 124
corn planting and tending, 83–84, 85
cornstalk education model, 81, 83–84
coronavirus, 88
Cottey College, 93
COVID-19 pandemic, 88
Creator, 53–54, 56, 57
Crownpoint Institute of Technology
(CIT), 77
Cultivating Indigenous Research Com-
munities for Leadership in Education
Alliance, 106
culture shock, 45, 93–94, 160
Custer Died for Your Sins (Deloria), 5
Cutler, Lynn, 116, 117

Dághá Ts'óósí (Slim Whiskers), 43
Dartmouth College, 165–66, 167
Davis, Jonathan, 109
Decolonizing Light, 162
Deloria, Vine, Jr., ix–x, 8, 73, 76, 107, 160,
171
Denny, Avery, 54, 68, 70
depression, 157–58, 159, 162, 167
Diné College, 53, 64, 71–72, 77–78, 80–
81, 134–35, 144
Diné People, 7, 29–30; 1868 Navajo
Treaty, 43, 129; Dilkon Chapter and
land use of, 109; educational support
for, 167; family traditions and child-
rearing by, 30, 32, 34, 38, 42–43,
128; –Hopi land dispute and forced
removal, 32, 33, 43–45; Long Walk of,
43–44, 45, 47, 80; philosophical and
educational framework of, 42, 81, 129,
132; size of reservation, 167; "T'áá hó
ájit'éego t'éiya" expression, 131; "T'áá
hwó ájit'éego t'éiya" expression of, 48;
"T'áá shí ànísht'éego t'éiyá ádoolnííł"
expression of, 29, 39; Twin Warriors

story of, 86, 133–34. *See also names of specific persons*; Navajo

Diné Policy Institute (DPI), 64

discrimination. *See* racism

disgrace, 45

dissertations: by Ali-Joseph, 22, 23, 26; by Badoni, 38, 39; by Blair, xv, 165; by Clark, 78, 79, 80, 81, 84; by Hale, 118, 121; by Lerma, 60, 63, 64, 67, 68–70; by Redhouse, 135, 139; by Spoonhunter, 103, 104; by Tsosie-Paddock, 45, 46, 50, 51; by White, 157, 159, 160. *See also* AIS program at UArizona; examination experiences

divorce, 127, 138, 139, 141, 144

Doing for Themselves (Hale), 108–9

domestic violence, 149, 150

Dozier, Edward P., 7

DPI. *See* Diné Policy Institute (DPI)

dreaming, 148, 159, 162

drug use, 152

education, xv–xvii; abuse during, 56; bullying and, 31–33; Choctaw culture on importance of, 18–19, 21–22, 27; Diné on, 42, 81, 129; Lerma's experience in, 56–57; Native families on children's, 112; White's experience in, 152–53, 155. *See also under* AIS; boarding schools; philosophical framework of Diné; storytelling

emotional stress, 45–46, 60–62, 80–82, 93, 134

English language, 49, 83

erasure: of language, 30, 33, 115; of relocation experience, 45–46

"Evaluation of Community-Based Land Use Planning Through Geodesign" (Hale et al.), 109

Evers, Larry, xvii, 109, 111, 113

examination experiences: of Badoni, 37–38; of Clark, 78; of Lerma, 54, 60–62, 68–69; of Spoonhunter, 101, 103–4; of Tsosie-Paddock, 46, 50. *See also* AIS program at UArizona; dissertations

exercise, 140, 141

family and kinship, 170; Ali-Joseph on, 16–28; Badoni on, 29–40; of Blair, 166–67; of Clark, 75, 80, 82, 84; of Hale, 120–22; of Lerma, 55–57, 68–69, 71–72; of Redhouse, 138, 141, 143; Tsosie-Paddock on, 41–50; of White, 148–52, 157–58

family management, 170; by Badoni, 29, 36, 37–38; by Clark, 78; by Lerma, 71; by Redhouse, 127; by Spoonhunter, 99, 100, 101, 102, 103, 105; of Tsosie-Paddock, 46–47. *See also* financial management; time management

fellowships, 58–59, 68, 105, 160. *See also* financial management

financial management: by Ali-Joseph, 18, 19, 24; by Badoni, 35; of Clark, 81, 84; by Lerma, 58–59, 67–68; by Spoonhunter, 104, 105; by Tsosie-Paddock, 46–47. *See also* family management; fellowships; graduate teaching assistantship (GTA); scholarships; time management

fire, as metaphor, xi, 63, 65, 167

First Peoples Studies program at Concordia University, 160

First Person, First Peoples (Garrod and Larimore), xv, 166

forced removal: of Choctaw, 18, 27; Navajo Long Walk, 43–44, 45, 47, 80; over Diné–Hopi land dispute, 32, 33, 43–45. *See also* boarding schools; land, relationship with the; second-generation relocatees

Ford Foundation, 7, 8

French language, 160

Garrod, Andrew, xv, 166

Gathering of the Nations, 103

gender differences: in graduate program enrollment, 10–11, 97; in tribal roles, 98

General Allotment Act ("Dawes Act," 1887), 87

General Appropriations Act (1870), 87

genocidal practices, 18, 27

geodesign workshops, 109

G.I. Bill, 131, 134, 135

Glacier National Park, 86, 91, 98, 99, 100

"Glacier National Park on Blackfoot Territory" (Spoonhunter), 100

Gorman, R. C., 77

graduate teaching assistantship (GTA), 48–49, 63, 101, 138, 171. See also financial management; scholarships

graduation day experiences: of Ali-Joseph, 24; of Clark, 79–80; Hale on, 112; of Lerma, 70; of Spoonhunter, 93, 104. See also AIS program at UArizona

Graham, Joe, 116

grief, 56, 158–59

Grijalva, Michelle, xvi

Guided by the Mountains (Lerma), 69–70

Guide to Native American Studies Programs in the United States and Canada (Nelson), 6

Hale, Michelle L., 13, 107–26, 165, 177

Hansen, Lori, 115

Harjo, Joy, 109, 111

Harris, Kamala, 111

Harvard Project on American Indian Economic Development, 119

Haudenosaunee culture, 159, 163

hepatitis C, 38

Hill, Roberta, 109

hogans (hooghans), 29–30, 33, 42

Holm, Tom: as AIS faculty, x, xvi, 9, 76; article by, 59; description of, 70, 101, 123; expressions of, 73; Lerma and, 54, 59, 61, 63, 69; on warrior culture, 136

Hoover Institute, 64

Hopi–Diné land dispute and forced removal, 32, 33, 43–45

House Made of Dawn (Momaday), 5

Hozhooji (Blessing Way), 81, 85

hunger, 83

hunting and gathering, 91, 99

illness, 38, 88. See also stress

"In Becoming Sa'ah Naaghai Bik'eh Hozhoon" (Clark), 78–79

inclusion, x, 125, 132. See also representation

Indian Civilization Act (1924), 87

Indian Civilization Act Fund (1819), 87

Indianness, expressions of, 75, 78–79, 83, 84–86. See also Navajo language; urban Indian populations; warrior identity and culture

Indian Placement Program (Mormons), 31

"Indian" stereotypes. See stereotypes

Indigenous Directions Leadership Council, 161

Indigenous Sovereignty in the 21st Century (Lerma), 70

Indigenous storytelling. See storytelling

Indigenous Studies. See under AIS

Institute of American Indian Arts, 99

internships, 116–18, 125, 153

IRB (Institutional Review Board), 50–51, 100, 106

Iverson, Peter, 125

Jackson, Jack C., Sr., 77, 86

Jacobs, Dan, 156–57, 163

Jim, Rex Lee, 81

job hunting, 39, 66, 68, 105

Jones, Brad, 58, 60, 62

journaling, 159

Kalt, Joe, 119

Kanien'kehá:ka (Mohawk), 148, 150–51, 161

Kanien'kéha language, 150, 161

Kemper, K., ix
kinship. *See* family and kinship
Kiowa Tribe, 88

LaDuke, Winona, 160
Laguna (Keresan) language, 115
Laguna Pueblo, 110, 116, 164
land, relationship with the, 42–44, 84–86,
    110, 163. *See also* forced removal
Landscape and Urban Planning (publica-
    tion), 109
land use planning, 108–9
language. *See* English language; French
    language; Navajo language; Spanish
    language
Larimore, Colleen, xv, 166
Lerma, Michael, x, xi, xii, 13, 53–73, 167,
    177
Lewis, Tommy, Jr., 77
Lewis and Clark National Forest, 100
lice, 31
livestock, 30, 31, 42–43, 65, 110
Lomawaima, Tsianina, x, xvi, 76, 157, 160
Lopez, Daniel, 109
Luna-Firebaugh, Eileen, xvii, 99, 101, 103,
    111, 124

Macarro, Holly Cook, 116, 117
Makil, Ivan, 116
Manuelito (chief), 129
Manuelito-Kerkvliet, Cassandra, 77
Marks, Nora, 109
Marshall Trilogy legal cases, 87
Martin, Robert, x, xvii, 76, 99, 101
Maze, Bill, 19
maze-of-life symbol, xi
McEnroe, John, 19
McGirt v. Oklahoma, 87
mentorship, 170–71; Clark on, 74–89;
    Lerma on, 53–73; Spoonhunter on,
    90–106
Meriam Report, 87
military service, 122, 127, 130–37, 144

Mills, Billy, 20, 27
Molina, Felipe, 109
Momaday, N. Scott, x, xvi, 5, 9, 109, 111,
    130, 160
Montana Indian Education for All Act
    (1999), 99
Morales, Fred, 57
Mormons, 31
Morris K. Udall Native American Con-
    gressional Internship, 116–18
Murray, John, 86, 96
Mvskogee Creek, 87

Na'gheiji (Protection Way), 81
name-calling, 32–33. *See also* bullying
naming practices, 38–39, 130
"Nan ikhvnanchi, nan ikhvnanchi, keyu
    hokma pi illachi" (Choctaw expres-
    sion), 18, 27
Naranjo-Morse, Nora, 109
National Collegiate Athletic Association,
    22
National Museum of the American Indian
    (NMAI), 95–96
National Native American Boarding
    School Healing Coalition, 161
National Park Service, 103
Native American Church, 86, 88, 134
Native American Connections (NAC), 122
Native American Culture Days, 20
Native American Graves Protection and
    Repatriation Act (NAGPRA, 1990), 94
Native American Student Association
    (UCD), 20
Native American Studies. *See under* AIS
Native American Studies program at
    NMSU, 40
Native American Studies program at
    UCD, 19–21
Native Nations Institute (NNI), 101, 106,
    116, 118–19, 124
Navajo. *See* Diné People
Navajo Code Talkers, 130, 133

Navajo Community College Act (1971), 77. *See also* Diné College

Navajo-Hopi Land Settlement Act (1974), 44

Navajo language: camaraderie through, 47; erasure of, 30, 115; identity and, 33, 43, 49–50, 83, 85–86, 142; teaching work of, 49, 51; used by Navajo Code Talkers, 130, 133. *See also* Diné People

Navajo Local Governance Act (LGA, 1998), 109

Navajo Long Walk, 43–44, 45, 47, 80. *See also* forced removal

Navajo Nation Higher Education Grant Fund Act (2004), 77–78

Navajo Nation-State of Arizona Transaction Privilege Act (H.B. 2676, 2016), 77

Navajo Technical University, 144

Navajo Treaty (1868), 43, 129

networking, 118, 138, 143, 145

New Mexico Public Education Department, 81

New Mexico State University (NMSU). *See* Native American Studies program at NMSU

Nicholas, Sheilah E., ix–xii, 164, 169, 177–78

Northern Arizona University (NAU). *See* Applied Indigenous Studies program at NAU

Ohen:ton Kariwahtekwen, 163

oil leases, 100

Oklahoma, 18–19, 87

O'odham People, xi

oral traditions, 43, 133–34, 138, 142–43, 177. *See also* storytelling

Ortiz, Simon, 109, 111

Osage Nation, 88

Otoe-Missouria Tribe, 88

Parezo, Nancy, xvi, 76, 99, 101, 161

Pascua Yaqui, 7

Paul, Alice, 9

pedophilia, 149. *See also* sexual abuse

Peoplehood (concept), 59–60, 64, 70

"Peoplehood: A Model for the Extension of Sovereignty in American Indian Studies" (Holm), 59

The People's History of the United States (Zinn), 36

perseverance, 52, 73, 80, 131, 144. *See also* resilience; resistance

persistence: Diné expressions on, 29, 39, 48; by Native families under colonialism, 52; by Redhouse, 145; by successful student graduates, 20, 140, 173; by Tsosie-Paddock's family, 44, 47. *See also* resistance

peyote meetings, 30

philosophical framework of Diné, 42, 81, 129, 132. *See also* education

physical abuse, 31, 56, 149, 152. *See also* bullying; sexual abuse

Pijawka, David, 109

Pima Community College (PCC), 144

Poetics and Politics series, 109–10, 157

poverty, 149, 151–52

powwows, 20, 64, 92, 97, 103, 121, 123, 167

pregnancy and child-rearing. *See* family management

Public Law 93-153, 33

racial justice, 125

racism, 32–33, 36–37, 156, 169. *See also* stereotypes

ranching. *See* livestock

Redhouse, Gregory I., 14, 127–46, 178

religious conversion, 31

relocation. *See* forced removal; second-generation relocatees

repatriation, 94–95, 96

representation, 20, 34, 114–15, 123, 125. *See also* inclusion

reservation system, 27, 57

resilience, 27, 85; of successful student graduates, 173; of Tsosie-Paddock's family, 44, 47. *See also* perseverance; self-determination

Resilience and Culture Through Sport program, 20, 27

resistance, 54, 57. *See also* perseverance; persistence

Rides at the Door, Roylene, 92

Robinson, Grammy, 17, 18

Roessel, Robert "Bob," 77, 80

running club, 92. *See also* sports

Running-Wolf, Tyson, 86

Sarris, Greg, 109

scholarships: for AIS students, 7; for athletes, 18, 19, 20, 22, 24; for Native students, 8. *See also* financial management

second-generation relocatees, 44–46, 50–52. *See also* forced removal; land, relationship with the

Sekaquaptewa, Emory, xvi–xvii, 8

self-determination, 22, 47, 87, 169, 173. *See also* resilience

Self-Determination Act (1975), 87

self-reliance, 108–9

service and giving back, 171–72; Hale on, 107–26; Redhouse on, 127–46; White on, 148–63

sexual abuse, 149, 158–59. *See also* physical abuse

shame, 45, 162

Sherman Indian School, 31

Silko, Leslie Marmon, 9, 109, 164

Smith, Kestrel A., 3–12, 178

Smithsonian Institution Museum of Natural History, 95

social justice, 125

Spanish language, 55–56

Spoonhunter, Tarissa, x, 13, 90–106, 178–79

sports, 16–26, 92

sports scholarships, 18, 19, 20, 22, 24

Stauss, Jay, x, xvi, 8, 76, 111, 113–14, 115, 123

stereotypes, 33, 34, 62, 141, 156, 169. *See also* racism

storytelling, ix–xii, xvi, 43, 86, 133–34, 164. *See also* education; oral traditions

stress, 45–46, 60–62, 80–82, 93, 134. *See also* illness

Survey of Earned Doctorates (National Science Foundation), 4

sweat lodge ceremonies, 140

The Sweet Smell of Home (Chana), xi

"T'áá hó ájit'éego t'éiya" (Diné expression), 131

"T'áá hwó ájit'éego t'éiya" (Diné expression), 48

"T'áá shí ànísht'éego t'éiyá ádoolnííł" (Diné expression), 29, 39

Tachine, Amanda, 143

Taigue, Michelle, 111

"Taking the Next Step" (Blair), 165

Tapahonso, Luci, x, xvii, 3, 76, 109, 110, 157

teaching experiences: of Badoni, 34–35, 36–37, 40; of Hale, 113–16, 125; of Redhouse, 134, 144; of White, 161–62

Tendoy, Merle, 92

tennis, 18–24, 27

Thomas, Robert K., x, 8, 53–54, 73, 107

Thomas, Wesley, 65

Thompson, Connie, 157

Timeche, Joan, 124

time management: by Badoni, 39; by Lerma, 65, 68; by Tsosie-Paddock, 51; by Williams, 66. *See also* family management; financial management

Tippeconnic Fox, Mary Jo, xv–xvii, 176–77; on AIS faculty, xvi, 76, 111, 113, 157; Hale and, 115, 121, 123

Tohono O'odham Community College (TOCC), 101, 102–3, 104–5

Tohono O'odham People, xi, 7, 102, 167
traditional regalia, 93, 104
Trail of Tears (1838), 18
transculturation theory, 144
travel, 154–55
Treaty of Dancing Rabbit Creek (1830),
    18
tribal college and university (TCU) move-
    ment, 165. See also *name of specific
    colleges*
Tribally Controlled Colleges and Universi-
    ties Assistance Act (1975–1978), 87
tribal registration processes, 90–91
Tsosie-Paddock, Aresta, 13, 41–52, 179
Tuba City Boarding School, 30–31, 41–42
Twin Warriors story (Diné), 86, 133–34

Udall Foundation, 116
United Keetoowah Band, 88
University of Alaska, 6
University of Arizona (UArizona). *See* AIS
    program at UArizona
University of Arizona/Sloan Indigenous
    Graduate Partnership (UA/SIGP), 10
University of California at Berkeley, 6
University of California at Davis (UCD),
    19. *See also* Native American Studies
    program at UCD
University of Minnesota, 6
University of Montana, 93–94
University of Wisconsin, 6
University of Wyoming, 105
urban Indian populations, 81–82, 98, 166.
    See also Indianness, expressions of

valley fever, 38
Velez, Maria Teresa, 58
veterans, 122, 127, 130–46
Veterans Education and Transition Ser-
    vices (VETS), 133, 135, 139

warrior identity and culture, 75, 88, 128–
    31, 134, 135–37. *See also* Indianness,
    expressions of; Twin Warriors story
    (Diné)
Washburn, Franci, xvii, 63
water rights, 100, 101, 102
watershed management, 100, 101
weaponry, 135–37
Welch, James, 109
Wentz, Elizabeth A., 109
White, Kalvin, 82
White, Louellyn, x, 14, 148–63, 167, 179
White, Mitchell Arionhawakon, 151
White, Skye Louis, 162
White House, 116–17
Wiche, Jeneen, 115
Wilkins, David E., 111, 123–24, 171
Williams, Robert, x, xvi, 66, 76, 157, 160,
    171
Willie, Charles "Vert," 77
Willie, Mary, xvi
Wind River Indian Reservation, 91, 105–6
Wounded Warrior Project, 134

Yazzie, Herb, 65
Yazzie, Robert, 54, 64–65, 70, 71

Zepeda, Ofelia, xvi, 109–10, 111